T0301609

Enforcing Cybersecurity in Developing and Emerging Economies

To the support and love of my reason for existence: Rana, Reem and Ruba; and to my life journey companion, Victor.
Zeinab Karake

Thank you, Marta Roskwitalska, for your support as a research assistant.

Enforcing Cybersecurity in Developing and Emerging Economies

Institutions, Laws and Policies

Zeinab Karake

Clinical Professor of Information Systems, Robert H. Smith School of Business, University of Maryland, College Park, USA

Rana A. Shalhoub

Fellowship Coordinator, Bitar Cosmetic Surgery Institute, USA

Huda Ayas

Associate Dean, The George Washington University, USA

Cheltenham, UK • Northampton, MA, USA

Published by
Edward Elgar Publishing Limited
The Lypiatts
15 Lansdown Road
Cheltenham
Glos GL50 2JA
UK

Edward Elgar Publishing, Inc.
William Pratt House
9 Dewey Court
Northampton
Massachusetts 01060
USA

A catalogue record for this book
is available from the British Library

Library of Congress Control Number: 2017931743

This book is available electronically in the **Elgar**online
Social and Political Science subject collection
DOI 10.4337/9781785361333

ISBN 978 1 78536 132 6 (cased)
ISBN 978 1 78536 133 3 (eBook)

Typeset by Columns Design XML Ltd, Reading
Printed and bound by CPI Group (UK) Ltd, Croydon, CR0 4YY

Contents

Chapter 1

INTRODUCTION

The advances of digital technology and the intertwined connections between computing and communications have set in motion many changes affecting and impacting the way we live. From 2000 to 2017, the Internet has expanded exponentially on a global level, and currently an estimated 3.7 billion people are connected to the Internet, which is close to 42 percent of the world's population. The technology has advanced so fast and has become more and more user friendly; at the same time, people around the world have become more and more sophisticated in the use of technology. These developments have also created unparalleled opportunities for cybercriminals in that criminal behaviors that were not imaginable a few years ago have become daily occurrences today. Digital technologies today make available to ordinary citizens tools that have the power and capability to inflict considerable damage, economic and social. As never before, and at insignificant cost, criminals can cause significant harm to individuals, companies and governments from unheard of locations worldwide.

In order to create a control mechanism over cyber space and some form of deterrence for cybercriminals, a number of countries around the world have reformed their existing laws and legislation to address cybercrimes; however, these have proven to provide vague and inefficient solutions. It is argued in this book that in order for ethical standards to be established in cyber space, penal legislation must be developed and adopted which is clear and transparent; in other words, new laws have to be legislated to deal with cybercrimes. In addition, since cybercrime is borderless, where offenders can aim their attacks at many people, systems and organizations in any country of the world regardless of their geographic location, international collaboration of law enforcement agencies and the creation of a common denominator for cyber laws in the different countries are critical. It is estimated that in 2016 cybercrime cost the global economy US$0.5 trillion and it is expected the cost will rise to US$7 trillion by 2021. United States' former Secretary of Defense,

Leon Panetta, cautioned of the rising threat of a 'cyber Pearl Harbor' (Panetta, 2012).

As information and computer technologies (ICTs) have developed, so have crimes related to their utilization; as a result of the move to the use of computer networks, new techniques of carrying out crimes have been exploited. Traditional laws were not developed with cyber society in mind. The main concern is the degree of relevance of legislations and their effectiveness in dealing with cybercrime. Traditional criminal laws describe qualified unethical behaviors that were developed over hundreds of years. The technological advancements of ICT networks have provided criminals with new opportunities to carry out attacks and commit fraud online. The costs incurred due to these attacks are considerable: loss of data and information, loss of revenues, losses associated with reputation and image of the entity affected, and damage to soft and hard infrastructure. Given the nature of cyber space in terms of lack of geographic boundaries, these attacks can cause inestimable devastation in a number of countries at once and attribution is a serious problem.

Several individuals have been engaged in the fight against computer crime from its early development. The pioneer in the area of computer crime is, by the account of many experts in the field, Donn B. Parker, a senior computer security consultant at the Stanford Research Institute in the United States. His journey with computer crime and cybersecurity started in the early 1970s; his first book on the subject was *Computer Crime* published in 1976. Parker was also the lead author of *Computer Crime: Criminal Justice Resource Manual* (1989), the first basic US federal manual for computer-related law enforcement.

In 1982, the Organisation for Economic Co-operation and Development (OECD) appointed an expert committee, the Information and Computer Communication Policy (ICCP) Committee, to discuss computer-related crimes and the need for changes in the legal systems. This committee presented its recommendations in 1986, stating that, given the nature of cybercrime, it was highly desirable to create some form of international cooperation to reduce and control such activity (OECD, 1986). In addition, it recommended that member countries change their penal legislation to cover cybercrimes. In 2012, the OECD published a seminal working paper entitled 'Cybersecurity policy making at a turning point: Analysing a new generation of national cybersecurity strategies for the Internet economy'. The paper covers a comparative analysis of national cybersecurity strategies for member OECD countries and reveals that in the majority of countries cybersecurity has become a national policy priority. What makes this paper stand out is that it pioneered a holistic approach to cybersecurity analyzing it from economic, social, educational, legal, technical and military aspects (OECD, 2012). In its 2017 *Digital Economy Outlook*, the OECD states that cybercrime incidents appear to be rising in terms of complexity, rate of occurrence and magnitude. According to the report, in May 2017 computers in 150 countries around the world were infected by WannaCry, malicious software (ransomware) that blocks access to the victim's data until a ransom is paid. This was devastating for both the public and private sectors; just as an example, manufacturing firms such as Nissan Motors and Renault stopped production at several sites. Operations at FedEx and Deutsche Bank were disrupted for a few days (Sharman, 2017). Cybercriminals have been very active both in developed and developing countries. While the developed world has moved at an early stage to enact laws and policies to deal with cybercrime, the developing world has been slow moving in this direction.

The 1980s and 1990s saw a great number of developing countries diversifying their economies from reliance on commodities and moving toward knowledge-based societies; to that end, there is a strong need for an appropriate legal foundation to govern cyber space and cybersecurity policies to create a framework for a cyber-safe society. The regulatory system, even in developed economies, has always had difficulties in keeping abreast with the advancement of technology. The author always refers to this phenomenon as 'the legal system being in a reactive mode, while the technological system is in a proactive mode.'

One of the most disturbing trends in recent years has been the surfacing of an advanced, well-developed underground economy in which spam software, credit card information and identity theft information are all available at affordable prices. Symantec, the prime security software company, raised red flags about what it calls the 'underground server' economy in November 2015, with the publication of a report that estimates nearly US$500 million worth of goods and information is available on online black markets. Credit card data accounted for the largest percentage of the information available for sale on these underground market servers; further, Symantec reports that identity theft information constitutes 16 percent and financial information accounts for 8 percent (Symantec, 2015). What is even more frightening than the accessibility of this information is its affordability! According to Symantec, bank account information is selling for US$10 to US$1000, while information about financial websites' exposure is promoted for an average of US$740. If all the information available on the servers were made use of successfully it would net in close to US$5 billion, the report estimates. A primary reason why this data is more broadly available is that hackers have taken hacking as a full-time job, earning a living by stealing information and putting it on the black market for sale on underground server systems. A previous study published by Symantec in 2014 states the average cost per cybercrime victim has increased, despite the fact that the number of victims has decreased. According to the report, the price associated with consumer cybercrime is US$113 billion annually; this is a 50 percent increase over 2012 (Symantec, 2014). According to Google, as many as 5.5 percent of unique IP addresses (amounting to 'millions of users') visiting Google pages included injected ads. Ad injectors are unwanted software that insert new ads or replace the ones already there and they have plagued the Internet for many years (Google, 2015). It is estimated that the cost associated with cybercrimes will reach US$6 trillion by 2021 (Symantec, 2014). In addition, in its 2016 report, Symantec found that 2015 saw a record-setting total of nine mega-breaches, and 429 million exposed identities. The report states that this number is underestimated because many entities either do not report the crimes or underreport them; Symantec provides a conservative estimate of unreported breaches that pushes the number of records lost to more than half a billion (Symantec, 2016). Another 2016 report published by Symantec indicates that ransomware was one of the major threats facing Internet users, both individuals and organizations. Attackers have sharpened and refined their ransomware activities using robust encryption and anonymous payment systems, such as Bitcoin, in order to create campaigns to treacherous worldwide malware. The ransomware activities are expected to increase in the near future (Symantec, 2017).

The rise of malware and underground servers has resulted in alarming financial disasters for a large number of businesses. The frequency and volume of those attacks have increased in recent years. *Newsweek* has termed 2014 the 'year of cyberattacks', starting with the attack on Sony, followed by Target, J.P. Morgan, Home Depot and others. These were only some of the many victims of cyberattacks in 2014; Staples, Healthcare.gov, Neiman Marcus, the University of Maryland System and many others also suffered cyberattacks that left many customers vulnerable (Tobias, 2014). Ransomware continues to lead the cybersecurity landscape in 2017, with businesses paying millions of dollars to release their encrypted files. Attacks such as WannaCry and NotPetya are taking over systems and data left, right and center, and disseminating new infections through a variety of proven methods. The continuation of this trend makes one thing very clear—ransomware is still leading the world of cybersecurity. Among industries, in 2017 education was the most attacked, followed by telecommunications, entertainment & media and financial services.

Given the less than optimal economic conditions in developing countries, financial crimes are expected to increase as cybercriminals take advantage of the predominant economic confusion and desperation of jobless people. The present global economic crisis will become a goldmine for cybercriminals and will most likely lead to more financial crimes in the next few years. Businesses and governmental agencies around the world are being pressurized by the economic downturn, and the insecurity facing them is compounded by significant added risks due to data leakage, data loss, and outside attacks, all of which have increased significantly over the past couple of years.

The growth of electronic commerce and activities in cyber space in the past few years has created a need for vibrant and effective regulatory mechanisms to further strengthen the legal infrastructure that is crucial to the success and security of cyber space. All of these regulatory mechanisms and the legal infrastructure come within the domain of cyber policies which will guide the regulatory environment. Creating an appropriate regulatory environment is important because it touches almost all aspects of transactions and activities concerning the Internet, the World Wide Web, and cyber space. Regulations also concern everyone; the most vigorous cyber gangs are using tried-and-true modus operandi to find Web applications containing major faults; they perform simple activities to break in, such as overloading a badly written program with too much input. Usually, the intruder aims at taking control of the victim's personal computer and using it to breed infections and perform illegal activities. Meanwhile, all of the victim's important data are gathered and traded. In the past few years, email, blog sites, social-network messages, search engine results, and popular webpages have become overloaded with such infections. In 2013 alone, 41.6 percent of user computers were attacked at least once; in order to conduct all these attacks over the Internet, cybercriminals used 10 604 273 unique hosts, which is 60.5 percent more than in 2012 (NDTV, 2016). One can only speculate the root cause of the proliferation of these attacks. Lately, phishers have been singling out smaller financial services companies and smaller banks worldwide, which may not be as prepared as the larger banking institutions; in addition, phishing software is becoming more and more sophisticated, allowing the hijacking of a larger pool of Internet technologies.

Cybercrime activities are coming in various forms and shapes. Crimes are carried on by individuals, governments and organized criminal rings.

Many governments, increasingly in the developing and newly industrial-ized nations, are carrying out cyber intelligence and offensive cyber activities. The majority of those activities are politically motivated, as in the case of the attack that targeted Sony Pictures Entertainment in 2014, where employee data, emails and unreleased movies were exposed.

It is important to note that the cost of cybercrimes is significant but is very difficult to measure, as many public and private sector entities in both developed and developing countries might be under cyberattack but are unaware of the cyber activities. As a result, there are no reliable cost figures based on recognized methodologies to measure the actual cost of those cybercriminal activities. The greatest cost component has to do with lost business, such as the cost associated with Nissan, FedEx and Renault stopping service and production back in May 2017.

IT TRENDS AND CYBERSECURITY

New trends in information technology (IT) development such as the diffusion of the Internet of Things (IoT), the move to the mobile platform, the widespread development of open source software, and the explosion of big data worldwide have added to the economic growth of countries falling in the developing/emerging domain but at the same time have increased cybersecurity concerns. As a set of related technologies, IoT includes the use of sensors, identification systems such as SIMs, chips and cards, and radio frequency identification (RFIDs), among others.

A recently published study authored collaboratively by Cisco Systems and the United Nations' International Telecommunication Union (ITU) estimates the number of networked devices at 25 billion worldwide by 2020, or as many as 50 billion if we consider RFID tags (ITU, 2015). This report states that in developing nations, IoT is helping meet all the sustainable developments goals set forth by the United Nations. Many examples are discussed in the study dealing with how developing/emerging countries are making use of IoT in many economic sectors, from health, utilities and agriculture, to disaster management. Just by way of examples, as of May 2017 Johns Hopkins University had 140 mobile health (mHealth) projects in developing countries. As of November 2017, the World Bank identified tens of projects in developing countries incorporating big data. A number of stakeholders are involved in implementing IoT projects in developing countries, including companies, NGOs, governments and universities. In advancing growth and development, IoT has improved the planning, delivery, implementation and monitoring of projects in various sectors in developing countries (Labrique, 2017). In the healthcare sector IoT is creating huge value-added in developing/emerging countries in healthcare. Nexleaf Analytics, a not-for-profit technology company supported by the Bill and Melinda Gates Foundation, is relying on the cloud to improve healthcare delivery in India (Nexleaf.org, 2017). During the transport of vaccines to remote areas for instance, Nexleaf monitors the temperature of vaccines via a device which uploads data to the cloud in real time. A server then sends warnings if and when the temperature exceeds acceptable levels.

Other examples of the use of advanced technologies such as IoT, Big Data and the Digital Mobile platform include applications in the utilities sector where a team at the Robotic Embedded Systems Laboratory of the University of Southern California tested a network of 48 manual arsenic biosensors to monitor water quality in Bangladesh. In Kenya, a team from Oxford University attached basic accelerometers (similar to those found in a mobile phone) to water pump handles that deliver data via Short Messaging Systems (SMS) to monitor water usage. Also in Kenya, M-KOPA installs solar home systems at a discount and charges households for the amount of electricity they use. The system disconnects the power if the meter runs out and the users can buy more with mobile payments. M-KOPA remotely monitors the efficiency of its systems and makes adjustments as needed.

Overall, the use of IoT has been shown to improve efficiency and enhance effectiveness. The technology is advancing social and economic growth in developing countries. As mentioned above, projects abound from healthcare to water sanitation, to electricity and agriculture. From a holistic perspective, the three areas that stand out in the use of IoT in development and growth are smart cities, water grids and smart power.

The above are only a few examples of how the development in information technology, especially IoT, is being utilized to achieve economic and social objectives in developing/emerging economies. With the enormous opportunities created by the technology, there are also great challenges associated with cybercrime. With the use of IoT, a large quantity of personal and corporate information will reside in the cloud where it interacts with a host of devices. The security chain could afford cybercriminals with a vulnerability to take advantage of systems by having access to and manipulating the data. Because there are so many devices that can be hacked, hackers can accomplish more.

The availability of advanced technologies in developing and emerging countries makes it critical for those countries to create a culture of cybersecurity awareness and to develop and implement quality cyber-security policies and strategies. As the diffusion of IoT in developing countries increases and becomes a modus operandi, decision makers in those countries have to be concerned about protecting the IT infrastructure. One possible explanation of why the adoption of IoT is growing rapidly in those countries is that the technology has moved from improving efficiency to the creation of new business models and products (ITU, 2015).

Given the importance of cybersecurity, and in trying to provide better metrics to measure infractions, Microsoft, in collaboration with a number of companies around the world, undertook the exercise of exploring predictive cybersecurity models in order to define and improve the understanding of the key technical and non-technical factors that contribute to cybersecurity (Microsoft, 2013). The study attempted to measure cybersecurity performance by using the diffusion rate of malware as a proxy for measuring cybersecurity performance. Malware infection rates were assessed on 600 million devices worldwide with the objective of defining the landscape of exploits, vulnerabilities, malware, and other intelligence data. This Microsoft study found that the diffusion of malware is negatively related to the levels of economic and social development of nations, concluding that more developed countries possess better cybersecurity. The model developed by Microsoft lumped countries into one of three categories of countries: (1) maximizers, countries with higher than expected cybersecurity performance; (2) aspirants, countries with an acceptable/expected cybersecurity performance and who are still developing cybersecurity capabilities; and (3) seekers, countries whose cybersecurity performance is below the model expected levels. Most developing countries were categorized seekers or in category 3. The Microsoft model also identified 11 key factors that can predict changes in global rates of malware; those factors included economic development factors, digital access factors, and institutional factors (Microsoft, 2013). As our study will demonstrate, economic, technological and institutional factors will determine the quality and comprehensiveness of cybersecurity policies and strategies of nations. The results will be presented in Chapter 5 of this book.

RESOURCE-BASED THEORY

The implications of the communication/cyber revolution are profound but still far from being evident for the developing/emerging world. Lower transaction and communication costs, combined with quality production of goods tend to entice many businesses to outsource to developing countries, however. The United Nations has been very active in promoting the diffusion of ICT as a means of economic development. A number of United Nations initiatives affirm that the difficulties associated with the digital revolution make it necessary for emerging and developing countries to identify the major challenges facing them as active participants in the knowledge economy. Specifically, these are the challenges they face in creating wealth and making optimum use of the new development opportunities offered by the information society in various priority sectors; the vitality of creating a trust framework through appropriate regulation of new social, economic and cultural phenomena; as well as prevention and control of the dangers and risks associated with the information revolution. Research has shown that the ability of those countries to be successful in getting on the information/knowledge society bandwagon is linked with possessing tangible and intangible resources. Of great importance is a legal structure that addresses criminal cyber activities. Deterrence and awareness are necessary conditions for the success of cyber laws; well-structured and well-designed cyber-security policies and strategies aiming at creating awareness and acting as a deterrent for cybercriminals are musts in this respect, above and beyond the necessary financial, human and political resources. To achieve a well governed cyber society, a country must possess tangible and intangible resources. In this book we construct and test a number of hypotheses dealing with the level of quality and comprehensiveness of a country's cybersecurity strategy and policy and its available resources. Those will be covered in Chapters 4 and 5.

The resource-based theory has been an area of interest over the years but it was only since the 1950s that this area of research was given noteworthy legitimacy (Lockett and Wild, 2014). This theory progressed into what is referred to in the literature as the VRIO framework (Barney et al., 2011). VRIO looks at the characteristics of resources possessed by firms, agencies, and in our case, countries. In order for an entity to create and sustain its competitive advantage it ought to possess resources which are valuable (V), rare (R), hard to imitate (I) and efficiently organized (O). The book assesses countries' financial, human and technological resources and their impact on the level of quality and comprehensiveness of their cybersecurity policies and strategies.

The resource-based view of the firm will be covered more comprehensively in Chapter 3 of this book. The following section will introduce deterrence theory and how it applies to cyber space.

DETERRENCE THEORY

Deterrence theory is based on the assumption that people choose to
engage in crimes and violate certain laws after they assess the benefits
and costs of their actions. The deterrence theory of punishment can be
traced back to the early works of classical philosophers such as Hobbes,
Beccaria and Bentham. These early philosophers addressed both the
effectiveness and fairness of punishment. Today, despite the merits of
deterrence theory, research based on the belief that punishment deters
criminals has been scarce. Four decades ago, research criminologist
Charles Tittle found support for the theory and established that punishment deters crime but that the gravity of punishment can only deter crime
when there is a high level of certainty that punishment will be executed
(Tittle, 1969).

From a holistic perspective, there are five different approaches to
deterrence identified in the literature. The two well-described approaches
to deterrence are *punishment* and *denial*, and the more recent identified
approaches include *association, norms and taboos* and *entanglement.*
Deterrence by punishment is based on a cause–effect relationship; in
other words, if a crime is committed then an appropriate punishment is
levied on the perpetrator. This is intended to deter the would-be criminal
from committing a crime for fear of being punished. Deterrence by
punishment will work only if the would-be criminal believes that the
punishment is highly probable and severe. Even though this form of
deterrence is straightforward and easy to understand, it is extremely
difficult to apply in cyber space, given the nature and complexity
involved. This will be discussed further in Chapter 3 of this book.

The second type of deterrence is that associated with denial. This type
of deterrence is based on either diminishing the perceived benefits a
criminal expects to gain from criminal activities, or creating high barriers
to entry, which would raise the costs and level of difficulty experienced
by would-be criminals. Under such conditions, the expectation is that the
would-be criminal would perceive the benefit of their action to be much
less than the associated cost so they would decide not to engage in their
criminal activities given the high likelihood of failure.

The remaining three approaches to deterrence are new and not as well
documented or tested as the classical approaches associated with punishment and denial. However, they are gaining importance and will be
covered in more detail in Chapter 3 along with the classical approaches.
Deterrence by association, the first of the three new approaches, is based
on creating an association between the criminal and the criminal activity;

it is basically making it possible to *name and shame* the perpetrator. The main idea here is to inflict a social damage/cost on the criminal. *Deterrence by norms and taboos* is the second of the three new approaches. Norms are thought of as a standard of acceptable behavior, or how people should act, while taboos are a description of inappropriate ways people should behave. Based on this approach, it is hoped that people will be deterred from engaging in criminal activities by having full understanding of the norms and taboos of a certain society. The last approach is *deterrence by entanglement.* Entanglement refers to the existence of a number of interdependencies that lead to a successful cyberattack but inflict great cost on both the attacker and the victim at the same time. All approaches will be discussed further in Chapter 3.

CYBERSECURITY POLICIES AND STRATEGIES

In analyzing the content of cybersecurity policies and strategies for the sample of developing/emerging economies, we will attempt to highlight the three main areas of capabilities critical to reducing the economic, political and social risks of cyber activities. These are: (1) prevention; (2) detection; and (3) response. Prevention deals with introducing fundamental measures dealing with identifying and placing responsibility for addressing cybercrime within the national boundaries and creating programs and activities to raise awareness for citizens. Education programs and civic activities are examples of ways to raise awareness.

Detection has to do with strengthening a country's technological detection measures; this entails investing in those technologies and being on the lookout for incidents and activities involving cybercrimes. Isolating unusual patterns in data traffic and trying to identify locations of the attacks are examples of detection. This is a very difficult activity due to the difficulty associated with attribution.

Response has to do with the development of a well-designed plan in dealing with possible attacks and the penalties associated with those crimes. In a nutshell, for a cybersecurity strategy to be effective, responses and the associated penalties have to be clearly stated and executed.

A study done by Luiijf et al. (2013) looked at published cybersecurity strategies of 19 countries, including developed and developing countries. The six developing countries included in their analysis were the Czech Republic, Estonia, India, Lithuania, South Africa and Uganda. Based on the content analysis performed on those strategies, the researchers concluded that large differences exist between the national focal points and approaches to cybersecurity. In addition, the analysis highlighted strengths and weaknesses of those strategies. The paper concludes that large differences exist between countries' national strategic objectives as stated in the cybersecurity document, including different visions like a safe, secure and resilient ICT environment, economic prosperity, national security, and defense. This study, however, stopped short of looking at the role of protecting children, or the approaches taken for deterrence, detection and/or response.

Based on the previously mentioned study, only 8 of the 19 countries have defined the notion of cybersecurity explicitly. Most of the strategies addressed economic prosperity aspects of the cyber space, but it was indicated that 18 of the 19 countries included in the study had no clear indication of the agency leading the cybersecurity initiatives. Further, 8 of the 19 countries have references to the cooperation between the private and public sectors in combating cybercriminal activities (Luiijf et al., 2013).

In this book we will look at the contents of national cybersecurity strategies and policies and identify if the document(s) addressed the following:

- coverage of the critical infrastructure of the country;
- reference to cybersecurity in what concerns the military and defense;
- reference to how cybersecurity affects the economic prosperity of citizens;
- reference to the role of globalization and necessity of international cooperation in this domain;
- reference to how cybersecurity is a necessary condition for national security;
- reference to how cybersecurity increases users' confidence in ICT;
- reference to how a secure cyber space affects social life;
- reference to the protection of children;
- reference to sources of cybercriminal activities including (h)activism, espionage, organized crimes, terrorism and cyberwars from nation states;
- reference to cyber laws.

The above list was constructed based on an extensive literature search and the authors' own points of view. For instance, reference to cyber laws was added to the list given its importance in prevention and response. The cybersecurity strategies and policies of the sample of developing countries will be evaluated based on the above components of content, and an index measuring the quality and comprehensiveness of the cybersecurity documents will be created based on the content analysis.

GLOBALIZATION OF CYBER SPACE

Cyber space and e-commerce have become a driving force for the globalization of the world economy, and countries that do not engage in e-commerce may put the competitiveness of their economies at risk. As a result, many firms and organizations in developing countries have become integral parts of global networks of production supply chains that increasingly use e-commerce mechanisms. Through these networks, entities in more developed countries induce developing-country enterprises to adopt new information technologies, organizational changes and business practices.

The diffusion of the use of cyber space in developing/emerging economies is relatively low. The main stumbling blocks are associated with regulatory, cultural and social factors, including (1) the lack of regulations dealing with data messages and recognition of electronic signatures; (2) the absence of specific legislation protecting consumers, intellectual property, personal data, information systems, and networks; (3) the dearth of appropriate fiscal and customs legislation covering electronic transactions; and (4) the absence and/or inadequacy of laws dealing with cybercrimes.

Moore's Law refers to the fact that today's technological advances are advancing at an accelerated pace. In addition, evidence from the breakthroughs in genetics and nanotechnology indicate that those developments are more pervasive and impactful. They are driving down computing and communications costs at a pace never seen in the history of humanity. Leading these transformations are the accelerated developments in ICT, biotechnology, and just-emerging nanotechnology. Information and communications technology involves innovations in hardware, software, telecommunications, database processing systems and microprocessors. In addition to the Internet of Things (IoT) is the diffusion of the mobile platform and the cloud. These innovations enable the processing and storage of enormous amounts of information, along with rapid distribution of information through communication networks. Moore's Law predicts the doubling of computing power every 12–18 months due to the speedy evolution of microprocessor technology.

Gilder's Law predicts the doubling of communications power every six months—a bandwidth explosion—due to advances in fiber optic network technologies. Individuals, households and institutions are linked in processing and executing a huge number of instructions in imperceptible timespans. This radically alters access to information and the structure of communication, thus extending the networked reach to all corners of the world. Today's technological revolution is associated with and fueled by another significant shift to economic globalization that is creating pockets of economic power around the world. Those two developments reinforce each other. Globalization boosts technological progress with the competition and incentives of the global marketplace and the world's financial and scientific resources. The global marketplace is based on technological changes, with technology being a driving force in market competition. Those developing countries that can create the necessary infrastructure will lead the group of countries standing in line to participate in new global business models of outsourcing, intermediation and supply and value chain integration. In developing countries, as the user base expands, this will lead to reduction in the cost structure, and as technologies are adapted to a country's local needs, the potential of cyber space will be unlimited. The organization of work must be revamped if national economies are to perform more effectively in a global market. Practitioners, theorists and futurists alike concur that the challenge for countries that want to maximize their global presence involves structuring relationships and the flow of secure information so that the right parties can obtain it at the right time. Information technology and e-commerce initiatives play critical roles in the strategy of global competition. Countries reap the biggest benefits not by superimposing computers on top of old work processes but by restructuring those processes and the national culture. This strategy is to move always in the direction of creating new and more advanced economic and business capacities. Through the standardization of messages and business processes, today's market makers will create interoperability among markets. They will serve also as guarantors of predictable, trustworthy behaviors among trading partners, giving entrepreneurs the confidence that they need to take their great ideas into the market and build virtual businesses. Another crucial step is to establish standard specifications for business processes—the ways in which messages are generated and acted upon once they are received.

Technology to support this vast interconnected global commerce network is maturing rapidly due, in large part, to the great progress being made in establishing standard specifications for building commerce messages dealing with contracts, purchase orders, invoices and so forth. These are mainly all activities associated with the inner and outer value chain. One of the global consequences of IT, however, is the international concern about the risks and dangers that developed as well as developing economies may face in the wide application of IT. One such risk may be found in the proliferation of criminal activities in cyber space.

REVAMPING THE LEGAL SYSTEM

Many studies suggest that the key determinants of economic development are the accumulation of physical and human capital and technological improvements. Traditional neoclassical growth theory emphasizes physical capital accumulation whereas endogenous growth theory presumes that investment in human capital and technological progress are the main sources of economic growth. More recently, and as an extension to neoclassical models, Mankiw et al. (1992) have shown that physical and human capital are important determinants of growth. Nevertheless, it remains an open question whether these factors are the real sources of economic development. There is reason to believe that if physical or human capital enrichment or technological improvements are taking place, the real growth factors must already have been unbound. Accordingly, physical and human capital and technology should be seen as proximate causes of growth. The changing value proposition in the knowledge economy is triggering a revolution in the way businesses and governments carry out their jobs.

The Internet always did have its own complicated ethics, and Internet-based ethics were set aside by old style management principles. This is radically shifting. Internet-based ethics are becoming the rules of the game. For example, not only does business-to-business supply-chain management provide huge efficiencies and significant bottom line enhancement but its deep integration allows partners to see into and through other organizations. As a consequence, decision makers are often privy to their competitors' internal strengths and weaknesses, trade secrets, unique know-how, market positioning, key personnel, and other valuable economic assets.

In summary, perhaps the most profound ethical changes in the New Economy are going on internally, inside the organization and at the firm level. In the New Economy, where knowledge, not equipment, drives profits, employees can no longer be considered 'outsiders'. They are the source of competitive advantage. The traditional command-and-control model of management is rapidly being replaced by decentralized teams of individuals motivated by their ownership in the corporation. Value in the New Economy is being fundamentally redefined. As a result, transparency and the rule of law are becoming two of the keys to success in the twenty-first century. In e-business circles, transparency is no longer a rhetorical word. It is the rule of the game. It is unarguably recognized that the IT revolution will have significant long-run effects on the economy and that the principal effects are more likely to be microeconomic than macroeconomic. As a result, the new information economy will require changes in the way the government provides property rights, institutional frameworks and 'rules of the game' that underpin the market economy. Two main reasons underlie these changes; first is the pace of technological progress in the IT sector, which is very rapid and will continue to be very rapid for the foreseeable future. For example, at the end of the 1950s, there were 2000 computers processing 10 000 instructions per second. Today, Gartner estimates that the overall shipments of devices including PCs and tablets will surpass 2.5 billion units (Gartner, 2014). Forrester Research (2008) predicted that the number of personal computers would reach 2 billion by the end of 2015. Forrester Research's forecast was based on the assumption that from 2003 to 2015 the total number of personal computers in the world would increase annually by 12 percent. By the end of 2014, there were more than 2 billion personal computers used worldwide (Quora.com, 2017). As the IT sector of the economy becomes a larger share of the total economy, the overall rate of productivity growth will increase toward the rate of productivity growth in the IT sector. Secondly, the computers, switches, cables and programs that are the products of today's leading sectors are general-purpose technologies. As a result, advances in high-technology affect all aspects of the economy, thereby leading to larger overall effects. These micro-economic effects will have long-lasting and far-reaching impacts on the economy. As a result, the role of the government in developed and developing economies needs to be re-examined. Since the creation of knowledge is cumulative, the importance of intellectual property rights becomes more critical in the new information economy. Three issues are interrelated: property rights over ideas; incentives to fund research and development; and the exchange of information among researchers.

The new information economy is 'Schumpeterian' rather than 'Smithian'. In a Schumpeterian economy, the production of goods exhibits increasing returns to scale. Under these conditions, the competitive equilibrium is not the likely outcome—setting price equal to marginal cost does not allow the firm to recover the large fixed costs. However, government regulation or government subsidies to cover fixed costs destroy the entrepreneurial spirit and replace it with 'group-think and red-tape defects of administrative bureaucracy' (Hakkio, 2001). In addition, when innovation becomes the principal source of wealth, temporary monopoly power and profits may be essential to stimulate innovation. In a Brookings study on the economic impact of the Internet, a group of scholars estimated that the increased use of the Internet could add 0.25 to 0.5 percent to productivity growth over the next five years (Brookings Institute, 2007). Most of the impacts come from reducing the cost of data-intensive transactions (ordering, invoicing, accounting and recruiting), from improved management of supply chains, from increased competition, and from increased efficiency of the wholesale and retail trade. In addition, many of the benefits of IT may result in improved standards of living, even though measured gross domestic product is unaffected.

The emergence of the information economy has been a key feature of faster productivity growth for many economies, developed and developing. Information technology has affected productivity in two ways. First, the IT sector itself has contributed directly to stronger productivity. Computers and other IT hardware have become better and cheaper, leading to increases in investment, employment and output of the IT sector. Secondly, advances in technology have also increased productivity in the more traditional sectors of the economy: financial services, business services, and the retail and distribution industries. In the US, economic policy has contributed to a revival in productivity growth. Policies to maintain domestic competition and increase international competition have been stressed. Funds have been provided to support basic research and education. Also, and most importantly, the mix of monetary and fiscal policy has lowered interest rates and encouraged investment. The information economy can improve the effectiveness of monetary policy by allowing the private sector to better anticipate future central bank actions. Central banks typically operate by affecting overnight interest rates. By affecting current overnight rates and, most importantly, by affecting market expectations of future rates, monetary policy can affect financial market prices such as long-term interest rates, exchange rates and equity prices. These prices will have the greatest effect on economic activity.

GLOBAL COOPERATION AND A THRIVING CYBER SPACE

Cyber space is one of the most complex legal frontlines today; the Internet diffusion has been growing at an increased rate between 2000 and 2017; it is estimated that Internet diffusion increased at an average rate of 290 percent globally, and presently an estimated 3.5 billion people per year are surfing the Internet. Developing/emerging countries in Africa and Asia have accounted for the largest chunk of the increase. The Internet diffusion rate was 7.3 percent in 2009; that number jumped to 49.7 percent in Asia and 29 percent in Africa in 2017 (statista.com, 2017). Cybersecurity and cybercrime, including enormous and synchronized attacks against countries' vital information infrastructure and attackers' misuse of the Internet, are activities of major concern to society in general and developing economies in particular. In addition, the costs associated with cyberattacks are substantial, not only when it comes to lost revenues and inconvenience caused by network inoperability but, and most recently, in cybercrimes they constitute a prime obstacle to the diffusion of e-commerce and e-government in developing economies. Thus governments have an important role in developing control mechanisms in the form of laws and legislation in order to minimize the rate and severity of cybercrimes to speed up Internet diffusion. Setting inappropriate policies and complementary services, particularly affecting the telecommunications sector, other infrastructure, human capital, and the investment environment, severely constrain Internet access in developing countries. The major impediment to the growth and success of cyber use in many developing and emerging economies is still poor telecommunications infrastructure. Required telecommunications facilities include transmission facilities connecting a country's domestic network to the greater Internet, the domestic Internet backbone, and connections from homes and businesses to the backbone network. The defects of domestic telecommunications services may be less important for the larger firms in developing countries; these firms may find it profitable to invest in telecommunications facilities (such as wireless) that bypass the local network. A growing number of African Internet sites, for instance, are hosted on servers in Europe or the US due to the poor infrastructure in those countries. Hence, even traffic that originates and terminates domestically can cost the same as international transmission.

The high cost of Internet access, the lack of local loop infrastructure necessary for basic dial-up modem access, and the poor quality of the local loop infrastructure that does exist all impede connections to the domestic backbone. Country comparisons show a strong relationship between usage price and Internet penetration. For many developing countries, the most important issue is the lack of telephone service to homes and businesses.

Despite increases in rates of telephone line penetration during the 1990s and the first half of the 2000s, the average number of telephone lines per capita was close to 5 percent for Africa. The most popular alternatives by which developing countries can overcome inadequate local loop infrastructure are shared facilities or wireless local loop. Shared facilities, which involve local entrepreneurs selling the use of a computer with Internet access, are a fast and relatively cheap way of increasing Internet use. Wireless and satellite technologies also provide an alternative to the high costs and inefficiencies of many domestic telecommunications systems. Although currently used primarily for voice, mobile phones are increasingly acting as better devices for many of the usual Internet applications. Cellular phones in some developing countries have experienced strong growth rates and relatively high penetration, similar to those in industrial countries. The United Arab Emirates (UAE) leads the Middle East and Africa in mobile phone penetration; in 2017, for instance, the mobile phone penetration rate was estimated at 228 percent. On average, however, for developing countries as a group, mobile phone penetration remains well below industrial-country levels. Poor infrastructure services (other than telecommunications) are an important constraint on the use of cyber space in developing economies. Frequent and long power interruptions can seriously interfere with data transmission and systems performance; to get around this problem, many Bangalore software firms are using their own generators or relying on portable solar power generators, for example (eMarketer, 2015). The lack of safeguards against fraud can severely restrict credit card purchases, the most common means of conducting transactions over the Internet. For example, many consumers in the Gulf countries of Saudi Arabia, UAE and Kuwait are unwilling to purchase goods over the Internet because credit card companies will not compensate holders for fraudulent use of cards (in many industrial countries, cardholders have only a limited exposure to loss). A critical mass of highly skilled labor is needed in developing countries to supply the necessary applications, provide support, and disseminate relevant technical knowledge for e-commerce. The workforce in many developing countries lacks a sufficient supply of these skills, and the demand for this specialized labor from industrial countries has further strained the supply of this labor in developing countries. Several regulatory impediments to the widespread adoption of cyber space activities exist in many developing countries. Duties and taxes on computer hardware and software and communication equipment increase the expense of connecting to the Internet. For example, a computer imported into some African countries may be taxed at rates exceeding 50 percent (UNCTAD, 2015). The overall environment for private sector activities is a significant determinant of Internet service diffusion. An open foreign direct investment regime helps promote technology diffusion, which is important to the growth of e-commerce. Government must provide a supportive legal framework for electronic transactions, including recognition of digital signatures; legal admissibility of electronic contracts; and the establishment of data storage requirements in paper form, intellectual property rights for digital content, liability of Internet service providers, privacy of personal data, and mechanisms for resolving disputes.

A number of international organizations have undertaken leadership in pushing toward cyber law development in both developing and developed economies. The International Telecommunication Union (ITU) is identified as a leader in this domain; it launched the Global Security Agenda in November 2007, and formed a High-Level Experts Group to look into the issues and develop proposals for long-term strategies to promote cybersecurity. This group is currently working with the International Multilateral Partnership Against Cyber-Threats (IMPACT), a group sponsored by the government of Malaysia, with the aim of putting together an early warning system for cyberattacks. Another initiative undertaken by the ITU is COP, Child Online Protection, to develop safe guiding principles of surfing the Internet for children. The ITU also developed the Global Cybersecurity Index (GCI) in April 2014; the index measures a country's readiness to combat cybercrimes in terms of legal, compliance and technical measures. The index also assesses the level of capacity building at the national level (ITU, 2014). In a nutshell, the GCI is a measure of each nation state's level of cybersecurity development; it essentially seeks to establish a framework of incentives to motivate countries in an attempt to strengthen their efforts in cybersecurity. The fundamental goal is to help create a worldwide culture of cybersecurity and help provide mechanisms to incorporate security at the highest levels of information and communication technologies.

The Council of Europe has developed what is thought by many to be the most comprehensive treaty to protect people against cybercriminals. It developed the Cybercrime Convention to resolve legal disputes and take forward a universal, collective system to take legal action against cybercriminals. The idea for the Convention on Cybercrime was founded on a number of studies carried out by the Council in 1989 and 1995. As a result, the Council created a committee to draft this convention; once it was completed, it opened for signing and ratification in November 2001. At the writing of this book, 47 countries have signed and/or ratified the convention, 29 of which can be classified as emerging economies (Council of Europe, 2015).

CYBERSECURITY AND THE LEGAL SYSTEM

The idea that technology is a catalyst of economic growth and development is shared by many all around the world. ICT is perceived to be a crucial element for economic growth, social equity and political stability. This view is a common denominator of many decision makers in emerging economies, where the diffusion of the Internet is high and the technology infrastructure is well developed as compared to other developing countries. Emerging economies' governments are infusing more money and deploying human and technical resources in an effort to increase Internet use and diffusion within their countries. A small country like Qatar with a population of about 2.2 million people, for instance, has a 97.4 percent Internet diffusion rate as of 31 December 2016, ranked second worldwide after Bermuda (Internetworldstat.com, 2017). Qatar has overtaken Singapore and many of the developed countries. In another Gulf Cooperation Country (GCC), the United Arab Emirates (UAE), where the Internet diffusion rate stands at 93 percent, broadband access is available via various means: ADSL, WiFi, Fiber to the Home (FttP), leased lines and mobile networks. In a large number of emerging economies, broadband has become much more commonplace in the past few years, as exhibited by the rising number of broadband subscriptions attributed to fiber. Brazil is another emerging economy that has placed a lot of faith in digitization; the 2016 Internet diffusion rate of Brazil stood at 66.4 percent.

Understanding the potential of making use of ICT for both social and economic development, many emerging countries have undertaken unwavering initiatives to develop their digital economies. In general, both governments and the private sectors have been effective in creating online services and contents that form the foundation of the digital economy. Governments of many of the emerging countries have made the development of the ICT industry a national priority and to this end they are marching in the direction of digitization. It is worth noting that, in addition to investing in the hardware side of the technology, many have developed the soft side of their digital economies, including instituting policies and streamlining business processes; these will be discussed further in the book. As an example, spending on IT products and services in the Middle East exceeded US$32 billion in 2014. Consumers, the public sector, and the communications and financial service sectors were the leading IT investors in the Middle East region, accounting for approximately 74 percent of the total IT spending in 2014. Public sector investments are geared toward improving government services, education and healthcare services; these sectors continue to be key drivers in the countries of the GCC (IDC, 2015). Saudi Arabia's spending on ICT alone is expected to exceed US$37 billion in 2015; healthcare and energy are the two sectors that will receive the lion's share of ICT investments in the kingdom.

With increased investment in ICT and more digitization, the threat of cyberattacks, hacktivism and cyberwars will undoubtedly increase. Unfortunately, while the development of information technology increases linearly, the risks associated with cyber space increase exponentially. In addition, while the development of the hard side of ICT increases steadily, policies and laws dealing with crimes associated with cyber space are lagging years behind. Risks associated with cyber warfare in emerging economies and the countries' capabilities to deal with those risks are, at best, based on guesswork. Cyber readiness, both offensive and defensive, is hard to evaluate and assess with any degree of accuracy. All we state at this juncture is that as sophisticated, digital technology becomes accessible, more and more cybercriminals will venture out. It is a known fact that the evolution and development of e-commerce and online financial transactions has given criminals new tools to move traditional crimes over to cyber space as new technology takes over older approaches (Sapa, 2013).

A report published in June 2014 states that the cost of cybercrime for the global economy has been estimated at US$445 billion yearly; close to 800 million people around the world had their personally identifying information (PII) and/or their identity stolen in 2013 (Williams, 2014). The total cost is estimated to surpass the US$6 trillion mark by 2021.

Despite the above stated statistics, an accurate assessment of cybercrime data and its financial cost is incalculable. Two factors lead to compounding this predicament: (1) the reluctance of businesses and governmental agencies to report cybercrimes, which can lead to reduced trust in governmental agencies and negative financial implications for businesses; (2) the fast development of technology, which makes cybercrimes hard to detect given the new methods used by cybercriminals to commit their acts.

Emerging and developing nations have been slow-moving in crafting and implementing cybersecurity laws, policies and strategies despite mounting international dangers to, and rising cyber threats on, Internet-connected systems globally. Being connected amplifies the negative impact of a cyberattack; as the number of cyberattacks increases linearly, the damage, socially, politically and economically, increases exponentially. While a number of countries around the world have taken some steps to develop their own laws and guidelines concerning domestic law enforcement, cybercrime by its very nature is often global and multi-national. In addition, many of the laws developed to deal with cyber-crimes do not have enough teeth and, as such, do not act as a deterrence to criminals. Just as an example, the UAE established special cybercrime units to deal with crimes within and outside its territory (Al-Jandaly, 2016). This is in addition to establishing dedicated police units to deal specifically with cybercrimes. These measures are value-adding but what is missing is the necessary training of those involved in combating cybercrimes and the required public awareness.

Given the many problems related to financial, social and political costs associated with an insecure cyber space, the development of cyber-security policies and strategies becomes a necessity both for emerging and developed economies. The prime objective is to minimize the negative impact that might hinder the growth and development of these economies.

At the time of writing this book, few developing and emerging economies possess suitable policies and practices geared to ensure a secure cyber space environment in an effort to support their public and private sectors and institutions and private individuals. The relatively high levels of diffusion of the Internet and worldwide networking, in addition to imperfect governance structure, make cybercrime a rich area for hackers and cybercriminals in emerging and developing countries, especially cyber terrorists. The authors maintain that the necessary legal structure aimed at dealing with cybercriminal activities lags five to ten years behind the advancement in technology and networking.

The literature on cybersecurity policy and strategies has been growing steadily over the past 15 years. Most of the literature, however, is geared toward the countries of the North. Given the prospective high rate of Internet diffusion in the countries of the South, especially in the countries in Africa, Asia and Latin America, it is imperative for us to turn our attention to crafting cybersecurity strategies in emerging and developing countries.

In developed countries, policy makers and legislatures have tried to levy severe penalties on cybercrime, including long jail terms and heavy financial fines, but, so far, those policies have not been successful in curbing the problem. Even in the most advanced countries, cyber laws have not measured up to cyberattacks and threats. In developing countries specific laws dealing with cybercrimes have not yet been fully crafted (Karake and Al Qasimi, 2010). On the international front, a number of NGOs have strived to standardize cybercrime laws in a number of countries. As an example, the Council of Europe's Convention on Cyber-crime helped establish some standards for cybercrime, including hacking, fraud, virus writing and child pornography. While the impact of these efforts has been minimal, as societies we need to keep supporting those global efforts since the global nature of the Internet dictates a global response. All developing nations—whether large, small, rich or poor—must develop well-structured strategies guided by international standards dealing with cybercrime laws and enforcement, in addition to proactive strategies aimed at minimizing the occurrence of those incidents.

One of the main challenges of enforcing cybercrime laws is jurisdiction; the cybercriminal, the intended target of the crime and the location where the attack originates are often in different locations. Consequently, enforcement dictates cooperation among a number of countries, which can be challenging and difficult to manage, especially if the actions taken by the cybercriminal are not considered to be a crime in one of the countries involved. Individuals in one nation can, via the Internet, violate a cybercrime law in another nation without physically being there. In addition, the country in which they reside may not have criminalized the action, so they would not physically be in a country where a law was broken, hence they will be protected from punishment for their crimes. The European Convention addresses the jurisdiction issue by making the country criminalize the unwanted actions and cooperate in the investigation of the crime. However, attribution remains difficult, but the Convention emphasizes the fact that more cooperation among countries would eventually lead to more attribution.

It is important to emphasize that laws and punishment alone do not deter cybercriminals; for cyber strategies and policies to be effective they must be proactive, in that, in addition to those defensive mechanisms, countries must use preventive techniques to increase the security of cyber space. Cooperation with other countries through the signing of treaties and the crafting of well-designed cybersecurity strategies and policies are two proactive approaches to curbing cyberattacks.

EXAMPLES OF CYBERATTACKS FROM GLOBAL POINTS OF VIEW

The cost associated with cyberattacks is extremely large; as an example, Estonia's online infrastructure suffered a severe attack that caused the interruption and the blocking of the functioning of its government institutions, public and private economic sectors, and the private use of computer networks by Estonian citizens for a few weeks. In April 2007, cyberattacks were elevated to warfare when it was claimed and later proven by the Estonians that a foreign government had launched a series of parallel and coordinated cyberattacks on the Estonian public and private sectors. Estonian banks, parliament, ministries, newspapers and TV were all paralyzed. The costs to Estonia, social, financial and political, were huge. However, something good came out of these cyberattacks: Estonia has spent the last few years becoming one of the most safeguarded countries against potential cybercrimes. Today, almost eight years later, the model developed by Estonia is being studied and applied by many countries looking to develop and build their national cybersecurity strategies and capabilities. This is of particular importance since the Estonians have a public–private business cybersecurity partnership model that is the envy of many countries (Rehman, 2013).

Another example that has been a target for cyberattacks is Iran. In the fall of 2010, it was reported that a new strain of malware was rapidly spreading on the Internet, with concentrations of the virus in Indonesia, India and Iran domains. After the discovery of this self-replicating worm (named Stuxnet), it was discovered that the worm was designed to target several previously unknown weaknesses in Windows, known as zero-day exploits, and alter the operation of Siemens Simatic process logic controller computers, which are used in power plants, production lines and other heavy industry. The danger of the virus was magnified by its capability of masking its presence while controlling and monitoring the infected systems. Stuxnet has been able to cause the destruction of about 1000 of the 5000 Iranian centrifuge enrichment devices. It was estimated that Stuxnet set back the Iranian nuclear program by two years.

Saudi Arabia's Aramco is another example. In August 2012, Aramco's computer network was attacked by a computer virus infecting more than 30 000 of its computer servers. The world's largest oil producer, with annual sales of more than US$200 billion, was crippled for a couple of weeks; it took the company (and the country) two weeks to go back to a semi-normal operational environment of its networks and somehow recover from the damage. Later named Shamoon, the virus caused substantial interruption to the world's largest oil producer. It was reported that both drilling and production data were lost, including data provided by multinational companies such as Santa Fe, Ocean and Schlumberger. The Shamoon virus also hit Aramco's management offices throughout the country as well as its offices worldwide (Houston and The Hague); the state-of-the-art Exploration and Petroleum Engineering Center in Dhahran were also affected. Up until the attack on Aramco, hacktivists had usually launched distributed denial of service (DDoS) attacks, in which they flood a website with requests until it crashes. However, the cyberattack on Aramco was the first substantial use of malware in a hacktivist attack.

The above-mentioned examples give an indication of the devastating economic cost of cyberattacks and the importance of creating a governance structure for cyber space both at the individual country level and at the international level.

CHAPTER OVERVIEW

Enforcing Cybersecurity in Developing and Emerging Economies: Institutions, Laws and Policies is a theory-based, empirical investigation to describe the linkage and determinants of the development, implementation of quality strategies and policies of national cybersecurity. The book's six chapters are organized as follows:

- **Chapter 1** has provided an overview of the entire book and has established the context for the whole book. Importance of the research at hand is emphasized, along with the theories used, the geographic area of implementation, the methods used, and the methodology applied.
- **Chapter 2** provides an overview of the move to the digital economy and the state of technology and security in cyber space. Coverage of the threat of cybercrime to economies and businesses is introduced in this chapter. The chapter also covers the recent technological development and its impact on facilitating cyber-criminal activities, especially in the financial, healthcare and energy sectors, the three industries most affected by cybercrimes.
- **Chapter 3** reviews the literature on the different approaches to cybersecurity including the economic-based approach, the political/social-based approach, the resource-based approach and the deterrence-based approach.
- **Chapter 4** is devoted to the content analysis of a number of emerging and developing countries' engagement in the information age and the importance of cybersecurity policies and strategies to those countries. This chapter will also cover the hypotheses to be tested in Chapter 5.
- **Chapter 5** is devoted to model testing, data analysis and presentation of the results; the analysis will reveal why some countries are more inclined to develop and implement what we refer to as mature national cybersecurity policies and strategies which will serve as a foundation for a mature cyber society.
- **Chapter 6** consists of a summary, concluding remarks, practical implications of findings, and recommendations for future research.

This book aims to take a step toward an empirical/theoretical framework for understanding the impact of mature cybersecurity policies and strategies and their determinants in terms of growth and development of emerging and developing economies.

Basically, a framework that is grounded in economic theory is developed. The framework uses core constructs that appear central to economic-based, social/political-based, resource-based and technology diffusion literature and provides a fine-grained understanding of cyber space adoption processes by public and private sector entities in developing and emerging countries. In so doing, this book considers how each exchange encounter is shaped by, and in turn shapes, relational characteristics, which form the bases for growth and development.

This book is aimed at the 'low to middle' level of rigor. It is not designed to compete with extremely sophisticated modeling or quantitatively oriented books. Actually, this book does not know of any competitor. This level of rigor makes the book attractive to any student, professional, practitioner, or policy maker interested in finding answers to questions such as:

1. What are the determinants to the development of quality and comprehensive cybersecurity policies and strategies?
2. What countries have been more vigilant in the development of cybersecurity policies and implementation of cybersecurity strategies?
3. What are the components of an ideal cybersecurity policy and strategy for developing economies?

The major thrust of the book, which evaluates the experience of cyber space policies and strategies, and their relation to cyber laws and regulations in developing and emerging economies from economic-based, political/social-based, and resource-based theory perspectives, is unique and innovative in nature.

The features of uniqueness and innovativeness, coupled with the radical changes in the use of governmental resources to improve the effectiveness and efficiency of an economy, and the effects of these changes on the economic structure of a country, make this book useful to many disciplines.

The book is inspired by a number of factors, including (1) the importance of the subject at hand and (2) the lack of empirical research on the subject. Most of the work done by others is descriptive in nature and applies mainly to developed, advanced economies. This book brings economic concepts into the picture of developing cybersecurity policies and strategies and adopting a cyber law model by using a number of theories as a vehicle of analysis.

CONCLUSION

The Internet and cyber space revolution is not only changing the technology of the workplace but is fundamentally redefining the way that countries design their growth and development strategies. Electronic governments and the B2B world with its e-markets, customer focus, and deeply integrated corporate and economic relationships are driving growth and development of economies at e-speed and creating value in different ways.

The key to survival in the relatively new world of cyber space depends upon governmental leaders' ability to adapt to a new, more collaborative, corporate-type and transparent competition model. This new reality presents major challenges to traditional ways of governing and leading economic growth and development. Economic development is the process of creating wealth by mobilizing human, financial, physical, natural and capital resources to produce (generate) marketable goods and services.

The government's role is to influence the process for the benefit of the various stakeholders in the country. Economic development, then, is fundamentally about enhancing the factors of productive capacity—land, labor, capital and technology—of a national, state or local economy.

Early economic development theory was but merely an extension of conventional economic theory that equated 'development' with growth and industrialization. As a result, Latin American, Asian and African countries were seen mostly as 'underdeveloped' countries, that is, 'primitive' versions of European nations that could, with time, 'develop' the institutions and standards of living of Europe and North America.

Economic growth is caused by improvements in the quantity and quality of the factors of production that a country has available, that is, land, labor, capital and enterprise. Conversely, economic decline may occur if the quantity or quality of any of the factors of production falls. Increases in the supply of labor can increase economic growth. Increases in the population can increase the number of young people entering the labor force.

Increases in the population can also lead to an increase in market demand, thus stimulating production. However, if the population grows at a faster rate than the level of GDP, the GDP per capita will fall. It is not simply the amount of labor and skills that will lead to economic growth.

It is often the quality of that labor. This will depend on the educational provision in countries. Improving the skills of the workforce is seen as an important key to economic growth. Many developing countries have made enormous efforts to provide universal primary education. As more and more capital is used, labor has to be better trained in the skills to use it. It should always be remembered that education spending involves an opportunity cost in terms of current consumption and thus it is often referred to as investment spending on human capital.

REFERENCES

Al-Jandaly, B. (2016). Dubai fares well against cyber criminals, *Gulf News*, 12 September, accessed 17 May 2017.

Barney, J., Ketchen, D. and Wright, M. (2011). The future of resource-based theory, *Journal of Management*, **37**(5): 1299–315.

Brookings Institute (2007). The effects of broadband deployment on output and employment: A cross-sectional analysis of US data, accessed 9 October 2016 at http://www3.brookings.edu/ views/papers/crandall/200706/itan.pdf.

Council of Europe (2015). Convention on Cybercrime, accessed at www.coe.int.

eMarketer (2015). United Arab Emirates leads Middle East and Africa in mobile phone penetration, accessed 20 December 2015 at http://www.emarketer. com/Article/United-Arab-Emirates-Leads-Middle-East-Africa-Mobile-Phone Penetration/1011971#sthash.GsgFRWwb.dpuf.

Forrester Research (2008). In 2008 the number of personal computers in the world will reach one billion, accessed 2 August 2016 at http://www.science-portal.org/in/7.

Gartner (2014). Gartner says worldwide traditional PC, tablet, ultramobile and mobile phone shipments on pace to grow 7.6 percent in 2014, accessed 23 July 2015 at http://www.gartner.com/newsroom/id/2645115.

Google (2015). Google's research on ad injecting malware shows millions of its visitors are affected, accessed 5 March 2016 at http://thenextweb.com/ insider/2015/05/07/googles-research-on-ad-injecting-malware-shows-millions-of-visitors-are-affected/#gref.

Hakkio, C.S. (2001). Economic policy for the information economy, accessed 11 September 2015 at www.kansascityfka.com/publicat/q5Sympos/2001/papers/ S02/Summ.pdf.

IDC (2015). Gulf Cooperation Council (GCC) Oil and Gas Vertical 2014–2019 IT Spending, accessed 5 March 2016 at https://www.idc.com/getdoc.jsp? containerId=CEMA23096.

International Telecommunication Union (ITU) (2014). *Global Cybersecurity Index (GSI)*, Geneva: United Nations.

International Telecommunication Union (ITU) (2015). *Regulation of the Internet of Things*, accessed 30 January 2018 at https://www.itu.int/en/ITU-D/ Conferences/GSR/Documents/GSR2015/Discussion_papers_and_Presentations/ GSR_DiscussionPaper_IoT.pdf.

Internetworldstat.com (2017). Usage and Population Statistics, accessed 3 November 2017 at http://www.internetworldstats.com.

Karake, Z. and Al Qasimi, L. (2010). *Cyber Law and Cyber Security in Developing and Emerging Economies*, Cheltenham, UK and Northampton, MA, USA: Edward Elgar Publishing.

Labrique, A. (2017). The mobile revolution: A catalyst for global health systems, accessed 1 February 2018 at https://webcache.googleusercontent.com/search ?q=cache:4D0WQq-ddPIJ:https://globalhealth.nd.edu/events/2017/03/21/the-mobile-revolution-a-catalyst-for-global-health-systems/+&cd=1&hl=en&ct= clnk&gl=us&client=safari.

Lockett, A. and Wild, A. (2014). Bringing history (back) into the resource-based view, *Business History*, **56**(3): 372–90.

Luiijf, E., Besseling, K. and De Graaf, P. (2013). Nineteen national cyber security strategies, *International Journal of Critical Infrastructures*, **9**(1/2): 3–31.

Mankiw, N.G., Romer, D. and Weil, D.N. (1992). A contribution to the empirics of economic growth, *Quarterly Journal of Economics*, **107**(2): 407–37.

Microsoft (2013). Linking cybersecurity policy and performance, Microsoft, February, accessed 17 December 2017 at http://aka.ms/securityatlas.

NDTV (2016). Cyber-security: A $35-billion opportunity, to create 1 million jobs: Nasscom, accessed October 2018 at https://gadgets.ndtv.com/internet/news/cyber-security-a-35-billion-opportunity-to-create-1-million-jobs-nasscom-827198.

Nexleaf.org (2017). Real-time data for immunization, accessed 12 December 2017 at http://nexleaf.org/impact/coldtrace-real-time-data/.

OECD (1986). *Computer-related Criminality: Analysis of the Legal Politics in the OECD Area*, ICCP report no. 10, Paris: OECD.

OECD (2012). *Cybersecurity Policy Making at a Turning Point: Analysing a New Generation of National Cybersecurity Strategies for the Internet Economy*, accessed 13 December 2017 at http://www.oecd.org/sti/ieconomy/cybersecurity %20policy%20making.pdf.

OECD (2017). OECD Digital Economy Outlook, accessed 20 December 2017 at http://www.keepeek.com/Digital-Asset-Management/oecd/science-and-technology/oecd-digital-economy-outlook-2017_9789264276284-en#page248.

Panetta, L. (2012). Remarks by Secretary Panetta on cybersecurity to the business executives for national security, New York City, 11 October.

Parker, D. (1979). *Ethical Conflicts in Computer Science and Technology*, Arlington, VA: AFIPS Press.

Parker, D. (1989). *Computer Crime: Criminal Justice Resource Manual*, Menlo Park, CA: SRI International.

Quora.com (2017). How many PC exist in the world?, accessed 16 January 2019 at https://www.quora.com/How-many-PC-exist-in-the-world.

Rehman, S. (2013). Estonia's lessons in cyberwarfare, *US News and World Report*, 14 January.

Sapa (2013). 70% of South Africans have fallen victim to cybercrime, accessed 5 March 2016 at http://www.timeslive.co.za/scitech/2013/11/04/70-of-south-africans-have-fallen-victim-to-cyber-crime.

Sharman, J. (2017). Cyber-attack that crippled the NHS systems hits Nissan car factory in Sunderland and Renault in France, *The Independent*, 13 May.

Statista.com (2017). Percentage of population using the Internet in the United States from 2000 to 2017, accessed 12 January 2018 at http://www.statista.com/statistics/209117/us-internet-penetration/.

Symantec (2014). 2013 Internet Security Threat Report, accessed 1 April 2016 at http://www.symantec.com/content/en/us/enterprise/other_resources/b-istr_main_report_v19_21291018.en-us.pdf.

Symantec (2015). Underground black market: Thriving trade in stolen data, malware, and attack services, November, accessed 2 April 2015 at http://www.symantec.com/connect/blogs/underground-black-market-thriving-trade-stolen-data-malware-and-attack-services.

Symantec (2016). 2015 Internet security threat report, accessed 2 April 2016 at https://www.symantec.com/security-center/threat-report.

Symantec (2017). 2017 Internet security threat report, accessed 22 December 2017 at https://www.websecurity.symantec.com/security-topics/istr-2017-infographic.

Tittle, C.R. (1969). Crime rates and legal sanctions, *Social Problems*, **16**: 409–23.

Tobias, S. (2014). 2014: The year in cyberattacks, *Newsweek*, 31 December.

UNCTAD (2015). At 11.4 per cent of the value of imports, African countries paid more for international transport than any other region in 2005–2014, New York: United Nations.

Williams, J. (2014). Net losses: Estimating the global cost of cybercrime. Center for Strategic and International Studies, June.

Chapter 2

INTRODUCTION

There is no doubt that the technology utilized by a great number of businesses, including financial institutions, especially in developing and emerging countries, is becoming more and more diverse, advanced and innovative. The rapid pace with which innovation in information technology has evolved has led people to rethink the way in which they handle their personal lives and direct their businesses. A recent report by the IDC (2018) estimates that the sale of smart mobile phones and other mobile devices will reach 2 billion items by 2022. Gartner indicates that by 2020 the 'Cloud Shift' will affect more than one trillion dollars in IT spending (Gartner, 2016). To put this into perspective, this is about 17 percent of the US GDP. In this age of the *Internet of Things* and the *cloud*, trust and security in cyber space have become the main ingredients.

The International Telecommunication Union (ITU) has identified five key factors to the success of a cybersecurity program at the national level: (1) a national strategy; (2) collaboration between government and industry; (3) a sound legal foundation to deter cybercrime; (4) a national incident management capability; and (5) a national awareness of the importance of cybersecurity (ITU, 2012).

Attacks and unauthorized uses on businesses and institutions include malicious activities such as theft or destruction of intellectual property, misuse and destruction by employees, and unauthorized access to information that leads to a loss of data integrity, as well as risks associated with viruses, spyware, worms and Trojan horses. These criminal activities weaken the trust of cyber users and lead to apprehension about using the Internet as a means to conduct business. Some of the cyberattacks are financially motivated, with the primary intention of embezzling money from targeted accounts; other attacks are state-sponsored, where hackers are motivated by their governments; hackers usually go after financial institutions in an effort to weaken the national infrastructure. Yet another type of attack is orchestrated and executed by hacktivists, who are motivated by political intentions. Hacktivists may, for instance, target financial institutions that support a government whose actions hackers are protesting against. All of these actions lead to erosion of trust in the financial sector in the country in question. Coupled with trust is the concept of deterrence. It is argued in this book that a well developed cybersecurity policy will act as a deterrent to would-be criminals.

When discussing 'trust', philosophers frequently refer to the party that displays trust in another as making itself vulnerable to the other party's behavior. The concepts of trust and security in cyber space have attracted a great deal of attention in recent management literature and empirical research. There has been discussion of what trust is, what it means, its impact on online activities, its contribution to the diffusion of activities in cyber space, and so on. Much of the literature has been in the organizational behavior field. More importantly, there has also been a growing use of the concept of trust in Internet-based businesses. The term *trust* is used by people concerned with information security and cyber space; the most popular domain for its usage has been research regarding authentication and the infrastructure for public key technology in a networked environment. The issue of how to exchange public keys and their certifications over the Internet has been important to the creators and users of public key application. However, the broader, more traditional usage of the word—beyond the specifications of certification formats for public keys—has increased with the rise of cyber activities.

The importance of trust in the use of the Internet as a means to transact business or a means of communication deserves special attention. The physical separation of the buyer and seller, the physical separation of the buyers and the merchandise, and the overall environment of perceived insecurity on the Internet provide unique challenges to Internet-based businesses to find ways in which to initiate and develop these cyber space relationships. Based on these limitations, the seller must develop a trustworthy relationship in order to make that initial sale, thus fostering customer loyalty. The lack of physical presence of the product and the physical distance between the buyer and seller make this a unique situation in which trust is of paramount importance. The development of this trust evolves over time as relationships grow between both parties. The pace at which customers are becoming connected to the Internet and the rate at which purchasing over the Internet is becoming conventional provide Internet-based businesses with greater opportunities in electronic commerce exchanges.

Business, as conducted online, is positioned to pump up in the next few years. Conventional marketing models, however, may not be sufficient to explain consumer behavior online. Such differences between store retailing and online retailing include the physical separation of the buyer and seller, the absence of a salesperson, the separation of the product and the buyer, and the ability of marketers to update product, price and distribution information immediately. These differences represent threats to e-marketers that must be overcome for consumers to initiate a purchase online.

Consumer loyalty is emerging as the marketplace currency for the twenty-first century. Marketers desire and seek it through building relationships with customers, yet it remains elusive. To acquire and hold this elusive currency would require a deep understanding of processes by which consumers maintain relational exchanges with providers, and how these processes in turn influence loyalty. This is especially the case for services as their inherent intangibility, heterogeneity and performance ambiguity pose challenges for forming and sustaining customer service provider relationships. Although this issue has received significant attention in the literature, some critical gaps remain. First, the literature has tended to view consumer relationships from the perspective of the marketer/service provider. Few researchers have used the consumers' perspective to examine relational exchanges. Likewise, much theoretical work for understanding relational exchanges in service contexts has been shaped by conceptualizations of exchange mechanisms involving inter-organizational partners (Berry, 1995). By contrast, theoretical work for inquisitive relational means from a consumer's perspective is not there. Thus, Buttle (1996) states that customers have no say in relationship marketing, and since relationships are intrinsically two-sided, this un-balanced focus is awkward. Second, the limited research that exists has tended mainly to attack either the economic or the psychological approach; as such, integrative endeavors have been lacking. For instance, researchers have had some success in using the economic principles of agency theory to understand contracts between consumers and providers. Equally, psychological approaches have tended to look at the role of consumer–provider trust in promoting relational exchanges and building trust (Garbarino and Johnson, 1999). Although both approaches have provided interesting findings, little attention has been given to how the economic and psychological approaches might work together to shape and influence consumer trust and loyalty in relational exchanges.

The Internet has proved of enormous potential benefit for consumers worldwide. Wider choice ranges, lower prices, and entirely new products have become available in many product categories such as books, CDs and travel packages, to consumers who are physically far away from the world's centers of traditional commerce. Amazon.com sells a large percentage of its products to foreign destinations. Trust can only exist if the consumer believes that the seller has both the ability and the motivation to deliver goods and services of the quality expected by the consumer.

This belief may be more difficult for an Internet-based business to create than it is for a conventional business. In cyber space, providers depend on an impersonal electronic storefront to act on their behalf. Additionally, the Internet lowers the resources required to enter and exit the marketplace. E-tailers face a situation in which consumer trust might be expected to be inherently low, and as such, certain strategies have to be developed and adopted to increase the level of trust in Internet-based businesses.

Notwithstanding the above, it is important to underline the very important fact that a multi-stakeholder cybersecurity policy-based model that includes government, private sector and civil society actors is a prescription for a safe, trusted and prosperous cyber space for countries in the North and the South.

CYBERCRIME IN THE FINANCIAL SECTOR

There is no doubt that one of the main targets of cybercrime is the banking/financial sector. As financial establishments move to digital networks like online banking and mobile transactions, the attack space grows, and there is more to protect. The banking sector environment is especially vulnerable to a wide range of cyber threats. Those in charge of information security have been investing significant resources in the implementation of diverse technologies designed to protect both data and information technology (IT) infrastructure from those threats. All of these investments can serve an important role in safeguarding today's highly IT-dependent financial institutions but, by themselves, they are insufficient. In fact, over-reliance on security technology can put a financial institution at risk because a large percentage of information security breaches are in reality the outcome of flawed human behaviors, rather than hardware or software weaknesses. The job of the regulatory agencies in these countries, dealing with developing, enacting and dictating rules and directions to cover all types of institutions, utilizing all kinds of technology to varying degrees, becomes a challenge. Major trends affecting the security issue in banking and financial institutions in emerging/developing countries are: (1) the increased complexity and coverage of technology; (2) the expansion of the number of financial institutions utilizing cutting-edge technologies; (3) the steady increase in

the number of cyber users, especially in conducting financial transactions; and (4) the lack of laws dealing with cybercrimes.

The main driver behind Internet banking is the massive benefits it
offers to customers and businesses. In addition to the reduction of
operational expenses, online banking leads to the creation of an
alternative distribution channel and provides banks with the opportunity
to increase their revenues by selling additional services. The diffusion
of cyber banking is slowed by a number of impediments, mainly
security in cyber space. When one considers banking in cyber space,
customer trust is absolutely vital and paramount; and, currently, this
trust is being focused more and more on technology-centered services.
Examples of issues associated with using cyber space to conduct
banking/financial activities include, but are not limited to, concern over
the hacking of passwords, theft of personally identifiable information
(PII), gaining access to a person's bank account number and credit card
number, and so on. It has to be emphasized here that in moving
forward, trust will be about ensuring the customer's investments, data
and identity are protected.

With respect to the state of the regulatory environment, the modus
operandi for agencies is playing catch-up at this point. Cybercrime laws
and regulation, especially when it comes to the financial/banking sector,
are not moving at the same pace as the technological advancement that
has taken place within the past ten years. More and more banking
services and transactions are moving away from the physical bricks-and-
mortar space to embracing a new business model based on the
philosophy of a customer gaining access to and utilizing his or her
finances whenever and wherever he or she wants. Mobile banking and in
general wireless data transmission appear as a target in the spotlight for
cybercriminals.

In 2016, Deloitte reports that cybersecurity was one of the major areas
for the financial sector and its institutions to deal with. To increase
cybersecurity, Deloitte's report calls for financial institutions to dedicate
more resources and adopt new ways, such as war gaming, drawing more
skilled experts, and increasing cooperation with private- and public-sector
entities. In addition, the report recommends improving investment in
detection hardware and expanding the authority of the chief information
security officer (CISO). A more recent survey of 40 banks by the New
York Department of Financial Services examined the role of third party
vendors and their notifications of cybersecurity breaches; the survey
found that only 30 percent of the institutions require third-party vendors
to provide them with information about cybersecurity breaches; the
concern here is that third-party vendors can provide a backdoor entrance

to hackers, allowing them to get hold of sensitive bank customer data. In addition, the survey found that fewer than half of the banks engage in on-site assessments of third party vendors. What was an eye opener in the survey was the role of US branches of foreign banks; it was found that those branches established tougher cybersecurity requirements than their domestic counterparts, by requiring multi-factor authentication—a process that involves more safeguards than a computer password (Deloitte, 2016).

The 2016 Global Economic Crime Survey published by PwC revealed that cybercrime has become the second most reported crime globally, stating that 54 percent of organizations worldwide have been hit by a form of cyberattack/crime in the past two years. The PwC study points out that one of the main targets of cybercriminal activities is the banking/financial sector. Banks from all over the world have been targets of cyberattacks (PwC, 2016).

Banks and financial institutions in developing and emerging countries are in need of more support and help when it comes to security and legislation. Security and data/information privacy, the global character of the provision of e-finance services, and entry by non-regulated new intermediaries are challenges faced by the financial regulators and financial services industry. The online environment leaves all the operations of a financial services firm susceptible to external and internal threats. Security of transactions and data privacy are increasingly matters of concern for regulators worldwide. Moreover, such threats can exist internally within the organization.

Pre-employment checks and security and continuous education become all the more pertinent in today's technology-intensive environment in which an employee can email enormous amounts of information in a matter of seconds. A report published by Verisign in 2015 alleges that Denial of Service (DoS) attacks are a global threat and not limited to any specific industry vertical, but the information technology and cloud verticals are prime targets because these services are used by multiple customers worldwide across both the private and public sectors (*PC Magazine*, 2016).

Spamming refers to the sending of unsolicited bulk messages to users. Although various techniques exist, the most common is email spam. Cybercriminals send out millions of emails to users, often including advertisements for services and/or products with malicious viruses attached to them. The first spam email appeared in 1978, but the frequency and maliciousness of spam have increased dramatically since. Recently, new data shows that 75 percent of all emails are spam email; China, the US and South Korea are the worst offenders. China topped the list, as the source of 23.1 percent of the world's spam, followed by the US (ranked second) with 19 percent of all spam, and South Korea, ranked third, with 13.9 percent of all spam (Stevenson, 2014).

The year of 2014 was full of stories of cybercriminal activities all around the world, with hackers, spammers and phishers causing chaos, and, in some cases, confusion among computer systems and consumers, causing credit and debit fraud numbers to soar. Experts and law enforcement officials worldwide who hunt down cybercrimes state that scams increased in the last half of 2014, as criminals took advantage of economic uncertainty and unease to attack both consumers and businesses. *BusinessWeek* termed 2014 the 'year of cybercrime'. Cybercriminals were engaged in sending out false emails and putting up bogus websites pretending to be banks, mortgage-service financial institutions, and even government agencies.

Mobile phones and Internet-based phone services have also been used to identify and attack victims, with the objective of stealing money or gaining information for identity theft. Cyber offensives on many banks doubled in 2014 in developed as well as emerging/developing countries around the world, including Mexico, Taiwan and Brazil. A 2014 study by McAfee found that cybercrime costs the global economy US$400 billion every year (McAfee, 2014). Although most of the financial sector institutions are protected by computer and network security defenses, such as spam filters and fraud-detection systems, that still leaves potentially millions of victims. Until recently, most cybercrimes were dispersed, with spam emails sent indiscriminately to thousands of computer users at once. Cyberattacks are one of the most serious threats facing the US today. In just the past two years, hackers have broken into computer systems at the White House, State Department and Pentagon; stolen millions of Americans' personal information from US companies; and disrupted the computer networks of some of America's most important companies.

Currently, criminals are beginning to identify specific targets through prior research, a tactic called 'spear phishing'. In these attacks, emails are targeting offices of wealthy families or their corporate money managers, for instance. Potential victims and/or their companies are addressed by name, and an email seems to be coming from an associate.

Cybercrimes are increasing exponentially; as mentioned above, 2014 will go down in history as a highpoint year for cybercriminals. The creativity of cybercriminals has demonstrated that no organization is safe, regardless of size or reputation, be it in the United States or other parts of the world. Entities affected include the likes of Sony, Apple, eBay, JP Morgan and Home Depot, to name just a few. The culmination of 2014 was with cybercriminals bringing down both the PlayStation Network and Xbox Live at Christmas. Just a few weeks into 2015, the US's second-largest insurer, Anthem, suffered a major breach.

In February 2016, The Bank of Bangladesh was targeted with one of the biggest cyberattacks of all time. Criminals were successful in hacking into the central bank's security system by masquerading as official banking authorities, and illegally transferred US$101 million of funds from its account at the Federal Reserve Bank of New York to accounts in two countries in Asia. Twenty million dollars were transferred to Sri Lanka, and the rest went to accounts in the Philippines (Jones, 2016). This incident is only one example of cyberattacks on the banking sector in developing/emerging countries. Banks in Asia have been the most vulnerable, with attacks in the Philippines, Vietnam, Thailand and Taiwan leading the way. Those attacks have led to losses in the billions of dollars in the continent.

In addition to countries in Asia, cybercriminals have targeted other banks in other parts of the world. Over a number of years the Carbanak gang, for instance, was able to steal around US$1 billion from close to 100 banks located in 30 countries worldwide. This activity covered hacking into the networks of each bank and masquerading as a legitimate agent before executing the transaction. The speed with which the Carbanak gang was able to move from bank to bank made their activity really difficult to track and detect (Jones, 2016).

The most dangerous and often ignored threat that financial institutions are facing and will face in the coming years is the threat of insiders. During economic downturns, employees are going to be more tempted to steal inside data, to sell it or use it for their own purposes. The insider threat will be more widespread where there are more disaffected players around badly secured data and information. Appropriate checks and balances of all employees, suppliers and contractors will help reduce this threat. Insiders constitute a permanent threat; they have access to data, information and systems and they know how the system and its security work. Most bank thieves and large-scale corporate frauds, and many of the most notorious and impressive criminal attacks, involve insiders. Insiders are especially pernicious attackers because they are trusted. They have access because they are supposed to have access. They have opportunity, and an understanding of the system, because they use it—or they designed, built or installed it. They are already inside the security system, making them much harder to defend against. In offices, employees are trusted people given access to facilities and resources, and allowed to act—sometimes broadly, sometimes narrowly—in the company's name. In stores, employees are allowed access to the back room and the cash register, and customers are trusted to walk into the store and touch the merchandise.

Replacing trusted people with computers does not make the problem go away, it just moves it around and makes it even more complex. The computer, software and network designers, implementers, coders, installers, maintainers, and so on are all trusted people.

Costs associated with criminal activities in the banking/financial sector amount to billions of dollars. This is only a portion of the total costs of global cybercrimes; one estimate put the cost of cybercriminal activities worldwide at US$6 trillion by 2021 (Jones, 2016).

CYBERCRIME AS AN INDUSTRY

Underground cyber markets have sanctioned the development of cybercrime into a money-spinning business (Samani et al., 2013). In this market, cybercrime service providers can offer buyers full control of the cyberattack or they can give full control of the process to others, allowing them to do the work for them. In this market, governments, individuals and businesses can be targeted (Samani et al., 2013).

A number of techniques are at the heart of cybercrime as a business, four notable techniques being: (1) Denial of Service (DoS) attacks; (2) Distributed Denial of Service (DDoS) attacks; (3) ransomware; and (4) identity theft. A recent report by American Banker states that DoS attacks against financial networks are increasing and they're costing banks as much as US$100 000 per hour (2015). In addition, the attacks are now expected to come in shorter, more severe gushes. In a survey of 510 companies, Neustar found that 91 percent of the firms that DDoS attacks reported that the threats hadn't decreased in the past year (2014), and nearly one-third said they lose more than US$100 000 in revenue per hour while DDoS attacks are going on. A Verisign report found that DDoS attacks against the financial industry doubled during 2014 to account for 15 percent of all attacks (PYMNTS.com, 2015).

Ransomware is a type of malware that locks access to its victim's computer to gain their information until a ransom is paid, unlike the Zeus Trojan. Malware, such as ransomware, gathers its victim's data by using a drive-by technique to install itself unknowingly to their computer.

Ransomware has been around for a number of years, but there has been an increase in the number of attacks and amount of damage caused. The year 2015 saw an increase in these types of cyberattacks, particularly against large organizations, because the payoffs are more substantial. The first six months of 2016 indicate that the number of ransomware incidents and the associated harm they cause will be much more severe in 2016 than in past years (FBI, 2016). Ransomware is a type of cyber extortion, whereby a ransomware program, such as Trojan, infects an institution system's hard drive and encrypts all common file types (.db2, .doc, .htm, .txt, .xls) on the system. It then leaves a text message instructing the institution how to contact the hacker to buy the key to unlock the files. Ransomware activities are not only flourishing, they are becoming more advanced. A few years ago, ransomware activities were typically carried out through spam emails, but because email systems became better at filtering out spam, cybercriminals turned to spear phishing emails targeting specific individuals (Komando.com, 2016).

Recently, a Kentucky critical care facility and a California hospital were victims of the Locky ransomware attack. The hospital paid hackers US$17 000 in undetectable bitcoins. In this instance, the hackers had locked up their computer system for 10 days using encryption. Apparently, the cost of a ransomware attack is much more than the amount of ransom paid; the amount of damage caused by ransomware hackers is mind-boggling. More than 42 percent of survey respondents said they worked for companies that had been victims of ransomware attacks. Some 72 percent of companies that were victimized could not access their computer systems, including patients' medical records, for two or more days; 32 percent could not access their system for at least five days.

One of the growing areas of identity theft is associated with the medical field; the frequency of medical identity theft continues to rise over the years. A recent report by the Ponemon Institute shows that medical identity theft in 2014 had doubled since the first study in 2000. In 2014 there were almost 500 000 more victims than in 2013 (Ponemon, 2014). The report indicates that the healthcare industry lags far behind the financial industry, which invested financial resources to detect fraud; this lag has impacted victims severely, forcing them to absorb the costs. According to the study, 65 percent of the victims had to pay an average of US$13 500 to resolve the issue.

Today data and information are the lifeblood of any firm or governmental agency, and as such must be protected, especially PII. Information classified as PII includes, but is not limited to: (1) full name; (2) national ID card; (3) credit card number; (4) telephone number; (5) address; (6) email; (7) financial account number; and (8) face and fingerprint information. All of this is information that can help a criminal or someone malicious to identify a person when it is combined.

There are no systematic data or statistics on the incidence of identity theft; with the exception of the United States, international statistics on identity-related cybercrime are not systematically collected, analyzed or published. Countries like Australia and the United Kingdom have recently developed various reports on identity theft that provide base-level statistics, but not on identity-related cybercrime. As with respect to emerging/developing countries, this kind of statistic does not exist. The efforts of the UNODC core group of experts on identity-related crime (UNODC, 2008) are laudable and it needs to specifically look further into identity-related cybercrime and provide solutions for its prevention and the protection of victims.

It is essential that law enforcement agencies, businesses, consumers and legislators understand the causes of data breaches, so they can be dealt with and the occurrence of these incidents minimized. It is only when one understands how data are exposed or stolen that one can avert further breaches through improved security procedures and safer information handling. Lost laptops and other digital media containing consumer data lead to 21 percent of data breaches, and 14 percent of breaches involve the accidental publishing of sensitive consumer data. Because these are accidental occurrences, they are difficult to prevent; however, banks can help minimize the likelihood with employee education. In the United States, for instance, customer data theft by company employees accounts for 15.6 percent of data breaches; and approximately two million identity thieves are hired every year using stolen credentials because of poor background screening processes (Morrow, 2008).

The problem is not so much recognizing the nature and severity of the problem caused by cyber-facilitated frauds of all kinds, but understanding just what to do to protect ourselves from them. Given the state of economic uncertainty in the world, identity theft does not seem to be a policing priority for most countries; there are insufficient numbers of trained personnel and specialists to deal with the amounts of fraud reported; consequently, a large number of reports dealing with identity theft go uninvestigated. In addition, some of the major frauds committed by employees and businesses go unreported or underreported. With the growth of online business, it has become common for users to disclose financial and personal information about themselves on websites that let other users identify them. In many cases, this information is used to target advertisements and promotions directly to users. The increased reach and richness of information collection has led to increased levels of fraud, identity theft, spam email, and junk faxes. The good news, though, is that the increase of international criminal activity in the form of identity theft and the like has been followed by an increase in court cases and judgments facilitated by the cooperation of international law enforcement agencies led by the United States. The face of cybercrime is global; in 2008, for instance, members of an international organized crime group operating a 'phishing' scheme in the United States, Canada, Pakistan, Portugal and Romania obtained private information to use in a credit card fraud. Among the financial institutions affected were Citibank, Capital One, JPMorgan Chase, Comerica Bank, Wells Fargo, eBay and PayPal. In another incident, hackers were arrested for infiltrating cash register terminals at Dave and Buster's restaurants in the United States to acquire credit card information, which was resold to others for criminal purposes. The hackers were prosecuted with the cooperation of the Turkish and German governments. A third case involves a Nigerian who installed a spyware program on a NASA employee's computer to capture personal data, such as bank account numbers, social security number, driver's license information, home address, and passwords to various computer accounts, as well as to intercept private electronic communications. Another incident involves a global criminal ring that smuggled counterfeit luxury goods into the United States from the People's Republic of China. Valued at more than US$100 million, the counterfeit handbags, wallets, purses and carry-on bags were labeled with such 'name' brands as Nike, Burberry, Chanel, Polo Ralph Lauren, and Baby Phat. The defendants paid more than US$500 000 in bribes to an undercover agent. Operation Phony Pharm investigated the illegal sale of anabolic steroids, human growth hormones, and other controlled substances over the Internet. Raw materials imported from China and manufactured in US, Canadian and Mexican underground laboratories were distributed through a MySpace profile and a website. Collaboration with Operation Raw Deal has resulted in the seizure of 56 steroid labs across the United States. The US operation took place in conjunction with enforcement operations in Mexico, Canada, China, Belgium, Australia, Germany, Denmark, Sweden and Thailand.

It is also projected that by 2021 the cost of cybercriminal activities will top US$6 trillion. Those studies are a wake-up call, especially in the existing environment of the current economic crisis; this will possibly lead to a global meltdown in vital information. Increased pressures on firms to cut costs and reduce staffing, especially in the information/ computer security area, have led to an increased opportunity for crime caused by weak security measures. The study calls for a corporate cultural change whereby companies would start looking at information security as a business enabler not as a cost center. The study further suggests that the ability to store data and information safely in the form of intellectual property is a key driver of security investment in Brazil, Japan and China. The study reports that 60 percent of Chinese survey participants cited 'safer storage' as a reason for storing intellectual property and other sensitive information outside their own country. The study sheds light on the impact of the current financial crisis on the state of securing intellectual property. Businesses are evidently concerned about the global financial crisis and its effect on the security of critical information such as intellectual property. The McAfee study reports that 39 percent of respondents surveyed consider their intellectual property to be at risk given the current economic conditions. The study also evaluated the commitment of the various countries to protecting critical information; the results suggest that emerging and developing countries are more enthused about protecting their valuable new wealth, as demonstrated by the money spent on protecting their intellectual property, than their Western counterparts. Results show that Brazil, China and India spent more money on security than Germany, the UK, the US and Japan, combined.

It is becoming evident to executives and policy makers around the world that intellectual property is an emerging target for cybercriminals, as evidenced by the increased number of attacks by what are being referred to as cyber mafia gangs. One trend shows that phishing techniques are becoming more and more sophisticated. Another trend highlights the danger of insiders and shows that employees steal intellectual property for the purpose of financial gain and to improve their competitive advantage.

A mounting number of employees and many executives believe that displaced employees are the main threat to critical infrastructure. Forty-two percent of those who responded to the McAfee survey believe displaced employees constitute the principal threat to critical information. In addition, it appears that China, Pakistan and Russia are still the main source of cyber threats for various legal, cultural and economic reasons.

The fastest growth in Internet users today is in developing and emerging countries—in Asia and Africa in particular. Nowadays, cyber space has become an inherent element of the development of any country, be it developed or developing. As technology continues to advance, the growth of cybercrimes will increase. Cybercriminals will endeavor to meet or even beat the evolution of technology and will continue to abuse the Internet for their personal gains. Among the most dangerous criminal activities are those centered with nation-state terrorist groups and hacktivist groups. Those groups have been growing in size, scope, reach and depth in the past few years. On the international scene, two countries are considered by many to be the two main hubs for emerging, growing organized cybercrime activities: China and Russia. As technology has continually changed, the adapting nature of cybercriminals has vigorously changed as well. Many of these groups have common attributes, but their aims have proven to be based on different political, economic, military and social bases.

Hacktivism essentially involves a number of distinct forms of cyber-crimes, such as website defacements, DoS attacks, DDoS attacks, intellectual property theft, and virtual sabotage. Hacktivists in the most part do not take an action for monetary gains; they mainly undertake their actions in an effort to convey an ethical message or in support of a social justice cause. 'To achieve their goals, cybercriminals offer everything necessary to arrange a cyber-fraud or to conduct a cyber-attack; the offer is very articulated and includes malicious code and also the infrastructure to control the spreading and operation of the malware' (Paganini, 2013, p. 1).

Cybercriminals are keeping pace with the advancement in technology and have been creating and using sophisticated malware, including the current trends in mobile communication, and current botnet trends. In addition to the use of fraud-as-a-service models, technology provides criminals with a larger variety of malware to use in their attacks. However, it has been stated that many cybercriminals still use old-fashioned malware that is easy to use to deliver the intended purpose. Cybercriminals use a number of methods to commit their crimes including social engineering, malicious software, botnets, worms, viruses and Trojan horses. Cybercrimes can affect all facets of life; they could mess up aircraft communications, delete satellite data, jumble traffic lights, impede the work in the financial sector, freeze a pacemaker, and break military command-and-control systems. The EC Council has a slogan: 'Hackers are here. Where are you?'. That should trigger a nation to frequently ask, 'Where are we?', a shout more to emerging and developing countries than it is for the developed world (EC Council, 2014).

China has the largest number of Internet users—more than 600 million in 2015—and was once listed as the second most cyber-targeted nation. Decision makers in the United States affirm that many of the cyberattacks on American companies are sponsored and supported by the Chinese government. China, on the other hand, asserts that it is a constant victim of cyberattacks from the Americans. The two countries have been negotiating, trying to reach a deal to curb cyberattacks, but recently the negotiations have become tricky after Edward Snowden's leaks that the US National Security Agency (NSA) has been spying around the world, even on American allies, such as Germany and France.

The Snowden leaks have also revealed that the NSA was spying on India. In the aftermath of these revelations, the Government of India publicized its first National Cyber Security Policy in July 2013 (Deity. org, 2013). The major objective of the policy was to help shape a more secure Indian cyber space for all parties involved: citizens, businesses, government, and international stakeholders.

Cybercrime service providers have created a new business, referred to as cybercrime-as-a-service (CaaS), mirroring other legal forms of *as-a-service* models such as software-as-a-service (SaaS); platform-as-a-service (PaaS), infrastructure-as-a-service (IaaS) and data-as-a-service (DaaS). Cybercrimes-as-a-service (CaaS) can be categorized as:

1.   crimeware-as-a-service;
2.   cybercrime infrastructure-as-a-service; and,
3.   hacking-as-a-service.

The above list of cybercrimes-as-a-service includes the finding and development of a toolset to help manipulate and exploit specific operations. Packages sold to criminals include tools that help to mask the malware from security software; card skimmers for financial fraud, or equipment that can be used to attack physical platforms are examples of crimeware-as-a-service (Samani et al., 2013).

Many other malware variants are available for sale. Rootkit services are a malicious code that conceals itself within an infected system to perform actions for which they are programmed. This can be for any attackers who want to acquire information located on their victim's computer. A particular malware service that has gained popularity is the development and use of ransomware viruses. This type of software forces its victims into performing specific actions, like entering payment information, by restricting them from conducting any activity until their information is entered into the system.

CYBERCRIME AND NATION STATES

Creative cyber activity threats continue to surface with the possibility of devastating global impact. Many of those threats are encouraged and financed by nation states. Threats come from both criminals and hostile countries, or nation states, especially China, Russia, Iran and North Korea. Nation-state hackers include government agencies, companies and businesses engaged in activities aimed at creating espionage networks to steal information or destroying and/or disrupting IT infrastructure in an effort to cripple political, economic or social structures. Some of the motivating factors of nation-state cybercriminal activities are military, political, civil disruption, propaganda, and/or industrial espionage.

Given the increase in nation states' involvement in cyberattacks, a number of countries have recently revealed their plans to increase offensive cyber competencies. This increase in competencies seems to have turned into a digital arms race that presents a major threat to the security of data in other countries (Zetter, 2015).

In addition, it is extremely difficult to assess attribution if an attack originated from a nation state given that it is extremely difficult to assess the forensic nature of the attack. Recently, it is believed that China and Russia employed state hackers and paid self-employed hackers to gain access to systems they consider important, but it was extremely difficult to attribute those attacks to the two states (Zetter, 2015). Russia and China lead those countries who 'view offensive cyber capabilities as an important geostrategic tool and will almost certainly continue developing them while simultaneously discussing normative frameworks to restrict such use' (USA Gov Policy, 2016).

Back in 2010, the discovery that the malware Stuxnet targeted Iran's nuclear program sparked international turmoil. To gain access to the Iranian industrial systems, the malware relied on 'zero day' vulnerabilities associated with flows in the Windows operating system. Those industrial control systems are computerized systems aimed at controlling and monitoring physical systems such as transportation, manufacturing, electricity and water. Stuxnet altered key components of the programmable logic controllers (PLCs) of the systems that controlled the centrifuges used in Uranium enrichment. In doing so, Stuxnet was able to manipulate the centrifuges at will while camouflaging those changes at the same time. Some estimates suggest that this attack on the Iranian nuclear facilities destroyed close to 1000 centrifuges, set back the Iranian nuclear program by at least two years, and cost the country billions of dollars yearly.

Given the role nation states play in cyber activities, it is important to understand their policies, strategies and philosophies as far as deterrence of cybercrime is concerned. The following sections cover cyber policies and strategies in the four countries identified with the main threat to Western democracies: China, Russia, Iran and North Korea, which are believed to pose the high-end cyber threats.

Cybersecurity and China

As far as involvement in cyberattacks by other nations is concerned, China is considered the leader in this category. The country has by far the highest level of cybercriminal activities. In terms of numbers, China is the largest Internet user in the world, with close to 1 billion Internet users in 2017. This figure is projected to grow to 1.14 billion by 2022 (Statista, 2017).

Those numbers are impressive given that the Internet became available in China in 1994, changing the country's economy tremendously (China-Daily, 2015). With China's open door economic policy, the country became a world leader in cybercriminal activities. As of 2015, 14 percent of all global cybercriminal attacks originated from China (ChinaDaily, 2015). China's primary objectives are mainly economic and technological espionage against Western countries, especially the United States.

As far as cybercrimes by Chinese citizens in China are concerned, the momentous growth of advanced technologies and high level of Internet penetration in the country, combined with the less than optimal cyber-security policy and measures necessary to protect them, has made China vulnerable to increased cyberattacks and cybercrimes. This will definitely lead to reputational consequences that could shatter the country's economic and technological development ambitions.

Since the Internet became commercially available in China in the mid-1990s, cybercriminal activities took various forms and were associated hand in hand with the high level of Internet penetration. These started in the form of *patriotic* hacking with the Green Army hacker group in 1997. In 1998, the Red Hacker Alliance surfaced and their activities were connected with the Jakarta riots, when Chinese nationals were accused of defacing websites in Indonesia in an effort to destabilize the country.

For-profit cybercriminal activities emerged at the start of the twenty-first century, focusing mainly on domestic activities and attacking Chinese IP addresses. The year 2001 was the first time that Chinese officials voiced concerns about domestic cybercriminal activities. Those activities increased exponentially in the mid-2000s, fueled by the high level of unemployment in the country, where a large number of young Chinese turned to cybercriminal activities as a means of economic survival. During that time, most Chinese hackers lacked technological sophistication and were relying on pre-packaged hacking tools offered on the black market. With time, cybercrime in China grew from simple phishing attempts against individuals to sophisticated attacks on financial institutions. A 2012 report indicated that 85 percent of all Chinese citizens were impacted by some form of cybercriminal activity (Norton, 2012). In 2015, the C2C e-commerce site Taoboa had more than twenty million of its consumers' accounts compromised due to cyber hacks. These hacks had a very negative economic impact, which was estimated at close to US$12 billion in 2015 (ChinaDaily, 2015).

In the last couple of years, China and the United States have been working collectively in an effort to curb cybercriminal activities. In 2016, both countries moved in the direction of narrowing the gap on fundamental issues dealing with cybercrimes, intellectual property (IP) theft, and cyber norms. Notwithstanding the positive development in collaboration, both countries still have a long road to walk. China's newly enacted Cybersecurity Law, which became effective in June 2017, raises legitimate concerns among the countries of the West, especially the United States. One of the main concerns is the fear that China's policies will limit market access for foreign companies. The new law calls for *Internet sovereignty*, defined as 'China's right to police the Internet within its borders and to participate in managing international cyberspace' (Lexology, 2017).

The new law also calls for technology providers to undergo security reviews to safeguard against hackers. Many Western governments, however, have voiced their concerns about the impact of the new law on the transfer of proprietary technology.

At one end of the spectrum, China's Cybersecurity Strategy recognizes the roles of government, industry, social organizations and the public in ensuring the success of cybersecurity. At the other end, the newly published and implemented cybersecurity policy still reasserts China's cyber sovereignty by affirming its right to control Internet use within its borders. This might create some complexity in the collaborative effort between China and other countries, especially the Western ones (Greenberg, 2017).

Notwithstanding China's emphasis of cyber sovereignty, Chinese leaders believe that protecting Chinese citizens against cyberattacks and defending the economy and the critical infrastructure against hacking come under the umbrella of protecting national security. As a result, the newly developed cyber laws, policies and strategies are implemented with an eye on national cyber sovereignty growth in cyber space. The newly implemented Cybersecurity Law (effective in June 2017) specifies the responsibilities of Internet Service Providers (ISPs) in dealing with censorship and providing support for law enforcement. It also requires ISPs to provide data on activities associated with critical industries such as transportation and banking.

Based on the above, the newly published Chinese cybersecurity policy law will remain a contentious issue between China and the Western economies. China's view states that governments must be in the driver's seat when it comes to managing the use of the Internet both domestically and internationally. This is believed to minimize the social and political disruption in the country. As mentioned above, the divergent views between China (and Russia) and Western democracies will add to the complexity of creating a shared governance agenda for cyber space. In a nutshell, China's cybersecurity strategy is based on a principle of 'active defense' and sets policy foundations for critical infrastructure protection, cryptography, dynamic monitoring, indigenous innovation, talent development, leadership, and funding based on this overarching principle.

Cybersecurity and Russia

The overwhelming majority of experts believe that Russia's cyber activities are mainly motivated by the desire to gain geopolitical leadership in an effort to gain more power. Added to this main objective, economic and financial gains are also motivating factors (Giles, 2012).

When it comes to cyber space, Russia's main concern is the threat associated with content of the Web. To the Russian government *Internet sovereignty*, defined as the ability of the state to have control over cyber space, is central to its objectives, in that having full control over its cyber space is considered a national priority for the country. To ensure this, Russia is pushing for the establishment of a new international doctrine. Not surprisingly, Russia's position is closely aligned with that of China (Kulikova, 2015).

After the collapse of the Soviet Union, Russia saw an opportunity to use cyber space to gain military, political and economic advantage. To accomplish this, Russia established four institutions which are in charge of information/cybersecurity operations: (1) the Security Council; (2) The Federal Agency for Government Communications and Information (FAPSI); (3) The State Technical Commission; and (4) the Russian Armed Forces (Bernik, 2014). While each of the above-mentioned institutions has its main charge, all of them deal with various facets of cyber activities.

Vladimir Putin, Russia's President, first announced plans to develop a national cybersecurity strategy in early 2000, and this national strategy was revamped by him in 2016. In addition to the revamped strategy, Russia was involved in negotiation with Western governments dealing with governance of cyber space; notable is the agreement signed by Presidents Obama and Putin in early 2016, which aims at the organization and exchange of information and reports on cyber incidents between the two countries (ISD, 2016).

The main goal of Russia's cybersecurity strategy up to 2020 is to protect online resources from hackers and cyber terrorists. It is primarily focused on protecting public networks and the State-Internet resource. The cybersecurity document states that all cyberattacks made on websites are deemed as attempts to seize power, classifying such hackers as criminals. Currently, Russia faces four main cybersecurity threats:

- the use of information technologies as weapons to achieve national objectives with the aim of carrying out hostile and aggressive acts;
- the use of information technology for terrorist purposes;
- the growing number of cybercrimes;
- the use of Internet technology for intervention in internal state affairs, disturbing public order, and stirring up national hatred (Gerden, 2016).

As indicated above, the Russian government controls the information that is accessed by its citizens. Even though there is no clear, defined private sector entity or agencies in charge of ensuring cybersecurity, the Kaspersky Lab, which is an international software security company based in Russia, has been working alongside the Russian government for years (NDTV, 2014). Along with the assistance of Kaspersky, the Russian government has introduced tough standards and regulations on cyber space (NDTV, 2014). These include laws requiring ISPs to store all personal data of Russian users at data centers in the country. Government officials have also cautioned business owners and Russian citizens not to use websites such as Google, because they use servers that are based in the United States (NDTV, 2014). In addition to Kaspersky, Russia is also working with private information security companies (which have not been named) that work closely with law enforcement authorities and to beef up their capabilities (NDTV, 2014).

The official Information Security Doctrine published by the Russian Federation (2008) refers to the overall balanced interests at the individual, society and state level, both domestic and foreign policy, and references four main national security strategies, or 'ingredients'. These include observing the constitutional rights and freedoms of its citizens in what concerns the use of information and the reinforcement of moral values in society, information support for the state policy of the Russian Federation, in addition to promoting modern information technology, boosting the national information industry, and protecting and securing information resources against unsanctioned access. Though there is no official mention of a National Cybersecurity document, philosophy, policy and strategies of national cybersecurity are all included in an official information security doctrine published by the Russian Federation itself. The document mentions how different aspects of activities have different information security threats, and in turn have different methods for combating the said threats.

As far as the economic impact of cybersecurity on the Russian Federation is concerned, the doctrine states that the financial sector, including banking, stock exchange and even tax information, are the areas that are most susceptible to information security threats. Some critical infrastructure strategies put in place by the Russian Federation stem from exercising state control over the creation, development and protection of systems and tools for gathering, processing, storage and transmission of statistical, financial, stock exchange, tax and customs information.

In the defense domain, the main targets for information security threats include the Russian armed forces, central military control agencies, and scientific research institutions like the Russian Ministry of Defense. The doctrine makes reference to internal threats, such as staff sabotaging or neglecting special-purpose information or telecommunication systems, or external threats like any intelligence activity for foreign entities. Some of the national defense strategies in place for this include systematically identifying threats and their sources to better target defensive efforts, creating and improving information protection tools, in particular military purpose automated control systems, conducting intelligence and electronic countermeasures, and training information security experts.

As far as the economic prosperity and the social life of its citizens are concerned, Russia's document indicates that improving information infrastructure will lead to the betterment of economic and social stability of the country's citizens. By improving its information infrastructure, Russia believes that it can ensure fairness of its constitutional system, and create an environment that could foster economic prosperity.

Although Russia's cyberattacks are hard to uncover, there is full agreement among experts worldwide from the private and public sectors that Russia was behind the cyberattacks in Estonia (2007), Georgia (2008) and the Ukraine (2014 to the present). In 2007, it took only a few minutes for the Estonian infrastructure to be crippled by a DDoS attack by institutional Russian hackers. In 2008, the Georgian Military Infrastructure was also crushed by a devastating cyberattack (DDoS) launched by Russian nationals. The first cyberattack on a power grid took place on 23 December 2015, when the Russians were successful in compromising a number of energy distribution companies in the Ukraine, leaving hundreds of thousands of people without electricity. The Russian attackers used various methods tailoring them to the targets intended. Spear phishing email messages were used to access the systems in question; once access was granted the hackers went ahead and installed the BlackEnergy malware to gain remote control over the infected servers and other devices.

Unsurprisingly, Russia's motivation for cyber activity is highly political, and is focused primarily on gaining and reinforcing its geopolitical power all over the world. It is not a secret that the educational system in Russia is behind its superiority in the cybersecurity domain; the country recruits and employs cyber warriors from top colleges and from its cybersecurity and cybercrime private sectors. In addition, Russia has many *patriotic hackers* who operate on the country's behalf. Those patriotic hackers are said to have been behind the attacks on Estonia, Georgia and the Ukraine. Although Russia poses a major cyber threat, it is not the only country that threatens Western democracies in cyber space. China, Iran and North Korea are also countries with robust cyberattack competencies.

Cybersecurity and Iran

The main objective of Iran's involvement in cyber space is to reaffirm its power over the Middle East, in general, and the Gulf Cooperation Council (GCC) in particular. In this quest, its cyber strategy has been focused on diminishing Western economic, military and political influence in the region, particularly that of the United States, which keeps close relationships with the Kingdom of Saudi Arabia and Israel. For Iran, maintaining dominance in the GCC region is paramount to its existence and survival. Iran's cybersecurity strategy falls under the auspices of the Islamic Revolutionary Guard Corps. In addition, after suffering a string of high-level cyberattacks on the nation's nuclear program and its oil ministry in 2010, Iran had strengthened its cybersecurity capabilities by creating a cyber council for safeguarding its domestic Internet resources and ensuring the control of the Iranian Revolutionary Guards; the policy is motivated by ensuring the sovereignty of the country. The operation against Iran's nuclear centrifuges which was the first 'weaponized' malware only led them to toughen their position and foster their cyber capabilities (Healey, 2016). This move was strongly criticized by human rights advocates on the grounds that it violates the human rights of the Iranian people.

According to a study by the Center for Strategic and International Studies (CSIS), Iran has an unpublished comprehensive cybersecurity strategy that includes the creation of what it calls a 'national information network' with cyber activities falling under both offensive and defensive dimensions (Lewis, 2014).

Cybersecurity and North Korea

In North Korea, the use of the Internet is only permitted for certain individuals upon approval and is actively monitored by the state for any hostile activity. North Korean citizens are restricted to the use of the intranet, known as Kwangmyong, which has no access or connection outside of the country's borders (HP Security Research, 2014).

Clarke and Knake (2010) argue that North Korea is a leading cyber power since it is very strong because its dependence on computer networks is very low, which leads to a very low level of vulnerability. Clarke and Knake classify North Korea as a strong cybersecurity hotbed at the defensive end of the spectrum as compared to the United States which is classified as having a high offensive ability as far as cybersecurity is concerned (Clarke and Knake, 2010).

A 2015 report by South Korea's Defense Ministry estimated that North Korea's *cyber army* had a crème de la crème force of close to 6000 hackers ready to attack. A large proportion of those hackers operate from remote locations in Southeast Asia and China. Added to that is North Korea's relationship with Russia and its arsenal of cybercriminals. North Korea's unsophisticated infrastructure and weak Internet connectivity make the country far less vulnerable than other countries to cyber retaliation (*The Guardian*, 2015).

The two attacks attributed to North Korea are the 2014 Sony hack and the massive 'WannaCry' Ransomware cyberattack of May 2017. The WannaCry ransomware targeted computers operating the Microsoft Windows operating system by encrypting data and asking for ransom payments in the Bitcoin cryptocurrency. The impact and ramifications of WannaCry were devastating economically and socially. The malicious software infected computers in healthcare sectors in a number of countries, leading to compromising critical healthcare systems and putting lives at risk. John Dickson (2015) indicated in an article on Dark Reading that the consequences of the Sony hack were the most devastating to date. The hack disrupted Sony's Information Systems for weeks, stopped a movie from being released on time, and caused Western governments to incur a lot of cost trying to get to the bottom of the hack. In addition, this attack is extremely concerning in that it was so sophisticated that 90 percent of Internet defenses in private industry might have not discovered it (Dickson, 2015). The Sony hack wiped clean data on thousands of computers and servers, and overwrote the data on the computers, leaving the computers as essentially dead shells (Elkind, 2015).

In summary, minimizing criminal behaviors by countries such as China, Russia, Iran and North Korea starts with cooperation among democratic countries and the development of cybersecurity strategies and policies which, if they do not stop the malicious behavior of those cybercriminals, minimize the negative consequences by adopting strategies and policies based on deterrence. It is also necessary for national governments and businesses to cooperate to diminish cyber risk and increase the cost to hackers by implementing policies based on deterrence. The Internet of Things (IoT), ransomware and mobile attacks, in addition to phishing and tax scams top the list of possible threats in the future, and countries all around the world need to collaborate in cybersecurity policies and strategies which will minimize the occurrence of cyberattacks and/or the negative consequences of those attacks when and if they happen. The book will conduct content analysis of cybersecurity policies of a number of developing countries and assess the level of readiness of those countries in the face of cyberattacks.

A Special Case: Edward Snowden Leaks and the Move to Localization

In the summer of 2013, Edward Snowden, a National Security Agency (NSA) subcontractor, uncovered information on attempts by American intelligence to perform mass electronic surveillance on a large scale, including taking hold of the communications of leaders in other countries, Brazilian President Dilma Rousseff, and German Chancellor Angela Merkel. The magnitude of the economic and political impact of the Snowden leaks will be mulled over for years to come. Snowden has his supporters and critics, but no one denies that his actions led to tension in international relations, and underscored the role Internet governance plays in foreign affairs.

Computers, information, and communications technology are increasingly becoming the foundation of developing and emerging economies, driving them on the path of economic growth and development. However, that same economic growth is threatened by a parallel increase in cyberattacks. Snowballing data breaches, theft of intellectual property, cyber terrorism, hacktivism and cyberattacks are causing huge costs and consequences for the economies of those countries. As a result, governments of those countries have to prepare to defend against growing cyber threats both through proactive and corrective policies, laws and strategies.

Cybercrime continues to evolve and develop, presenting one of the most critical national security dangers, not only in the United States and Europe, but globally. Consequently, cybersecurity is not a concern of individual countries; it is a big problem for the world community as a whole to deal with.

The Edward Snowden incident has impacted the way developing and emerging countries view and perceive the privacy and security of their data when it is stored and managed by American companies on United States soil. As a matter of fact, trust in American businesses has been affected negatively since the initial reports suggested that the US NSA was directly monitoring the servers of some US companies for the purpose of obtaining data for national security investigations (Lyon, 2014). Several of those companies denied knowledge of being active participants in the surveillance. Delving into the nature of the relationship between the NSA and those companies is beyond the scope of this book; all we can fairly state is that there were a number of security ramifications associated with this action which weakened the foundation of trust between customers, the US government, and businesses all around the world.

The impact of the NSA spying is not merely political nor is it confined within the borders of the United States; many economists believe the most devastating impact is economic (Miller, 2014). Since the Snowden leaks, many American companies have reported declining sales in international markets such as China and Brazil. A number of American companies ventured early on to discuss the damaging economic impact of the spying program on their companies; Cisco was one of the pioneering companies to openly discuss the consequences of the NSA actions on its business in November 2013. Based on Cisco's account, the company estimated it lost close to 18 percent of orders from China and suffered a 25 percent decline in orders in the Brazilian market (Durden, 2014). Other companies, such as IBM, Microsoft and Hewlett-Packard, followed suit and reported in late 2013 that sales were down in some emerging countries as a result of the spying revelations (Ante, 2013).

The Snowden impact has also been suspected to be a major reason for swaying Brazil to award a US$4.5 billion contract in December 2013 to Saab over Boeing, an American company that had previously been the frontrunner in a deal to replace Brazil's fleet of fighter jets (Meyer, 2014). As a result of the Snowden revelations, Brazil, India and Russia have moved in the direction of considering data localization proposals that could impact US business interests negatively by introducing new compliance rules and deterring American companies from entering into new markets because of high compliance costs. To regain trust, many American companies started to adopt policies allowing their customers to store their data on servers located in their countries (Microsoft is an example). IBM is supposedly investing over a billion dollars to build overseas data centers in order to reassure foreign customers that their data is protected from NSA surveillance (Kontzer, 2014). Emerging and developing countries are proposing legislation in order to ensure that data of their customers and citizens are protected; as an example, Brazil has proposed that companies such as Facebook and Google set up local data centers so that they can abide by Brazilian privacy laws. Another country has moved on the same path: India. The Indian government has drafted a policy which require companies to maintain part of their IT infrastructure in-country and give local authorities access to the encrypted data on their servers for criminal investigations; in addition, the new Indian policy will prevent local data from being moved out of the country. The data nationalization provision in Brazil was defeated, and was substituted by a claim for universal jurisdiction over all data produced by Brazilians that meant that data might be subject to Brazilian law, regardless of where it was stored internationally (Hill, 2014).

The government of India has drafted and approved policies that require storage of all data within the country as well as guaranteeing that it has local control and management of servers. The government of India has traditionally had an interest in data localization and has, since the 2008 Mumbai attack, been entangled in a public dispute with Research in Motion (RIM), mainly over requests for localized data storage and encryption keys in order to gain access to BlackBerry communications. A number of proposals before the Indian government were set forth to prevent data on Indian citizens, government organizations, and businesses from being moved out of the country, forcing foreign companies to ensure that it was all stored on local servers. In October 2013, the Indian government also announced that it would be implementing an internal email policy to avoid relying on major American email service providers such as Gmail, Yahoo, and Outlook.com. It has been reported that government workers were not only advised not to use Gmail, but also to avoid using computers altogether when typing up sensitive documents (Technologyguide.com, 2013).

Brazil is another country that had one of the strongest reactions to the NSA revelations. In September 2013, the Brazilian government approved a number of policies geared at better protection from the NSA surveillance. These policies include domestic Internet bandwidth and international Internet connectivity as well as encouraging domestic content production and the use of network equipment built in Brazil. One of the actions taken by the Brazilian government is its intent to abandon Microsoft Outlook in favor of a domestic email system that relies on data centers located only in Brazil. In addition, in February 2014, Brazil indicated its intention to build its own undersea cables so that data can move between Brazil and the European Union without going through the United States. Brazilian and Spanish companies were contracted to lay fiber optic cables that will connect Brazil and Portugal directly. Additional fiber optic cables such as this one can improve routing efficiency and speeds, but only if they come without routing restrictions (Emmott, 2014).

As of June 2015, both India and Brazil have put their data localization proposals on hold, while Russia moved in the opposite direction, towards developing costly legislation: a new law on data, which requires Russians' personal data to be stored on servers located within Russia, will cost around US$5.7 billion, according to estimates from the European Center for International Political Economy (ECIPE, 2015). This makes up about 0.025 percent of the Russian economy. In addition, in July 2014, Vladimir Putin signed a law that will require websites and businesses to store all Russians' personal data on servers located inside Russia. The law took effect on 1 September 2015. In anticipation of the new Russian law, in early April 2015, two US-based pure play companies, eBay and PayPal, agreed to transfer the personal data of their Russian users to servers based in Russia.

In 2014, the European Center for International Political Economy undertook a study to assess the costs associated with data localization laws in a number of developing and emerging economies, including Brazil, China and Vietnam; the findings (published in May 2014) found that these costs are 0.2 percent of GDP for Brazil, 1.1 percent for China, and 1.7 percent for Vietnam.

In addition to Brazil and China, Brunei and Vietnam have also outlined their own data control proposals. Proponents and supporters of these proposals maintain that these policies would provide more protection because local servers can be controlled by local authorities and can give governments both access to and legal jurisdiction over the data being stored on them.

CYBERSECURITY POLICY: A MUST!

A national cyber policy is a must in any country; developing a cyber policy might be easier than implementing and operationalizing it. A policy might call on the protection of critical infrastructure in a country, but how to implement the policy in order to protect power grids, nuclear plants, defense systems, and communication and telecommunication networks is a totally different matter. As an example, the cybersecurity policy of the government of India calls for the recruitment and training of half a million cybersecurity professionals by 2018; this is easier said than done. As of the writing of this book (late 2018), the country has created an army of 64 000 cybersecurity professionals. In June 2015, India signed a memorandum of understanding (MoU) with Symantec to develop cybersecurity certified professionals. This MoU aims at increasing the number of cybersecurity professionals in the country from 63 200 to a million; the focus will be on training and creating new job opportunities in the field of cybersecurity.

The European Community Council (ECC), with almost 100 countries as members, is a top certification body for information security professionals, and the owner/creator of the famous Certified Ethical Hacker (CEH) and similar programs. The ECC states that most emerging and developing countries are poorly equipped to handle cyber intrusions owing to a 'serious shortage' of skilled professionals.

Cyberattacks do not focus on civilian targets only; in addition to the vulnerability of critical civilian infrastructures, there are obvious military risks to computer and communications systems. Former US Secretary of Defense, Leon Panetta, warned of the risk of a 'cyber-Pearl Harbor', stating that the Third World War will take place in cyber space and not on the battlefields (*New York Times*, 2012), and many future conflicts will move to cyber space. State-sponsored cyberattacks, hacks, and cyber-terrorism activities are on the rise and they essentially cause large-scale interruptions of computer networks. Waging wars in cyber space is more harmful than waging war on the battlefields because in today's attacks, the victimized country is clueless about who is the instigator.

Cybercrimes in developing and emerging economies have been increasing over the past few years; this level of growth of cybercrime activities has been driven by a number of factors which will be discussed later in this chapter. The main driver, however, is the recent increase in Internet diffusion in developing and emerging economies. Just to illustrate, the Internet penetration rate in the African continent jumped from 10 percent in 2010 to more than 27 percent by the end of December 2014. As for Asia and the Pacific, the Internet penetration rate jumped from 26 percent to more than 47 percent over the same period (ITU, 2016). Cybercrimes in the Asia/Pacific region are on the rise; China is mainly considered a source of cybercrimes and a hub for activities in that part of the world.

The growth of the Internet brought with it the realization by citizens in developing and emerging countries that it is an incredible force for social change and economic growth. This increase of Internet use has brought lots of benefits to these countries as well as a number of challenges associated, mainly, with cybercriminal activities. One of the main challenges is the lack of awareness among the population of users of the various risks associated with cybersecurity and cybercrimes. The major types of cybercriminal activities that exist in developing and emerging countries are software piracy, identity theft, malicious software, intellectual property theft, social engineering and financial fraud.

The diffusion of the Internet of Things (IoT) is a technical term that provides Internet connectivity among devices without human interference, facilitating machine-to-machine (M2M) communication between individuals (entities) that use mobile communication networks. Even though the IoT has increased the efficiency, effectiveness, convenience and productivity of individuals, it has added a layer of anxiety as far as cybersecurity is concerned. This added layer of anxiety has increased the level of network vulnerabilities. To minimize the devastating consequences of cyberattacks associated with the IoT, countries have to exert a huge effort in developing both offensive and defensive national-level cybersecurity measures aimed at protecting their critical infrastructure from cybercriminals (Kim et al., 2017).

Central to ensuring a safe cyber space is the development of a comprehensive cybersecurity policy and strategy at the national level based on both defensive and offensive spectrums. A country has to be ready to defend itself against cyberattacks and at the same time has to be proactive in creating the necessary environment both technically and socially. The following is a set of common denominators for national cybersecurity policies and strategies. The list is not exhaustive by any stretch of the imagination. The area of research is still in its infancy and it is expected to grow exponentially in the near future.

The first area of proactive cybersecurity policy is the development of national cybersecurity capabilities inclusive of cultural, technical, social and human elements. Raising awareness at the national level is key, in addition to being open to international cooperation in this domain. By achieving good national cybersecurity, countries will be better able to contribute to the global effort. An example of regional cooperation is that of the ASEAN countries; those countries are trying to minimize cyber risks by raising the level of regional capacity and cooperation in cybersecurity. They have created an ASEAN Cyber Capacity Building Program (ACCP) aiming at instilling cyber norms in the region and building technical cyber capacities. The ASEAN countries have also reaffirmed the critical role that regional cooperation plays in addressing cybersecurity challenges. In March 2017, the countries developed the ASEAN Cybersecurity Cooperation Strategy (United Nations, 2017). Notwithstanding the effort of the ASEAN countries in collaborating in the cybersecurity domain, the countries still have a long way to go in building their capacities and creating the necessary social and cultural environments.

Central to an effective cybersecurity policy is the call for better coordination and a more integrated approach at the national level. The policy must indicate a clear allocation of responsibilities among the various agencies and create a high level of public awareness. Estonia has been avant-garde in this domain; their cybersecurity policy states it is necessary to acknowledge cyber threats more widely and to improve interdepartmental coordination in an effort to prevent and combat cyber-attacks (Republic of Estonia, 2017). This is a necessity for both the private and public sectors. It is recommended that one central agency be in charge of coordinating all cyber activities in an effort to centralize controls and responsibilities. Based on Estonia's experience, much of the activities concerning cybersecurity, its vulnerabilities and mitigation rest with the private sector. A telling example of public and private sector cooperation is the volunteer cybersecurity department of the Estonian Defense League (Republic of Estonia, 2017). National governments must develop robust systems that more efficiently distribute resources and cybersecurity expertise in their countries.

Creating a culture of cybersecurity is key to a successful national cybersecurity policy. Development of curricula specializing in cyber-security at schools and universities should be a priority for local governments. Further to increase awareness at the national level, confer-ences and forums should be organized frequently. Those meetings must address the economic, social and political importance of a cybersecurity education. Whether we morally agree or disagree with the activities of the Russian and North Korean regimes in cyber space, the two countries are great examples of how to cultivate cybersecurity professionals. Chapter 3 will address the ways and means the two countries, among others, achieve this objective. Given the dearth of cybersecurity profes-sionals, governments in developing and emerging economies need to step up efforts to develop expertise and grow an energetic security ecosystem.

Lastly the cybersecurity policy needs to address defense issues at the national level. Cyber terrorism is alive and well, and as Leon Panetta indicated, countries might be facing a 'cyber-Pearl Harbor' (*New York Times*, 2012).

Another pressing development contributing to the risk of cybersecurity is the development of smart cities all around the globe. Many of those cities have been established in developing/emerging countries such as Singapore, Abu Dhabi, Cape Town and Buenos Aires, to name a few. A known fact is that the rate of urbanization is growing at an unprecedented scale. This is a worldwide phenomenon where people are relocating from rural areas towards the cities, triggering an explosion of cities' popula-tions. It is expected that 60 percent of the world population will reside in cities by 2030. This percentage will climb to 70 percent by 2050 (*The Guardian*, 2017).

A number of initiatives worldwide have contributed to the rise and growth of smart cities aimed at addressing the needs of businesses, institutions and citizens, through effective and efficient delivery of services. IBM has defined a smart city from a data perspective as 'one that makes optimal use of all the interconnected information available today to better understand and control its operations and optimize the use of limited resources' (Cosgrove, 2011).

Even though the *Smart City* industry is still in its infancy, it is one of the fastest-growing segments of governments around the world and is estimated to reach US$775 billion by 2021; leading the way is investment in North America, followed by Europe. Asia-Pacific countries and Latin American countries are also making strides in this domain (Maddox, 2017).

The smart city prospect of facilitating the implementation of a connected environment for all residents is realized through the post-PC era; that is, the increased penetration rates of the IoT, the mobile platform and the cloud. There are many smart city models worldwide, but the United States National Institute of Standards and Technology (NIST) model is the most widely used and has a high level of maturity. The NIST smart cities framework comprises four industry verticals: (1) smart buildings, including the need for connectivity and provision of integrated service; (2) smart transportation; this includes the facilitation of smart transport, smart charging, smart traffic and smart parking; (3) smart infrastructure; this comprises the development and provision of smart water, smart lighting, and smart waste management; and (4) smart energy; this includes increasing energy efficiency, reducing emissions and providing smart meters. This model is based on the premise of providing intelligent connectivity within and across city verticals (Koenig, 2016).

The following contains some examples of countries in the emerging/ developing world ranked in the top 100 of smart cities by the 2017 IESE Cities in Motion Index (IESE, 2017). All of those countries are part of our sample of countries subject to our analysis. One of the objectives of our analysis is to assess the adequacy of those countries' cybersecurity policies in dealing with the risks generated by the high level of connectivity those countries are subjected to. Leading the list of developing/ emerging countries with smart cities is Seoul, South Korea, which ranks 7th overall, followed by Singapore, ranking number 22 overall on the Index of Smart Cities and 2nd among developing and emerging economies. Singapore is followed by Taipei Taiwan, which ranks 56th overall and 3rd among the developing/emerging economies. The United Arab

Emirates follows Taiwan, with the city of Abu Dhabi taking 64th place and the city of Dubai 66th place on the list overall. Hungary ranks 67th on the list, followed by Slovenia and Lithuania, which rank 70th and 71st respectively. Among the South American countries, Argentina (Buenos Aires) ranks 83rd and it tops the list in South America, followed by Chile (85th), and Columbia (96th). Among the African countries South Africa and Tunis top the list there, with Cape Town ranking number 133 and Tunis taking 137th position.

We will use the Smart City Index ranking to assess any relationship between whether countries have smart city initiatives and the comprehensiveness and quality of the cybersecurity policies in those countries. Chapter 5 of the book is dedicated to this analysis.

DRIVERS BEHIND CYBERCRIMES IN DEVELOPING COUNTRIES

The growth of Internet diffusion and penetration, added to lack of awareness and less-than-ideal cyber laws and policies, are among the main drivers behind cybercrimes in developing and emerging countries. The following are the major drivers behind the high level of cyber-criminal activities, especially in emerging and developing countries.

Internet Penetration is on the Rise

As mentioned above, the rate of Internet penetration has been on an upward path socially in the past five years. There has been a major increase in Internet accounts in many developing and emerging economies. As of 2017, it is estimated we have 3.5 billion Internet users around the world, as opposed to 2 billion users in 2011 (Internetsociety. org, 2017). The number of Internet users is growing rapidly and is estimated to reach 5 billion people, using 50 billion devices, by 2020. Most of the growth of Internet users over the past five years is accounted for by developing and emerging economies; sub-Saharan Africa was the leading area of growth, with a 32 percent compound average growth rate (CAGR), followed by the Emerging Asia Pacific countries with 21 percent, the Middle East and North Africa with 19 percent, and Latin America with 13 percent. Compared to the countries of Western Europe that registered a CAGR of 4 percent, and North America with 2 percent, developing and emerging economies have been adding Internet users at an exponential rate (Internetsociety.org, 2015). The diffusion of fiber optics and wireless broadband in the countries of Africa, Asia and Latin

America has engendered a growth of Internet users and led to the establishment of Internet cafés enabling citizens to surf the Internet for a fee but simultaneously breeding various types of cybercriminal activities.

Mobile and smart phones are the main medium for Internet surfing in developing and emerging economies. In 2015, the mobile phone penetration rate was 203 percent in the United Arab Emirates, 130 percent in Iran, 113 percent in Egypt, 105 percent in Thailand, 110 percent in Peru, 140 percent in Argentina, and 108 percent in Romania. These penetration rates are higher than those of some developed countries, such as Japan with 95 percent, the United States with 103 percent, and Canada with 80 percent (ITU, 2015).

These high levels of Internet and mobile phone penetration in emerging and developed countries have increased the opportunities for cybercriminals to take advantage of users who are not sophisticated enough to protect themselves against cyberattacks.

Awareness Programs Are Inadequate

In many of the developed countries, cybersecurity awareness is a top priority; the US Department of Homeland Security (DHS), for instance, has developed a number of programs aimed at reminding citizens of the importance of protecting their individual identities, finances and privacy, in addition to protecting the national security of the country, critical infrastructure and economy. These awareness programs are based on the principle that cybersecurity is a responsibility shared by all—the public sector, the private sector and the general public. Such programs are missing from the majority of developing and emerging economies. Users in these countries must be aware that criminals can access their bank accounts online; they can steal their PII; they can infect their computers with viruses and worms; and they can take their computers hostage for ransom. Governments of developing and emerging countries must create training programs to make users aware of how to update antivirus software installed on their systems; how to enable automated patches on their operating systems; that they should be careful in opening email attachments or clicking on URLs in unsolicited emails; how to create and use strong passwords; and how to avoid putting out PII on social media platforms.

A major reason why cybersecurity awareness has not been a priority for the governments of developing and emerging economies is because of the lack of resources. Governments and private sectors should invest more in information infrastructure security, employees' awareness and compliance.

Cyber Legal Structure Is Absent, or Weak at Best

The rule of law is a requirement for stability and economic prosperity in any country; laws geared toward governing cyber space are a necessary component to preserve the integrity of cyber space and minimize criminal activities. Cyber laws act as deterrents to criminals, especially when the laws have enough teeth and long arms. The vast majority of developing and emerging countries do not possess the necessary cyber laws because of a lack of awareness on the part of the legislators and, furthermore, absence of cyber laws from governments' priority lists.

Preventing cybercrime involves the enforcement of security policies in the private and public sectors and fighting cybercrime involves the enactment of laws to guide law enforcement and the judiciary system in prosecuting cases effectively. The unavailability of a legal framework for prosecuting cybercrime means there are no guidelines for law enforcement to follow when investigating cybercrime. Karake and Al Qasimi (2010) carried out a content analysis of cyber laws in a number of emerging and developing countries; the authors show that the content of those cyber laws in the majority of the countries examined are inadequate and/or deficient.

Technical Skill-Set Is Deficient

Developing and emerging economies suffer from the scarcity of trained cybersecurity professionals and personnel with the necessary technical know-how to manage and maintain information technology systems. It seems there is a disproportionality between the growth of Internet diffusion and number of users, on the one hand, and the development of a trained, skilled labor force to guarantee the security of the information technology systems, on the other. An increase in broadband access will give Internet access to more users in developing and emerging economies; if and when the proliferation of IT training of these users does not match the growth and distribution of the broadband access, the existent lack of IT know-how may be exploited (Grobler and Van Vuuren, 2010). The maintenance of network infrastructure will be negatively affected as a result of the inadequacy of IT professionals in emerging and developing countries. Developing and emerging economies need strong institutions to deal with cybersecurity, and this requires training in cybersecurity to deal with the future challenges of cybercrime.

Cybercrimes are also amplified by the shortage of e-forensic skills and know-how in the developing world, in addition to the pervasive use of pirated software that is more susceptible to attacks by viruses, malware and Trojans. Under these conditions, controlling cybercrimes becomes more daring and problematic. Experts believe that the rapid growth of consumer PC markets in developing countries like India, Brazil, China, Malaysia and Pakistan has been contributing more to the rising piracy rates (Herhalt, 2011). China has spent US$19 billion on pirated software in 2009, whereas India has spent only US$2 billion on the unlicensed software market value (Herhalt, 2011). Similarly, cybersecurity is a major challenge for the GCC countries, where 50 percent of software is pirated (Ghauri, 2014). Software piracy has infested computers and servers in most developing and emerging economies; in Romania, for instance, nearly two-thirds of computers run at least one pirated software program; the value of pirated software in Romania reached US$208 million in 2013 (Fuscutean, 2014).

Economic, Financial and Political Triggers

Many of the developing and emerging economies have undergone years of economic turmoil, *coups d'état*, corruption and poverty, making it difficult for their governments to zoom in on cybersecurity as a priority. According to Frank and Odunayo (2013), online fraud is seen as the popularly accepted means of economic sustenance by the youths involved. The corruption of the political leadership has enhanced the growth of an Internet crime subculture. The value placed on wealth accumulation has been a major factor in the involvement of youths in online fraud (Frank and Odunayo, 2013). Economic hardship has helped fuel the cybercrime industry. The lack of job opportunities on the continent has contributed to the cybercrime industry using Internet cafés and any available Internet access to commit crime for financial gain.

The frequency and magnitude of cybercrimes in developing and emerging countries can be damaging to online transactions, e-business and e-commerce. In Africa, for instance, it is estimated that more than 100 million PCs are infected with Trojans, worms and viruses (Grobler and Van Vuuren, 2010). Malware infestation is partly caused by the inability of people in those countries to pay for antivirus protection and by the high rate of pirated software.

The major motive for hacktivism all over the world is political; the word 'hacktivism' is derived from hacking and activism. Hacktivists, or politically motivated hackers, are different from other types of cyber-criminals in that their activities, directed against governments and corporations, are motivated by the quest of social change, as opposed to seeking monetary rewards and/or having access to intellectual property. Hacktivists are described as adversaries of the power elite, and they aim to use technology to foster their own agendas. Given their stands against governments, hacktivists have been described by the media as criminals and dangers to society. Since most hacktivists' actions target governments and corporate authorities, hacktivism has been classed as cyber terrorism. It is essential, however, to differentiate between hacktivism and cyber terrorism, which uses violent means to accomplish its objective; even though both use cyber space as a tool to achieve their objectives, their reasons are somewhat different. Fitri (2011) clarifies the difference between hacktivism and cyber terrorism by stating that while cyber terrorism aims at destruction, hacktivism is aimed at disruption.

Malicious economic cybercrime has become a serious issue for many developing and emerging economies. Because Internet and smart phone usage is growing faster in those countries than in the developed part of the world, with increasing connectivity rates, Internet penetration rates and mobile phones diffusion rates, risks to citizens are now that much greater. This is because these new commodities have enabled and extended the reach of cybercriminals all around the world. These criminal organizations, among other online criminals, use computer hacking and other digital strategies to gain financially, socially or politically. Cyber policies and strategies aimed at dealing with cyber space and cyber-criminal activities are practically non-existent in many developing and emerging economies. It is imperative for those countries to have well designed policies and articulated strategies to raise awareness, increase preventive measures and to couple their strategies with well-articulated laws for punitive measures.

With the rise of cybercrime, governments and the private sector in developing and emerging economies look for new ways to protect against hacking and practices such as malware and phishing; costs associated with cybercrime amount to billions of dollars, with cybercriminals being able to be engaged in many criminal activities from defacing government sites, to stealing credit card information from bank customers, to having access to confidential data. Cybersecurity policies and programs, cyber defense hubs, and new cyber laws comprise some of the key strategies of governments and companies.

FERTILE GROUND FOR CYBERCRIMES

The economies of many developing/emerging countries are far from being stable, and cybercrimes will definitely add to the instability of these economies. Having said that, it is fair to state that, similar to developed economies, in addition to the social, cultural and political effects, cybercrime's biggest impact in those countries is economic in nature; loss of trust, loss of data, theft of intellectual property and so on impact consumer confidence and consequently the overall economy. Cyberattacks can originate from any part of the world and it has been documented that their impacts are mainly damaging to emerging and developing countries (LeClaire, 2013).

Most developing countries lack the financial resources to earmark funds for the protection of their cyber space. In situations where a country has to deal with a cyberattack, resources are apportioned from other development projects to address instances of cybercrime, leading to the cancellation of critical projects. Theft of money from central banks of government through electronic crime creates a hole in developing and emerging countries' economies because it affects the countries' abilities to invest in infrastructure programs. In addition, these cyberattacks dissuade foreign investors from investing in those countries largely because of the weaknesses of the IT infrastructure (Olowu, 2009). Smart phone users in developing and emerging economies are apprehensive when it comes to transacting online. As mentioned earlier, many e-commerce transactions in these countries use smart phones as a medium because of the scarcity and/or unreliability of wired infrastructure. For users in these countries who depend on inexpensive mobile phones for the whole shebang from banking to deterring criminal activities, network security is almost an afterthought (Sternstein, 2013). Citizens of those countries use their smart phones to deal with their daily activities; the less-than-secure environments in which users operate have created a host of opportunities for cybercriminals.

Unsecure cyber space in emerging and developing economies will impact the whole world. In developed countries, the Internet is regulated and managed by a set of rules and regulations in an effort to minimize abuse and criminal conduct. Public and private sector institutions in developed countries are bound by certain policies aimed at protecting their networks from cyberattacks. The interdependencies of countries on the Internet create a major security concern especially from those countries that lack the necessary rules and controls. Everyone on the Internet is connected and weak security anywhere puts other users at risk; therefore, investing in developing cyber defenses in the developing world will help improve cybersecurity everywhere (Paller, 2008).

Policies, strategies and laws that have been created and implemented in developed countries have helped deter prospective hackers from partaking in cybercrime. The lack of policies, strategies and laws in the developing world lead to creating a fertile environment for cybercriminals. Not only can attacks be launched from any country or location in the world, it is also very hard to track suspicious devices and locations. Further, trying to take legal action against cybercriminals without the legal framework and infrastructure that permits investigations to be conducted will be a senseless exercise (Karake and Al Qasimi, 2010). Many governments and decision makers in the developing world are aware of the extent to which cyber space vulnerabilities prevent them from capitalizing on the advantages associated with the use of the Internet; nonetheless, they do not have the necessary resources or skill-set to minimize these vulnerabilities. In a nutshell, awareness of the risks associated with an unsecure cyber space is one thing; doing something about it is a totally different ball game.

CONCLUSION

This chapter has presented an overview of the literature on cybersecurity issues and the role of cybersecurity policies in enhancing cyber activities. The term 'malware' (*mal*icious soft*ware*) refers to a program with malicious intention planned to damage the machine on which it operates or the network over which it communicates. The growth in the complexity of modern computing systems makes it difficult, if not impossible, to evade bugs, which, in turn, leads to an increase of the likelihood of malware attacks, acting on the vulnerabilities of the system. Consequently, the threat of malware attacks is an inevitable problem in computer security, and therefore it is critical to discover the existence of malicious codes in software systems. Information is the lifeblood of any public or private entity, and it must be protected, especially PII. There are many ways in which customer information can be stolen: dumpster diving, social engineering, phishing, pharming.

There are a staggering number of ways that information could be taken from computer networks and released outside an organization's boundaries. Whether using an MP3 player, CD-ROM, a digital camera or USBs, today's employees could easily take a significant chunk of an organization's intellectual property out of the door in their back pocket. These types of devices are effectively very portable, very high-capacity hard drives; someone could take away up to 60 gigabytes of data on a USB stick. Observing current computer security practices in banking and financial institutions leads one to question whether the level of cybersecurity in these institutions is adequate. Each week brings yet another news story of a major security breach; one reason for our failure in what concerns cyber privacy and security is that these problems are difficult to resolve.

In systems development, in the haste toward releasing a product, there is little economic motivation to spend the time properly designing privacy and security into systems. While a number of developed countries have enacted, passed and enforced laws that require notification in the case of data exposure, and call for the criminalization of hackers and system attackers, legal and policy systems simply have not kept up with the advancement of technology. While information and communication technology keep evolving at an ever-increasing pace, our networked systems pose new threats and present new challenges.

The battle against the majority of malware has been somehow sorted out. Today the biggest danger is not to the company's hardware or software, it is rather related to soft issues related to people, mainly insiders, who are trying to compromise our data and information. The list of targets of cyberattackers is a mile long, ranging from individuals, banking and financial institutions, communication systems, infrastructures, government agencies, hospitals, universities, and many others. Recently we have been witnessing the move to cyber terrorism against sovereign nations, as evidenced by the examples of Estonia, Iran and Saudi Arabia. The growing intricacy and interdependence of the various networks of these entities make them more susceptible to cyberattacks and increase the reach, depth and range of an attack's effects. A recent study by Symantec, the world's largest maker of security software, found that the fraud industry is worth a potential US$7 billion. McAfee's more recent study estimates the loss of intellectual property and adjusting the damage at about US$1 trillion.

The relationship between systems' security and trust is well documented; it is demonstrated that the common denominator between the trust dimensions presented in the literature is the emphasis on issues that may directly influence the trust in an individual or an organization. In addition, the focus is on unidirectional trust dimensions. Research has been dedicated to regard trust as a unidirectional and direct relationship concept, though some authors have lately emphasized the importance of mutuality between firms in a business relationship. Still, trust is often regarded as an isolated phenomenon in a marketing channel context, despite the fact that we know that other indirect factors certainly or most probably are important and will influence the trust in a dyadic business relationship.

Trust is based on competence, goodwill and behavior. In order to build trust a wide scope of information is needed as different types of information (rational–emotional, economic–social, tacit–explicit) affect the trust experienced. Even in the business context the emotional level has a great impact on organizational trust building. Personal feelings and emotions are intertwined with more rational factors. In order to be able to communicate needs and expectations precisely and efficiently, both rational and emotional information is needed. Overly emotional information is not believable since it may seem subjective, lacking facts. Purely rational information of objective facts lacks emotional depth, ensuring the other party of the commitment and true intentions of the speaker.

Trust in cyber space relates to certain expectations about the intentions of the exchange partner. Often referred to as the 'expectancy' conceptualization of trust, it focuses on one's belief that the exchange partner will act in a manner that is responsible. In addition, trust in electronic commerce relates to one's rationale to rely on the exchange partner accepting the contentious disadvantage. This concentrates on one's predisposition toward exchange partners. Undeniably, these conceptualizations are linked, since behavioral intentions entail weighing expectations of a business associate's behaviors against a person's susceptibility in the exchange. In the marketing literature, however, researchers have argued against combining the expectancy and behavioral conceptualizations of trust, presumably because keeping them separate provides opportunities to study trust processes. This notion is strongly held up in the management literature as well.

REFERENCES

American Banker (2015) DDoS attacks against banks increasing, accessed at https://www.bankinfosecurity.com/ddos-a-8497.
Ante, S.E. (2013). Qualcomm CEO says NSA fallout impacted China business, *Wall Street Journal*, 22 November.
Bernik, I. (2014). *Cybercrime and Cyberwarfare*, Hoboken, NJ: Wiley.
Berry, Leonard L. (1995). Retailers with a future, *Marketing Management*, 5(Spring): 39–46.
Buttle, Frances (1996). Unserviceable concepts in service marketing, *Quarterly Review of Marketing*, 11(3): 8–14.
ChinaDaily (2015). Chinese mobile app startups set sail for overseas markets, accessed at http://www.chinadaily.com.cn/business/tech/2016-10/28/content_27202593.htm.
Clarke, R.A. and Knake, R.K. (2010). *Cyber War: The Next Threat to National Security and What To Do About It?* New York: HarperCollins.
Cosgrove, M., Harthoorn, W., Hogan, J., Jabbar, R., Kehoe, M., Meegan, J. and Nesbitt, P. (2011). Smarter Cities series: Introducing the IBM city operations and management solutions, IBM Corporation, accessed 23 March 2016 at http://www.redbooks.ibm.com/redpapers/pdfs/redp4734.pdf.

Deity.org (2013). National cyber security policy of India, accessed 13 April 2015 at http://meity.gov.in/sites/upload_files/dit/files/National%20Cyber%20Security%20Policy%20(1).pdf.

Deloitte (2016). Cybersecurity and a one million data scientist shortfall are trends shaping business in 2016, accessed 12 July 2016 at http://www2.deloitte.com/us/en/pages/about-deloitte/articles/press-releases/analytics-trends-shaping-business-in-2016.html.

Dickson, J. (2015). 6 ways the Sony Hack changes everything, accessed 13 June 2017 at https://webcache.googleusercontent.com/search?q=cache:mpPp7aKu5cgJ:https://www.denimgroup.com/resources/article/6-ways-the-sony-hack-changes-everything/+&cd=2&hl=en&ct=clnk&gl=us&client=safari.

Durden, T. (2014). First Cisco and Microsoft, now IBM: China orders banks to remove high-end IBM servers, accessed 19 June 2015 at http://www.zerohedge.com/news/2014-05-27/first-microsoft-now-ibm-china-orders-banks-remove-high-end-ibm-servers.

EC Council (2014). Hackers are here, where are you?, accessed 29 April 2017 at http://www.logiciel-inc.com/cehweb/docs/ceh-faq.pdf.

ECIPE (2015). Data localization in Russia: A self-imposed sanction, accessed 23 January 2016 at http://ecipe.org/publications/data-localisation-russia-self-imposed-sanction/.

Elkind, P. (2015). Inside the hack of the century, accessed at http://webcache.googleusercontent.com/search?q=cache:BjlBvtTJxyAJ:fortune.com/sony-hack-part-1/+&cd=1&hl=en&ct=clnk&gl=us&client=safari.

Emmott, R. (2014). Brazil, Europe plan undersea cable to skirt U.S. spying, accessed 29 January 2016 at http://www.reuters.com/article/us-eu-brazil-idUSBREA1N0PL20140224.

Federal Bureau of Investigation (2016). Incidents of ransomware on the rise. accessed 13 January 2017 at https://www.fbi.gov/news/stories/2016/april/incidents-of-ransomware-on-the-rise/incidents-of-ransomware-on-the-rise.

Fitri, N. (2011). Democracy discourses through the Internet communication: Understanding the hacktivism for the global changing world, accessed 17 December 2015 at http://www.arifyildirim.com/ilt510/nofia.fitri.pdf.

Frank, I. and Odunayo, E. (2013). Approach to cyber security issues in Nigeria: Challenges and solution, accessed 19 December 2015 at http://ijcrsee.com/index.php/ijcrsee/article/view/11/114.

Fuscutean, A. (2014). The mix of poverty and piracy that turned Romania into Europe's software development powerhouse, accessed 11 February 2016 at http://www.zdnet.com/article/the-mix-of-poverty-and-piracy-that-turned-romania-into-europes-software-development-powerhouse/.

Garbarino, E. and Johnson, M. (1999), The different roles of satisfaction, trust and commitment in customer relationships, *Journal of Marketing*, **63**(April): 70–87.

Gartner (2016). Gartner says by 2020 'cloud shift' will affect more than $1 trillion in IT spending, accessed 19 July 2016 at http://www.gartner.com/newsroom/id/3384720.

Gerden, E. (2016). Russia revamps its Infosec strategy, *SC Magazine UK*, 1 January 2015, online 24 April 2016.

Ghauri, I. (2014). Electronic Crimes Act: Cybercrime to be made non-cognisable offence, accessed 12 February 2016 at http://tribune.com.pk/story/672721/ electronic-crimes-act-cybercrime-to-be-made-non-cognisable-offence/.

Giles, K. (2012). Russian cyber security: Concepts and current activity. London: Chatham House.

Greenberg, A. (2017). How an entire nation became Russia's test lab for cyberwar, 20 June, accessed at https://www.wired.com/story/russian-hackers-attack-ukraine/.

Grobler, M. and Van Vuuren, J. (2010). Broadband broadens scope for cyber-crime in Africa, accessed 10 November 2015 at http://icsa.cs.up.ac.za/issa/ 2010/Proceedings/Full/28_Paper.pdf.

Healey, J. (2016). Winning and losing in cyberspace, in Proceedings of the 8th International Conference on Cyber Conflict, Tallinn: NATO CCD COE.

Herhalt, J. (2011). Cybercrime: A growing challenge for governments, accessed 30 November 2015 at https://www.kpmg.com/Global/en/IssuesAndInsights/ ArticlesPublications/Documents/cyber-crime.pdf.

Hill, J. (2014). The growth of data localization post-Snowden, accessed 10 June 2015 at https://www.lawfareblog.com/jonah-force-hill-growth-data-localization-post-snowden-lawfare-research-paper-series.

HP Security Research (2014). Profiling an enigma: The mystery of North Korea's cyber threat landscape, August, accessed at http://h30499.www3.hp. com/hpeb/attachments/hpeb/off-by-on-software-security-blog/388/2/HPSR%20 SecurityBriefing_Episode16_NorthKorea.pdf.

IDC (2018). Worldwide mobile phone forecast, 2018–2022, accessed 30 March 2018 at https://www.idc.com/getdoc.jsp?containerId=US43624018.

IESE (2017). Cities in Motion index, accessed 18 February 2018 at http://www. ieseinsight.com/fichaMaterial.aspx?pk=140223&idi=2&origen=3&idioma=2.

Information Security Doctrine of the Russian Republic (2008). Accessed 29 May 2016 at https://info.publicintelligence.net/RU-InformationSecurity-2000.pdf.

International Telecommunication Union (ITU) (2012). ITU: National Cyber-security strategy guide, accessed at http://www.itu.int/ITUD/cyb/cybersecurity/ docs/ITUNationalCybersecurityStrategyGuide.pdf.

International Telecommunication Union (ITU) (2015). Measuring the infor-mation society report, accessed 14 May 2017 at https://www.itu.int/en/ITU-D/ Statistics/Documents/publications/misr2015/MISR2015-ES-E.pdf.

International Telecommunication Union (ITU) (2016). ICT facts and figures, accessed 30 June 2016 at http://www.itu.int/en/ITU-D/Statistics/Pages/facts/ default.aspx.

Internetsociety.org (2015). Global Internet Report 2015, accessed 12 June 2016 at https://www.internetsociety.org/globalinternetreport/2015/.

Internetsociety.org (2017). Global Internet Report 2017, accessed 2 December 2017 at http://www.internetsociety.org/globalinternetreport/.

ISD (2016). Obama–Putin cybersecurity, accessed at https://www.fedscoop.com/ obama-putin-g20-cybersecurity-2016/.

Jones, A. (2016). Cybercrime: The growing threat to global banking, accessed 3 November 2017 at https://internationalbanker.com/banking/cybercrime-growing-threat-global-banking/.

Karake, Z. and Al Qasimi, L. (2010). *Cyber Law and Cyber Security in Developing and Emerging Economies*, Cheltenham, UK and Northampton, MA, USA: Edward Elgar Publishing.

Kim, K., Kim, I.J. and Kim, L. (2017). National cyber security enhancement scheme for intelligent surveillance capacity with public IoT environment, *Journal of Supercomputing*, **73**(3): 1140–51.

Koenig, M. (2016). NIST IoT-enabled smart city framework, accessed 29 October 2017 at https://s3.amazonaws.com/nist-sgcps/smartcityframework/files/GCTCTechJamKickoff/MichalKoenig_NIST_24_March_2016.pdf.

Komando.com (2016). True cost of a ransomware attack is a lot more than the ransom you pay, accessed at http://www.komando.com/happening-now/352145/true-cost-of-a-ransomware-attack-is-a-lot-more-than-the-ransom-you-pay.

Kontzer, T. (2014). IBM spends $1.2 billion on new cloud datacenters, accessed 22 July 2015 at http://www.networkcomputing.com/data-centers/ibm-spends-12-billion-new-cloud-datacenters/421885746.

Kulikova, A. (2015). China–Russia cyber-security pact: Should the US be concerned? *Russia Direct*, 21 May, accessed at http://www.russia-direct.org/analysis/china-russia-cyber-security-pact-should-us-be-concerned.

LeClaire, J. (2013). What the $500 billion cybercrime estimate means for enterprises, accessed at http://www.sci-tech-today.com/story.xhtml?story_id=010000CF25Q0.

Lewis, A. (2014). Cybersecurity and stability in the Gulf, accessed 30 October 2017 at https://webcache.googleusercontent.com/search?q=cache:qTsI69-l8SsJ:https://www.csis.org/analysis/cybersecurity-and-stability-gulf+&cd=5&hl=en&ct=clnk&gl=us&client=safari.

Lexology (2017). China data protection update, accessed at https://www.lexology.com/library/detail.aspx?g=4700ec39-245c-47cc-bd5f-268f5f02aa85.

Lyon, D. (2014). Surveillance, Snowden, and Big Data: Capacities, consequences, critique, *Big Data & Society*, accessed 3 December 2017 at http://bds.sagepub.com/content/1/2/2053951714541861.short.

Maddox, T. (2017). Smart city technology set to reach $775 billion by 2021, accessed 1 February 2018 at https://www.techrepublic.com/article/smart-city-technology-market-set-to-reach-775-billion-by-2021/.

McAfee (2014). McAfee Internet Security 2014, accessed 12 May 2016 at https://download.mcafee.com/products/manuals/en-us/MIS_DataSheet_2014.pdf.

Meyer, P.J. (2014). Brazil: Political and economic situation and U.S. relations, accessed 21 June 2016 at http://fpc.state.gov/documents/organization/225120.pdf.

Miller, C. (2014). Revelations of N.S.A. spying cost U.S. tech companies, accessed 30 June 2016 at http://www.nytimes.com/2014/03/22/business/fallout-from-snowden-hurting-bottom-line-of-tech-companies.html?_r=0.

Morrow, B. (2008). No one is immune, *Texas Banking*, **97**(11): 16–17.

NDTV (2014). Kremlin wants to 'protect Russian cyberspace from unpredictable west', *NDTV.com*, 19 September, accessed 28 April 2016 at http://www.ndtv.com/world-news/kremlin-wants-to-protect-russian-cyberspace-from-unpredictable-west-668317.

New York Times (2012). Panetta warns of dire threat of cyberattack on U.S., 12 October, accessed 1 July 2017 at http://www.nytimes.com/2012/10/12/world/panetta-warns-of-dire-threat-of-cyberattack.html.

Norton (2012). Norton Internet Security 2012 v19.8.0, accessed at https://www.techadvisor.co.uk/download/security/norton-internet-security-2012-v1980-324 9307/.

Olowu, D. (2009). Cyber-crimes and the boundaries of domestic legal responses: Case for an inclusionary framework for Africa. *Journal of Information, Law and Technology*, accessed 27 January 2016 at https://warwick.ac.uk/fac/soc/law/elj/jilt/2009_1/olowu/.

Paganini, P. (2013). China is also a victim of cyber attacks, accessed 5 July 2015 at http://securityaffairs.co/wordpress/13070/malware/cncert-china-is-also-a-victim-of-cyber-attacks.html.

Paller, A. (2008). The changing face of cyber crime: Top cyber menaces for 2008 and promising initiatives to fight back, accessed 12 March 2016 at https://www.sans.org/summit-archives/file/summit-archive-1493742282.pdf.

PC Magazine (2016). DDoS attacks Skyrocket in 2015, 11 March, accessed 2 April 2016 at http://www.pcmag.com/article2/0,2817,2500698,00.asp.

Ponemon (2014). The aftermath of a data breach: Consumer sentiment, accessed 21 April 2015 at http://www.ponemon.org/local/upload/file/Consumer%20Study%20on%20Aftermath%20of%20a%20Breach%20FINAL%202.pdf.

PwC (2016). Global Economic Crime Survey, accessed at https://www.pwc.com/gx/en/services/advisory/forensics/economic-crime-survey.html.

PYMNTS.com (2015). DDOS attacks cost banks ups to $100 K per hour, accessed at http://www.pymnts.com/news/2015/ddos-attacks-cost-banks-up-to-100k-per-hour/.

Republic of Estonia (2017). Cyber security, Republic of Estonia: Ministry of Economic Affairs and Communications, accessed at https://www.mkm.ee/en/objectives-activities/information-society/cyber-security.

Samani, R., Paget, F. and Hart, M. (2013). Digital laundry: An analysis of online currencies, and their use in cybercrime, White paper, McAfee® Labs, accessed 5 March 2015 at http://www.mcafee.com/de/resources/white-papers/wp-digital-laundry.pdf.

Statista (2017). Number of Internet users in China, accessed at https://www.statista.com/statistics/278417/number-of-internet-users-in-china/.

Sternstein, A. (2013). Pentagon will require security standards for critical infrastructure networks, accessed 15 January 2016 at https://www.nextgov.com/cybersecurity/2013/02/pentagon-will-require-security-standards-critical-infrastructure-networks/61328/.

Stevenson, A. (2014). Three quarters of world's email traffic is spam, accessed 20 June 2015 at http://ec2-75-101-158-109.compute-1.amazonaws.com/news/stories/5535-three-quarters-of-world-s-email-traffic-is-spam.

Technologyguide.com (2013). Email showdown: Gmail vs. Yahoo! vs. Outlook vs. the Field, accessed 29 April 2015 at http://www.technologyguide.com/feature/email-client-comparison-gmail-yahoo-mail-microsoft-outlook/.

The Guardian (2015). North Korea has 6,000-strong cyber-army, says South, 6 January, accessed at https://webcache.googleusercontent.com/search?q=

cache:aRfY-QMONCMJ:https://www.theguardian.com/world/2015/jan/06/north-korea-6000-strong-cyber-army-south-korea+&cd=2&hl=en&ct=clnk&gl=us&client=safari.

The Guardian (2017). The new smart city – from hi-tech sensors to social innovation, accessed 21 January 2018 at https://www.theguardian.com/sustainable-business/smart-cities-sensors-social-innovation.

United Nations (2017). Statement on behalf the members of the Southeast Asian nations, accessed 17 August 2017 at https://www.mfa.gov.sg/content/mfa/overseasmission/newyork/nyemb_statements/first_committee/2017/201710/press_20171023.html.

UNODC (2008). Report of the second meeting of the core group of experts on identity-related crime, Vienna, 2–3 June, accessed 21 September 2017 at www.unodc.org/documents/organized- crime/Final_Report_ID_C.pdf.

USA gov policy.com (2016). Director Clapper on cyber and tech threats, accessed at http://www.usagovpolicy.com/director-clapper-on-cyber-and-tech-threats/.

Zetter, K. (2015). We're at cyberwar: A global guide to nation-state digital attacks, accessed 10 January 2018 at https://www.wired.com/2015/09/cyberwar-global-guide-nation-state-digital-attacks/.

Chapter 3

INTRODUCTION

In the past 20 years, the nature of countries' wealth has changed significantly. Looking from a closer, down to earth perspective, currently 80 percent of the value of Fortune 500 companies consists of intellectual property (IP) and other intangibles. Related to this increased growth of 'digitization' of assets is a mounting level of digitization risk. The negative impact of this risk is not associated only with the digitization of developed countries and advanced economies, but it is more harmful to developing, less advanced nations as they are increasingly becoming an active economic agent in the world economy. This makes cybersecurity for them a top priority of the list of issues they are facing.

The economics of cybersecurity has not so far been on the radar screen of many economic theorists, practitioners and researchers. Examining economics journals, one notices a scarcity of papers dealing with the economics of cyber space, cybersecurity and cyber sovereignty. This shortage of published articles is most probably due to the rapidly changing nature, impact and frequency of cybersecurity threats.

In addition, determining the return on investment in cybersecurity is extremely difficult. It is not easy to assess the likelihood that an attack will succeed and wreak havoc on a country's infrastructure. It is also extremely difficult to assess the monetary damages in case an attack happens to succeed. Most developing countries are cash starved and need to allocate their resources to bare necessities, economic and social programs. To the majority of decision makers in those countries, investing in securing their cyber space is viewed as a luxury they cannot afford; they would rather concentrate on feeding their people and creating jobs for them.

Insights from psychology and behavioral economics point to the fact that human judgment is often biased, and this is more pronounced when it comes to investing in programs to secure cyber space. Many leaders use inappropriate decision models to help them determine where and how to invest. As an example, decisions to invest in programs aimed at raising cybersecurity awareness might suffer because of the misconception that cyber defense is a fortification process: fortifying your systems using firewalls will keep cybercriminals away. The shortcoming of this approach is the implicit assumption that cybersecurity is a finite problem that can be solved at a data point rather than looking at it as an ongoing process. Regardless of how fortified the country's IT infrastructure may be, cybercriminals will find a way to infiltrate those systems.

Looking at what is available based on the different economic theories, some work has focused on the expanded concept of sustained competitive advantage as it relates to cybersecurity; this, simply put, is the idea that some forms of competitive advantage are very difficult to imitate and can therefore lead to persistent superior economic performance of developed, advanced economies. The authors of this book argue that countries with a well established national cybersecurity policy and well formulated sets of cyber laws have more sustained competitive advantage than those countries lacking well designed cybersecurity policies and laws. Popular theories of competitive advantage in strategic management research, based on industrial organization economics (Porter, 1980; 1985) and the resource-based view (RBV) of the firm (Barney, 1991; Conner, 1991), predict that factors that sustain competitive advantages will generate superior economic performance that continues and persists over time.

In addition to the RBV, this book argues that well established cybersecurity policies and strategies by countries will form some kind of a barrier for cybercriminals to deter them from engaging in cyberattacks. However, coupling deterrence theory to cybersecurity policy and protection of a country's critical infrastructure is not as easy as it sounds. In other words, deterrence does not come in one flavor and does not have the same impact all over the world; it is not one size fits all! Based on the literature of classical deterrence theory, researchers have identified four different types of deterrence theory (Marinelli, 2017), which will be discussed later in this chapter.

The RBV is one of the latest strategic management concepts to be enthusiastically embraced by information technology (IT) and information management scholars. It is maintained that the RBV holds much promise as a framework for understanding strategic information/ knowledge economy issues including the security of cyber space and the behavior of cybercriminals and their associated activities. This chapter charts the development of the RBV from its origins in early economic models of imperfect competition, through the work of evolutionary economists to the contributions of strategy economics scholars over the past two decades. This broad literature base has given rise to a great deal of ambiguity, inconsistent use of nomenclature, and several overlapping classification representations. The book seeks to draw together common themes of sustainable competitive advantage and the RBV theory, and how they relate to the concept and application of cybersecurity.

In addition to the RBV theory, two other approaches were advanced to assess cybersecurity; the two approaches are the economic and the public goods approaches. Those will be covered in addition to the resource-based approach. Then we will move to cover deterrence theory and the four approaches associated with it. The chapter concludes by noting some important conceptual and methodological issues that need to be addressed by future research adopting the RBV and the deterrence theory perspectives of cybersecurity.

THE ECONOMIC APPROACH TO CYBERSECURITY

Strategies, goals and objectives of cybersecurity are sometimes achieved through economic incentives that might be positive or negative. The diffusion of ubiquitous environments, advanced computing technologies, and multifaceted networks facilitate globally distributed access to data and information repositories to countries around the world, and the economic impact of a cyberattack might have negative consequences for a large number of countries.

The objective of economic approaches to cybersecurity is mainly the alignment of economic incentives with actions taken to improve a country's cybersecurity infrastructure. A few years back, Moore (2009) concluded that a system's security was negatively impacted when the parties in charge of protecting both the hard and soft infrastructures were not punished as a result of their failure to protect that system. One of the noteworthy findings was the absence of disclosure of data breaches by parties involved (both from the private and public sectors) seeking to avoid a decrease in market value of a specific economic entity or a country as a whole (Moore, 2009). Two recommendations were advanced by Moore (2009): (1) make the Internet Service Providers (ISPs) responsible and accountable for eliminating malware infecting computers connected through their systems; and (2) require disclosure of security incidents such as data theft, cyber espionage, and control system intrusions.

The very nature of cybercrime being conducted over the Internet has made it a global problem. A more recent study found a positive correlation between lower rates of software piracy in a country and considerably lower rates of malware on the nation's networks (Kleiner et al., 2013). An important question for researchers is the extent to which national cybersecurity strategies have taken into account relevant economic principles when drafting their strategies and policies.

Anderson et al. (2012) indicate that cybercriminal activities can be classified under three categories: traditional crime, transitional crime, and new crimes related specifically to the use of the Internet. By way of examples, traditional crimes involve tax fraud; transitional crimes include those that were traditionally committed offline, such as credit card fraud, but those crimes have moved online for accessibility and convenience; and criminal activity, such as botnets, are new crimes which depend on the Internet and do not exist offline. All of those criminal activities carry a huge economic load in terms of cost and scale.

Notwithstanding the cost and scale related to cybercriminal activities, the main challenge to an economic model is the difficulty in determining the cost associated with the externalities associated with the Internet. This has to do with the perception of both business providers and consumers. In 2007, Gordon testified before the US Congress that it is challenging to assess the costs associated with customers' perceptions of cyber (in)security and the liabilities stemming from data breaches. If we project this to the global scene, this could be amplified as more and more people avoid investing in a country with weak cybersecurity practices. The economic losses associated with lack of investment in countries due to cybersecurity and cybercrime issues are huge but very difficult to measure.

A second challenge associated with the economic model is the difficulty in determining the costs and benefits involved in securing a country's technological infrastructure. Gordon and Loeb (2007) under-lined the risks associated with making a business case for cybersecurity as it compares to risks associated with other business-related challenges. So far, no reliable methods are available to help determine the total magnitude of weaknesses, vulnerabilities and exposures in a system or the probability of a system penetration by a cybercriminal actor (Garfin-kel, 2012). In the absence of cost–benefit assessments, it is difficult to justify more spending on cybersecurity since this does not necessarily mean this will lead to more secure, or profitable space (Garfinkel, 2012).

Garvey et al. (2012) present a macro-analytic method for assessing the economic-benefit return on investments in improving cybersecurity. They dubbed the method *Table Top Approach*. Among a number of competing investments in cybersecurity, this method identifies sets of Pareto efficient cost–benefit investments, based on measuring their economic returns and capturing tangible and intangible advantages of counter-measures that strengthen cybersecurity.

The Table Top Approach took a different view from the other two economic approaches known in the literature. The first of those approaches requires in-depth knowledge about the network infrastructure and the strategies of the cyberattacker. This approach, based on techniques from operations research and network science, is referred to as the *Network Infrastructure Approach*. The other approach, referred to as the *Multi-criteria Risk and Decision Science Approach*, is based on in-depth knowledge of information networks and being cognizant of the ability of the attacker to compromise a system's security. The Table Top Approach falls under the multi-criteria methods category, but has a number of different attributes: (1) it incorporates monetized and unmonitored costs of cyber activity events when searching for Pareto optimal mixes of investments; (2) then, it derives economic measures of the various combinations of investments and their interactions with cyber events and intrusions; (3) finally, the method provides a cybersecurity event matrix which registers cyber incidents and their impacts and likelihood of occurrence (Garvey et al., 2012).

In evaluating the above three stated economic approaches, it is fair to state that all of them are far from being easy to comprehend, use and implement. This is not a surprise given that the knowledge about cybersecurity attacks is at best imperfect, not to say uncertain. Subsequently, a fully-based economic justification for investing in cybersecurity measures may be difficult to sell to investors, governmental officials and/or citizens.

THE PUBLIC GOODS APPROACH TO CYBERSECURITY

Another leading approach to national cybersecurity policy emerged from the concept of the Internet and cyber space as public goods. Recently, several authors have adopted and advanced the public good model approach to cybersecurity. The literature has for some time now drawn comparisons between cyberattacks and a public health epidemic. It is believed that a country's 'cyber health' is as much a public good as a country's public health. The socioeconomic negative effect of a cyberattack can be as devastating for a country as an attack by an unknown virus on the public health system. Given that what is always said in the cybersecurity literature, a system is as strong as its weakest link, the parallels between the two systems (*cyber* and *health*) become evident when one assesses the impact of the massive ransomware cyberattack that hit nearly 100 countries around the world, and where more than 45 000 attacks were recorded; that is an epidemic (Wong and Solon, 2017).

Looking at a public good, one can assert that it possesses two attributes: (1) non-rivalrous, where the use of the good by one individual does not limit the amount of good available for consumption by others; and (2) non-excludable, meaning when no paying consumers can be prevented from accessing the public good. Proponents of this approach argue that, similar to public health, cybersecurity is a public good: it is non-rivalrous and non-excludable. For instance, once a system is secure, individuals cannot be excluded from the benefits of that secure cyber space. In addition, a user who benefits from the cybersecurity of a network does not reduce the opportunity for others to benefit from the same network (Schneider et al., 2016). As such, the use of a system's cybersecurity does not diminish the security for others, and all participants enjoy the same access to the system's security.

The role of governments in protecting the common good in the public health system by establishing quarantines or developing vaccination requirements for school attendance provided the metaphor for this approach to cybersecurity strategy. In the public health model, improved cybersecurity is the desired public good. Put differently, cybersecurity is the desired positive state in the loosely interconnected cyber network (Mulligan and Schneider, 2012).

Public health and cybersecurity as public goods are both deeply dependent on a number of environmental determinants. A main consideration in one's physical or digital health is the environment in which one lives. As reported by the World Health Organization (WHO), 25 percent of death and diseases worldwide are caused by environmental factors. Similarly, in cyber space, a user is exposed to environmental vulnerabilities in the form of cyberattacks, computer viruses and other digital threats caused by a connected digital device.

As public goods, both cybersecurity and public health are subject to interdependencies between individuals, agents and entities. An example of these interdependencies is a virus, which exists in both the physical and cyber environments. Vaccinated individuals are less likely to spread diseases because they are more resistant to viruses. By the same token, a 'healthy' connected device in cyber space is less likely to be devastated by a cyberattack, or to be subject to data breaches than an 'unhealthy' device.

Based on the concept that cybersecurity is a public good, it is argued that improvements in any area will benefit all participants, beneficiaries and users in the network. Extending from the ideas of immunization and quarantine to protect the population from contagious diseases, Charney (2012) advanced the public health model as a means of shifting from purely defensive strategies to an alternative that seeks to improve the security of each system connected to the global network; that is, equip the system with more preventive measures. Devices that are connected to the network must be secured to prevent risk to others in the global common space; this mirrors the public health focus of preventing the spread of infections (Sales, 2013).

Given the cross-border nature of the most serious cybercriminal activities, in addition to understanding cybercrime from a public good perspective, it is also important to understand the importance of cyber-security issues from the international relations perspective. The fact that most countries' critical infrastructures are connected to the Internet, cyber threat has become increasingly recognized as a legitimate security issue associated with national security (Kshetri, 2013). Looking at this from a macro perspective, it is understandable that all countries should protect their infrastructures from cybercrimes and should mitigate the risks associated with exposure to cybercriminal activities in order to have a safer cyber space for all.

As far as developing, less advanced countries are concerned, they are faced with the dilemma of needing to use IT to continue their growth and development, and their inability to fully protect their infrastructure. With this in mind, there are many issues that decision makers in those countries need to keep on the front burner. First, decision makers in developing countries need to understand that cybersecurity is both an internal and external risk issue on the one hand, and it is both a technical and conceptual/behavioral issue on the other hand. Thinking of cyber-security only from a technical perspective is not complete and/or sound. As a matter of fact, the main vulnerability in cyber infrastructure is associated with the soft element in people using and managing those systems. In addition, countries need to acknowledge that risk is associ-ated with external, international agents who might prove to be a detriment to the country's infrastructure. As such, countries need to: (1) invest in cybersecurity expertise as most of the developing countries lack the needed expertise to assess the risks associated with cyberattacks; (2) revamp their legal systems and put teeth into existing laws in order to increase the level of deterrence and help protect their cyber infrastruc-ture; and finally (3) have the necessary technical and human resources to help assess the damage inflicted by and the cost associated with the attack, and provide ways and means of handling the negative conse-quences of an attack, in case of an imminent cyberattack.

Also based on the public good approach, Asllani et al. (2013) discussed the role of the public sector in enhancing cybersecurity, arguing that treating cybersecurity as a public good makes it the responsibility of the federal government. Looking at the operational risk element of cybersecurity, Biener et al. (2015) discussed the widening gap in economics research when it comes to cybersecurity insurance, which they referred to as a public good given the voluntary investment associated with self-protection. The practice of cyber insurance as a risk transfer mechanism and as a way to deal with the problem of under-investments in cybersecurity has been gaining importance in the literature lately. The bulk of the literature has focused on determining the power of cyber insurance in improving infrastructure cybersecurity (Pal et al., 2014).

Notwithstanding the fact that the public good approach is gaining momentum, it is still a long way to convince those in charge of investing in cybersecurity to adopt it. Two reasons can be advanced for the lack of enthusiasm on the decision makers' side: (1) the lack of resources to invest in fortifying a country's infrastructure; and (2) the existing antiquated laws which do not provide those decision makers the necessary ammunition to force the ISPs and those in charge of the networks to create an immune cyber space and to penalize them if they do not comply.

RESOURCE-BASED APPROACH TO CYBERSECURITY

A central principle of the RBV is that performance is a function of an entity's unique resource bundle. Resources are broadly defined to encompass specific assets as well as human competencies and intangibles. Ideally, managers will strive to build up resources that are valuable, rare, without substitutes, and structured in a manner so that the organization's resources are unique and difficult to replicate by competitors.

Accumulating such resources requires that significant acquisition barriers be overcome. Thus, decision makers/managers who overcome these barriers place their countries/organizations in a desirable competitive position. Over time, the most successful countries/organizations may develop such a strong competitive advantage that their competitors will cease their attempts toward imitation through resource accumulation.

The RBV is primarily interested in the extent to which strategies are distinctive and different. Differences that yield superior performance for an organization and a superb comparative advantage for a country are determined by the distinct abilities of an entity and its decision makers/ managers to accumulate and implement strategic resources. Thus, while generic strategies may be used to label an entity's basic strategic focus, broad generalizations alone are not useful for understanding differences that lead to a sustained competitive/comparative advantage. The resource-based theory provides an explanation to understand why entities do obtain strategic advantage and are able to keep it. The theory has been used previously in IT to explain how information technology could be used to gain competitive advantage. It also gives an interesting framework to assess whether an activity should be kept internally or outsourced. It focuses on the strategic resources that entities develop and nurture.

Even though they are not always readily discernible, these resources are important investments for organizations and countries alike, and as such should be leveraged for strategic advantage. The key elements on which the resource-based theory is constructed are simple deviations from the perfect market environment. Resource-based theory argues that, in many situations, three hypotheses of a perfect market are not met: economic entities are constrained by their past choices (history matters); the resources are not perfectly mobile; and expertise is not easy to reproduce or imitate. These elements are discussed in sequence, and can be applied at the macro level to a country's economy.

Recent work in the area of resource-based strategy has sought to more clearly explicate the role of resource value in determining firm competitiveness and performance (Barney, 2001). Bowman and Ambrosini (2000, p. 1) note that 'a more precise and rounded underpinning theory of value is required to help us identify "valuable resources"'. These authors then proceed to set out a process model that distinguishes between creating new 'use value' and capturing 'exchange value'. We are concerned with both the 'use value' and the 'exchange value' in this book, as 'use value' of goods is perceived by potential buyers and 'exchange value' is perceived as a key determinant in the profitability of resource-based strategies. As we focus mostly on managers' perceptions of value in this chapter, we specifically define value to be that (or those) characteristics of a good that makes the firm better off (more capable, more efficient, more effective, and so on) with the good than without it. These characteristics are embodied in the components of our model discussed later. Naturally, there are several ways to define 'value' in this context (Bowman and Ambrosini, 2000), but to us the 'use value' perceived by managers is more important than the perceived value inherent in the good under consideration. Valuable resource bundles are heterogeneous not so much because of inert physical characteristics of the assets but because of their unique employment in the creation of use value. The uniqueness of such employment arises from the initial perceptual differences upon which our model elaborates.

These perceptual insights cannot be easily transferred across the boundaries of economic entities. What implications does this have for price and value? Resource-based scholars suggest that value/price discrepancies form the first step in the development of sustainable competitive advantages, as some firms 'see' opportunities that elude others (Barney, 1986). Above-normal returns accrue in such scenarios as ultimate values are not fully imputed into the costs of procurement (Rumelt, 1987). Sellers in the resource-based scenario may fail to recognize this value, and thus fail to incorporate true asset value into the prices they charge (Barney, 2001). Competitors may also fail to grasp these insights and therefore will provide less than adequate competition necessary to drive the knowledge-rich firm's returns to 'normal' levels. It is this learned, tacit valuation capability that provides the potential for resource-based competitive advantage.

Viewed from a growth perspective, resource-based theory is concerned with the origin, evolution and sustainability of firms. Firms experiencing the highest growth have added new competencies sequentially, often over extended periods of time (Hall, 1992; 1993). Although everyone seems to agree that resources are developed in a complex, path-dependent process, no resource-based theorist has explained or predicted this growth path. With the exception of work investigating the direction of firm diversification (Montgomery and Hariharan, 1991), analysis of the sequential development process of a firm's resource base over time is lacking in the literature. Resource-based sequencing is important for achieving sustainable growth (Heene and Sanchez, 1997). In a changing environment, firms must continuously invent and upgrade their resources and capabilities if they are to maintain and sustain their competitive advantage and growth. Firms need to maintain the VRIS attributes of their resources (Valuable, Rare, hard to Imitate, and hard to Substitute).

Looking at this from a country's perspective, it is safe to state that countries cannot simply buy these resources and capabilities without investing heavily and incurring lots of expenses, which in most cases they do not have. This is because the resources and capabilities are built over time in a path-dependent process that makes them inextricably interwoven into a specific economy. This facet of resources and capabilities development makes it theoretically impossible for competing countries to imitate completely.

As indicated above, the RBV framework identifies four attributes for assessing whether a resource has the potential to generate sustainable competitive advantage. On the one hand, Barney and Hesterly (2012) state that sustainable competitive advantage will occur only if acquired resources possess the following attributes: they are valuable, rare, imperfectly imitable, and hard to substitute. On the other hand, powerful forces for change are re-mapping the economic and business environment and have also led to a key alteration in adopted processes. The fundamental drivers of change comprise globalization, higher degrees of complexity, new technology, intense competition, volatile customer demands, and movements in the economic and political structure. These evolutions mean economic entities/countries must strive to learn quickly, respond faster, and proactively adapt and shape their structure. Economic entities are beginning to perceive that the conventional product-based competitive/comparative advantages are transient and that the only sustainable competitive advantages they possess are their resources. This means a greater focus, in practice, on intangible assets; what that means to developing countries is more emphasis on raising awareness, creating and increasing cybersecurity training, and in general, developing well crafted cybersecurity policies and strategies. To improve competitive momentum and to endure over time in a competitive market, economic entities need to measure, assess and manage their strategic potential with incomparable efficacy.

In 2015, Wu et al. redefined the foundation of the RBV of the firm and they recommended some guidelines on how to link the governing cyber activities of entities and economic/financial performances of the entities in question.

Bahl and Wali (2014) looked at employees' perception of information technology security and the quality of service provided to customers in Indian Software Service Providers. Luiijf et al. (2013) suggested that top executives implement cybersecurity to protect companies from cyber-criminal activities that will compromise the integrity and confidentiality of available data and information in their units and may lead to great economic and financial losses.

Burton (2015) identified and discussed the challenges that small, developing countries face in trying to deal with cybersecurity issues. The author also indicated the risks associated with the growing cyberattacks both on the public and the private sectors in New Zealand. As an economic entity, New Zealand is still trying to find the point of equilibrium where cyber policies protect its citizens without compromising their privacy. Looking at cybersecurity risks associated with emerging technologies, Ali et al. (2015) studied risks associated with the diffusion of cloud technology. They noted that cloud security risks are related to problems associated with the architectural, contractual and legal levels of the systems and associated infrastructure.

Oluga et al. (2014) explored the fundamental criminal activities associated with cyber space and indicated that looking at those activities from a resource based view, cybercriminals disseminate different forms of cybercrimes, including: cyber gaming; cyber journalism; cyber broadcasting; cyber advertising; cyber politics; cyber medicine; cyber governance; cyber tourism; cyber evangelism; cyber mobilization; cyber commerce; cyber learning; cyber entertainment; and cyber socialization. Based on the authors' classification, major modern-day cybercrimes and threats are: cyber harassment; cyber defamation; cyber impersonation; cyber prostitution; cyber child porn; cyber gambling; cyber fraud; cyber murder; cyber warfare; cyber espionage; cyber terrorism; cyber spoofing; cyber service denial; cyber piracy; cyber-jacking; cyber malware; illicit cyber business; and cyber blackmail (Oluga et al., 2014). Defining each type of cybercriminal activities is beyond the scope of this book.

Robinson et al. (2015) surveyed the current state of research in the area of cyber warfare. They classified research in the area of cyber warfare into a number of categories including: early warning systems; ethics of cyber warfare; applying existing laws to cyber warfare; conducting cyber warfare; cyber weapons; attribution problems; cyber defense and deterrence; conceptualizing cyber warfare; and nations' perspectives.

Examining the above-mentioned studies, especially Oluga et al. (2014) and Robinson et al. (2015), it can be inferred that having the appropriate resources to deal with the above-listed crimes and developing the appropriate policies and strategies to minimize their negative impact at all levels, economically, politically, culturally and socially, constitute the necessary conditions for success, especially in the developing/emerging world.

Intrinsic Resources

Taking an inward look at a country and its intrinsic resources such as the cultural, political and economic sub-systems, in addition to the regulatory framework, and the social variables involved will help us assess the level of the country's economic growth and development. Supposedly, the level of economic development of the country will be associated with a higher interest in strategic issues in IT management and cybersecurity investment. In addition to investment in IT infrastructure and protection of cyber space, among the strategic issues in IT we can mention I-based business process redesign, planning, and managing telecommunications networks, improving information systems strategic planning, and so on. On the other hand, issues such as the scarcity of qualified human resources and obsolescence of computing equipment are still of great importance in developing and less advanced countries (Okunoye, 2014). A few countries such as the United Arab Emirates have developed very useful policies and adopted strategies to (1) develop their indigenous workforce through training and education, and (2) attract talents from neighboring countries by facilitating movement of skills into the country (Karake and Al Qasimi, 2003).

Extrinsic Resources

The authors maintain that external resources and forces impact the development of cybersecurity strategies and policies and the level of investment in cybersecurity. Three extrinsic factors were identified as sources of synergy impacting cybersecurity investment, and deemed vital in contributing to the development of an effective IT infrastructure, an efficient investment in cybersecurity, and the protection of cyber space. These are first, a country's being part of an economic block, that is, members of a sub-regional integration group such as the Association of Southeast Asian Nations (ASEAN) or the Gulf Cooperation Council (GCC). Being an active member in those groups creates some kind of synergy and causes a trickle-down effect. It is believed that sub-regional integration groups facilitate cooperation, encourage synergies, avoid duplication of efforts and pool their initiatives in a way that will create value-added. Secondly, countries which are subject to a hostile environment and being under the constant risk of their systems being compromised by a bigger power will be motivated to fortify their cyber space and invest both in tangible and intangible resources to strengthen their cybersecurity. A good example here is the countries of Estonia and Georgia: both countries' infrastructures were attacked and compromised by the Russians in 2007 and 2015 respectively. Reactively, these external forces led both countries to invest heavily in cybersecurity and strengthen their technological infrastructures. Thirdly, sometimes requirements placed by NGOs and international regulatory bodies act as external forces pressuring countries to invest in cybersecurity and to strengthen their technological infrastructures. The International Communication Union (ITU) and the United Nations Conference on Trade and Development (UNCTAD) are examples of those international bodies. It is important to mention here that, given the interconnected nature of the world, if a country is to be an active participant and engage in international trade, and attract foreign direct investment (FDI), it needs to show that its systems are protected.

Based on the second Global Cybersecurity Index (GCI) published in 2017 by the ITU, only close to about half of all countries in the world have a cybersecurity strategy or are in the process of developing one, and only 38 percent of countries around the world have a published cybersecurity strategy. The report states that more effort is needed in this important area since having a well devised cybersecurity strategy and policy sends a loud message that governments place digital risks on the high priority list. Among the countries, the top-10 list in the ITU report includes Singapore and Malaysia; in addition, in January 2018, a report published by A.T. Kearny (Ganapathy, 2018) found that in addition to Singapore and Malaysia, the Philippines and Thailand were the top countries in the ASEAN region when it comes to cybersecurity. The common denominator among those four countries is that they are members of the ASEAN regional pack; in addition, they established the Asia Pacific Regional Intelligence Center to help them cooperate in the cybersecurity area and share intelligence about activities in cyber space. Being members of this center creates a host of extrinsic synergies affecting those countries' outlooks and approaches regarding cybersecurity.

Tangible versus Intangible Resources

Resources come in two broad categories: tangibles, or property-based, and intangibles, or knowledge-based. Some resources, such as patents, cannot be imitated since they are protected by property rights; knowledge-based barriers protect the majority of intangible resources. When an economic entity has exclusive ownership of a valuable resource that cannot be legally imitated by other competitors, it controls that resource. This economic entity will attain superior returns until market conditions change to diminish the return on that resource. Any competitor wanting to acquire the resource will have to offer the discounted future value of its expected economic returns. Examples of tangible resources are enforceable long-term contracts that monopolize scarce resources such as exclusive rights to a valuable technology, or exclusive access to distribution channels.

Tangible resources provide economic entities with a protection from competition by generating assets that are not available to other competing economic agents—at least not under equally favorable terms (Franco and Haase, 2013). Further, most competing economic agents will be aware of the value of a competitor's tangible resources, and they may even have the necessary knowledge to create identical resources. However, those newcomers either lack the legal right or the necessary skill-set to imitate effectively. It might be argued that in order for tangible resources to produce above-average economic return, they require protection from exclusionary legal contracts, trade restrictions, or first-mover pre-emption (Karake and Al Qasimi, 2010).

As an intangible resource, tacit knowledge acts as a barrier protecting resources from being imitated. Those resources cannot be imitated by other economic agents because they are less identifiable and are difficult to understand because they involve talents that are elusive and whose connection with results is difficult to discern (Kabir, 2013). Intangible resources often take the form of particular skills: technical, creative and collaborative. For example, some economic agents have the technical and creative skill-sets to develop competitive products and market them successfully. Others may have the collaborative or integrative skills that help experts to work and learn together very effectively (Eyring et al., 2011).

Intangible resources allow economic agents to dominate not by market control or by eliminating competition, but by giving their entities the skills to adapt their offerings to market needs and to deal with competitive challenges. The high return on those skills is credited to the fact that competition is ignorant of why a certain economic agent is successful. It is often hard to know to realize why those intangible resources may have what Lippman and Rumelt (1982) called 'uncertain imitability': they are protected from imitation not by legal or financial barriers, but by knowledge barriers.

The advantages of tangible and intangible resources are quite different. Existing laws allow an economic agent to control the resources it needs to gain a competitive edge. They may, for example, have exclusive access to certain supplies or markets, keeping those out of the control of competing economic agents. Intangible resources are better directed at responding and adapting to the challenges facing an economic agent. As an example, creative skills can be utilized to interpret market characteristics and respond to developing market trends. It is important to note that tangible and intangible resources might be interdependent and reinforce each other. As a matter of fact, in many instances intangible resources lead to the development of tangible resources. However, while the benefits of intangible resources are quite specific, and thus the resources are appropriate mostly for the environment for which they were developed, intangible resources, including skill-sets, can be transferred from one economic agent to another. In other words, intangible, knowledge-based resources often tend to be less specific and more flexible.

Some tangible resources are in the form of systems and their interwoven components; these typically include physical and economic agents' physical infrastructure. By themselves, most concrete facilities are easily imitable: thus, much of their value relies on their role within and their links to an integrated system whose synergy is hard to duplicate. This is true of some integrated supply, manufacturing and distribution systems. The units of a distribution network, for example, may be valuable because of their connection with a steady source of supply or with economies of administration and promotion engendered by a well respected parent company (Brumagin, 1994).

Predictable settings do not typically call for as deep or extensive set of skills for product or process innovation and adaptation as do uncertain and changing environments. Some economic agents not only have a depth of technical, functional and creative expertise, but they are also adept at integrating and coordinating that expertise. They invest in collaborative efforts that promote adaptation and flexibility. Indeed, it is not just skills in any one domain, but rather the way skills from several domains complement one another in an economic setting that gives many agents their competitive advantage (Hall, 1993). Being an intangible resource, the set of collaborative skills is most likely subject to uncertain imitability. According to Reed and DeFillippi, 'ambiguity may be derived from the complexity of skills and/or resource interactions within competencies and from interaction between competencies' (1990: 93). The systemic nature of coordinative skills makes certain intangible resources more valuable to a certain economic agent than to its competitors. Collaborative skills typically do not develop through programmed or routine activity. Instead, they require nurturing from a history of challenging product development projects. These long-term projects force specialists from different angles of an economy to work together intensively on a complex set of problems. And such interaction broadens both the technical and social knowledge of economic actors and promotes ever more effective collaboration.

The above arguments suggest that team building is apt to be more necessary, more rewarding, and perhaps even more likely in uncertain than in predictable environments. Collaborative talents are robust—they apply to a wide variety of situations and products. In contrast with fixed routines, teamwork enables companies to handle complex and changing contingencies (Thompson, 1967). Moreover, 'unlike physical assets, competencies do not deteriorate as they are applied and shared ... They grow' (Prahalad and Hamel, 1990: 82). Collaborative skills not only remain useful under changing environments, but they also help firms to adapt and develop new products for evolving markets (Lawrence and Lorsch, 1967; Thompson, 1967). Indeed, the flexibility born of multi-functional collaboration will help firms to respond quickly to market changes and challenges (Mahoney and Pandian, 1992). In stable environments, on the other hand, the returns to collaborative and adaptive skills may be small. Where tasks are unvarying, coordination can be routinized very efficiently, and thus coordinative or team skills will be less important (Thompson, 1967). Moreover, when customer tastes and rivals' strategies are stable, there is little need to constantly redesign or adapt products. In such contexts, the benefits of intensive collaboration may not justify the costs.

Another side to the RBV has to do with the New Institutional Economics approach which attempts to incorporate a theory of institutions into economics. However, in contrast to the many earlier attempts to topple or take the place of neoclassical theory, the New Institutional Economics builds on, amends and broadens neoclassical theory to allow it to come to grips and deal with an entire range of issues beyond its domain. What it maintains and builds on is the fundamental assumption of scarcity and hence competition. What it leaves behind is instrumental rationality—the assumption of neoclassical economics that has made it an institution-free theory. Institutions are formed to reduce uncertainty in human exchange. Together with the technology utilized, they determine the costs of transacting. Coase (1937) made the central connection between institutions, transaction costs and neoclassical theory. As he stated, 'the neoclassical result of efficient markets only obtains when it is costless to transact; when it is costly to transact, institutions matter' (p. 391). And because a large part of our national income is devoted to transacting, institutions and specifically property rights are crucial determinants of the efficiency of markets. Practically, there is still a tendency for the resource-based theory and the branches of New Institutional Economics to be used in isolation from one another. For example, much research in financial economics still assumes away firm heterogeneity, except perhaps for industry membership, and concentrates upon the agency problem, while some strategy research ignores agency considerations as belonging to a lower level or strategy implementation dimension. This division is far from universal and it was seen above that the analysis of corporate refocusing issues has drawn liberally upon both traditions. However, one consequence of the bifurcation is the relative neglect of governance–RBV interactions. It was noted earlier that the internal governance devices adopted by the firm (the composition of its board, the control systems covering its divisional management and so on) do not merely have implications for the level of agency costs, but have implications for the optimal configuration of the firm's activities.

The firm's governance mechanisms (both internal and external) are to be considered as a relevant resource. For example, in the USA or UK these could include the skills of the non-executive directors and in Germany could include the firm's interlocking directorships with suppliers and customers and its banker relationships (Cable and Dirrheimer, 1983). Similarly, the firm's set of transactional arrangements with suppliers and customers is not simply a cost-minimizing device, in terms of transaction cost economics (TCE), but a resource that may yield competitive advantage. In general, this suggests that firms may need to secure an appropriate fit between the set of activities undertaken and the governance mechanisms and transactional arrangements in place. For example, external factors, such as the debt–equity funding mix and the extent of equity ownership concentration, may influence the optimal mix of activities (Demsetz and Lehn, 1985). Similarly, internal factors, including the choice between strategic and financial control systems, may determine the appropriate extent of diversification. The authors share the view that in the early stages of market development, institutional theory is unmatched in illuminating the impact on government strategies. This is because government and societal pressures are stronger in developing economies than in developed countries. Institutional theory underlines the influences of the social and organizational behavior of organizations. These systems might be internal or external to the company, and they do affect an organization's processes and decision making. Perspectives derived to examine these institutional pressures have both an economic orientation and a sociological orientation. This new theory focuses on the interaction of institutions and organizations resulting from market imperfections (Harris et al., 1995). North (1990) maintains that institutions provide the rules of the game that shape interactions in societies and that economic entities are the players constrained by those rules (formal and informal). The role of institutions in an economy is to reduce information costs and information asymmetry through minimizing uncertainty and crafting a stable structure that facilitates interactions. Palmer et al. (1993) examined the institutional constraints on American corporations in developing countries. The authors tested the institutional, political and economic accounts of adoption of the multidivisional form (MDF) among large US industrial corporations in the 1960s, most notably by elaborating the institutional account. Their results suggested that institutional processes, including coercive and normative dynamics, substantially underpinned the MDF's diffusion during the 1960s. Firms producing in industries that had shunned the MDF earlier in the twentieth century were slow to adopt this form in the 1960s, an effect mediated by the percentage of firms in a corporation's sector using the MDF at the time. Firms with high debt-to-equity ratios, whose chief executives had elite business school degrees, and whose directors had non-directional corporate board contracts with the directors of MDF firms, adopted the MDF more frequently than other firms. Peng and Heath (1996) argued that the internal growth of transition economies is limited by institutional constraints. As a result, it was concluded that a network-based growth strategy was more appropriate in developing economies. Child and Lu (1996) maintained that economic reform of large state-owned enterprises was moving very slowly because of relational and cultural constraints. Following the same rationale Suhomlinova (1999) found that government institutions had a negative impact on Russian enterprise reform. In a study done on Chinese enterprises, Lau (1998) concluded that market and political forces were the institutional constraints that hindered the effective functioning of chief executive officers (CEOs) in these enterprises. Many firms in developing and emerging economies are influenced by existing institutional mechanisms and realities.

From a strategic perspective, institutions can also facilitate the process of strategy formulation, alignment and implementation. Enterprises can play a more active role in an institutional environment when these institutional mechanisms allow them to maneuver and move beyond imposed constraints. A number of studies dealing with institutional effects on developing countries have focused mostly on state-owned enterprises.

In 1996, Lee and Miller studied the changes of institutional mechanisms and their impact on firms in various industries in Korea (Lee and Miller, 1996). They found that firms benefited to various degrees from a number of institutional and cultural changes in the country. Soulsby and Clark (1996) showed how institutional changes in the Czech Republic have led to a revamping of how managers think about and do their jobs in terms of acquiring new strategic thinking skills and other managerial techniques which are more appropriate to their new semi-open market environment. In an earlier article, Jefferson and Rawski (1995) concluded that the success of industrial reform in China was attributed to relaxing institutional constraints, market-leaning institutional change, development of property rights, and gradual relaxation of state ownership and control. In the case of China, these institutional changes provided appropriate incentives and the necessary changes in corporate culture that motivated firms and enabled them to take steps forward. The number of studies using resource-based and institutional perspectives in developing economies is scarce, even though some theorists have argued that these perspectives are the most applicable for explaining economic behavior in developing economies. Characterized by trends toward market liberalization and privatization but still heavily regulated, developing and emerging economies provide the necessary institutional and resource influences in testing the theories.

DEVELOPING ECONOMIES AND RBV

Until recently, little research using a RBV framework had examined strategy differences in the social context of developing economies. As with most resources that create competitive advantage, resources for competitive advantage in developing economies are, on the whole, intangible. However, they are not necessarily market or product specific, as might be expected. Although some qualifications are standard regardless of the level of development (for instance, first-mover advantages), others are particularly important in developing economies. Global and multinational firms that are able to manage some of the imperfect conditions in developing economies benefit from being first movers; some of the benefits include economic advantages of sales volume, knowledge of domestic regulatory environments and economies of scale. In general, many of the developing countries use the economics of free markets as the primary engine for growth. Hoskisson et al. (2000) investigated two groups of emerging and developing countries: (1) the developing countries in Asia, Latin America, Africa, and the Middle East; and (2) the transition countries in the former Soviet Union and China. Both private and public enterprises have had to take different paths and use different strategies in dealing with the two distinct groups of developing countries. The research has examined the different strategies and implementation paths used by private and public businesses from a number of theoretical perspectives. One of these perspectives is the RBV of the firm.

In most developing and emerging economies, the postcolonial period saw the materialization of a state-centric form of governance, especially due to the lack of private capital and the absence of sophisticated market forces. More significantly, the role of the state expanded a great deal as a result of governments' national developmental agendas. Furthermore, many economic entities were brought under the management of the state through gigantic nationalization programs in order to end foreign economic dominance (cases in point are Egypt and Algeria). These programs brought with them immediate needs for basic services such as education and health that had to be provided by government in the absence of private sector initiatives (Haque, 2002). In fact, most of these initiatives were often supported by international aid agencies prior to the 1980s. But since the early 1980s the mode of governance has changed in developing and emerging countries. This is due to the impact of globalization demanding the substitution of state agencies by market-driven mechanisms supported by economic policies and institutions under a new political economy model.

In responding to the New Political Economy, developing and emerging governments have attempted to reduce the range of public governance through various measures such as privatization, deregulation and downsizing, and to restructure its functions by emphasizing the state's role as a facilitator while assigning the main role to the private sector (UNCTAD, 2015). For instance, as a result of pressure from international agencies such as the World Bank and the International Monetary Fund, gigantic privatization and deregulation initiatives have been undertaken in most Asian, African and Latin American countries. Some of the well-known examples include Argentina, Brazil, Chile, Indonesia, Malaysia, Mexico, Nigeria, Pakistan, the Philippines, South Korea and Thailand. In these countries different approaches of privatization have been adopted in major sectors such as telecommunications, airlines, electricity, petroleum, automobiles, television, fertilizers, tobacco, banking, insurance, and so on. This unparalleled process of privatization has significantly reduced the state's economic control in these countries. In addition, most governments have also taken initiatives to directly downsize the public sector to create greater avenues for the private sector. For example, under the influence of the World Bank and the Asian Development Bank, Malaysia has implemented measures to downsize the public sector; the Philippines has adopted the strategy of 'streamlining the bureaucracy' to reduce staff by 5–10 percent; Singapore has applied a zero-manpower growth policy in order to ultimately reduce the number of public employees by 10 percent, and Thailand has put on hold new employment (Borst and Lako, 2017). Similarly, India has decided to downsize the public sector by reducing public employment by 30 percent, and Sri Lanka has introduced an early retirement policy and retrenched thousands of government employees. In Latin America, governments started to reduce or freeze public sector employment twenty years ago; examples are Argentina, Bolivia, Brazil and Mexico. A recent study shows that between the early 1980s and 1990s, as a percentage of total population, the number of central government employees decreased from 2.6 to 1.1 percent in Asia, 1.8 to 1.1 percent in Africa, and 2.4 to 1.5 percent in Latin America (Schiavo-Campo, 1998: 465). These downsizing exercises express the growing tendency of developing and emerging economies to reorganize public governance in line with the overall agenda for its diminishing role in socioeconomic activities. In recent years, the governments in

India, Malaysia, Pakistan, Singapore, Sri Lanka and Thailand have de-emphasized the role of public bureaucracy as the primary actor in socioeconomic development, redefining its role to facilitate or enable the business sector to take more active initiatives to deliver services. According to the World Bank (2015), in Arab countries such as Algeria and Jordan the recent structural adjustment programs have led to a greater role for private enterprises and investors, while the public sector has to enable rather than constrain such enterprises and investors. The overall objective of this restructuring of the role of public governance vis-à-vis business sector management has been to reduce the prominence of interventionist states and to expand the sphere of national and global market forces.

In line with the assumption of the New Political Economy, there have emerged a number of reform initiatives to restructure the organization and management of public governance based on the experiences of the private sector. The trends are toward commercializing government entities, adopting corporate practices, managing public agencies like private companies, and forming partnerships with business enterprises. These worldwide trends in restructuring governance can be observed today in many Asian, African and Latin American countries. More specifically, various government ministries and departments have been converted into businesslike 'autonomous agencies' enjoying considerable operational autonomy in financial, personnel and administrative matters. Following the examples of developed nations, many developing and emerging countries have introduced these structural changes in governance. In South Asia, Pakistan has introduced such a structure in specific sectors such as railway, telephone and rural energy. In Southeast Asia, Singapore has introduced the most complete program to convert almost all government departments into autonomous agencies based on comprehensive restructuring of the budget and personnel systems. In various degrees, managerial autonomy in governance has also emerged in Indonesia, Malaysia, the Philippines and Thailand. These new structural movements in governance represent an unmatched shift from the traditional bureaucratic model practiced in developing countries. In addition to these internal restructuring initiatives, there have been external structural changes, especially in terms of increasing partnership between the public and private sectors. In embarking on new projects, initiating new policies, and delivering services, such public–private partnership or alliance has expanded in Asian countries including India, Indonesia, Malaysia, Pakistan, the Philippines, Singapore, Thailand and Vietnam, although this deeper public–private alliance often creates potential for conflict of interest between public agencies and business firms. The number of joint ventures has also increased in various African and Latin American countries such as Argentina, Mexico and South Africa. This business-like restructuring of public agencies and expansion of public–private collaboration implies diminishing boundaries between the public and private sectors.

DETERRENCE THEORY

Deterrence is grounded in military theory and it dates back to the 1920s when the first flight bombers were perceived to be irresistible as far as defensive measures were concerned. There is no one single definition of deterrence, but the term's origin comes from the Latin *deterrere*, and, as defined by Webster, it means 'to discourage and turn aside or restrain by fear'. This definition underlines the two perceptions of proactive deterrence: (1) the would-be cybercriminal will be discouraged by the would-be victim's defenses; and (2) the criminal will be restrained for fear of retaliation.

Deterrence is generally viewed in terms of leading opponents to believe that a specific action would provoke a strong response resulting in intolerable damage that would be more damaging than any likely benefit. As a process, deterrence possesses a number of dynamic attributes allowing continuous feedback, identifying who will be deterred, and how they will be deterred. Within this frame of reference, and as far as deterrence in cyber space is concerned, this may include legal responses, international collaboration, and successfully secured communication lines among the parties involve (Kshetri, 2013).

It is important to stress at the outset that laws and policies and their associated penalties only deter would-be cybercriminals if three conditions are present:

* fear of penalty;
* possibility of being apprehended;
* likelihood of associated penalty being applied.

The most controversial aspect of deterrence theory is related to nuclear proliferation. Under these circumstances, countries try to arm themselves with many nuclear arsenals in an effort to accomplish nuclear parity with other countries to diminish conflict and maintain stability. Applied to cyber space, deterrence focuses on pushing potential cybercriminals to think twice before engaging in criminal activities. The main thesis here is to make would-be cybercriminals pay great attention to the penalties associated with their actions, as well as the punishment that might come from any legal responses. Many theorists and practitioners still have their doubts about whether cyber deterrence is effective in the long run. To be able to shed some light on the effectiveness of cyber deterrence, one must understand the theories or concepts behind effective deterrence strategies and how they apply to cybercriminal activities.

The basis of cyber deterrence goes back to the early time of Operation Desert Storm in 1991. During that time, the United States pursued what was called 'information warfare' against the Iraqi forces, shattering Iraq's military communications infrastructure. This was the first significant cyber deterrence activity in recent memory. This was followed by other cyberattacks such as the one on Estonia in 2007, and the one on Georgia in 2008. Attention then turned to deterring cyberattacks that have strategic and political significances (Stevens, 2012). In the past decade, many attacks were launched by nation states against other nation states; noteworthy are the attacks on Georgia and the Ukraine in 2014 and 2015.

Based on existing theories, there are two main types of deterrence: (1) deterrence associated with denial which aims specifically at convincing would-be cybercriminals that they won't succeed, at least without massive effort and cost beyond what they are willing to invest; and (2) deterrence associated with punishment intending to make sure that, if they decide to engage in cybercriminal activities, the criminals know there will be a forceful response to their actions and that they might sustain more damaging consequences than they are willing to endure. To discourage would-be criminals from launching offensive acts, deterrence theory identifies two techniques, as described by Libicki (2009), deterrence by denial, or passive deterrence; and deterrence by punishment, or active deterrence.

Passive Cyber Deterrence/Deterrence by Denial

Passive cybersecurity addresses deterrence principally through the norms of denial; that is, trying to stop attackers before they engage in cybercriminal activities and reach their aims, or in the case of an attack, minimize the harmful consequences on the cyber infrastructure. From a cyber space perspective, denial or passive deterrence includes those actions taken to secure a country's infrastructure, both hard and soft, from cybercriminal activities or to build robust networks that reduce the damaging impact of the cybercriminal activity. These measures are necessary to ensure a secure cybersecurity infrastructure but they are not sufficient in the sense that they do not carry a sizeable influence in aggressively discouraging cyberattacks. They can, however, make it harder for the cybercriminal to have a damaging impact on the cyber infrastructure of a country.

Deterrence by denial involves increasing login security, securing data and boosting communications, protecting systems against viruses, worms, Trojan horses and other malware, and ensuring that systems are securely equipped to reduce vulnerability and weaknesses when they are attacked. These precautions are vital when one considers the prevalence of the Internet of Things (IoT) in societies worldwide. Cybersecurity expert Bruce Schneier (2017) appropriately describes the pervasiveness of insecure IoT devices as a market failure similar to pollution. As far as security of IoT devices is concerned, Schneier argues that device manufacturers are to blame. He suggests levying more regulations on manufacturers to motivate them to produce devices with higher security standards, or holding them accountable when their products are the sources responsible for launching cyberattacks on a country's cyber infrastructure or compromising a nation's systems.

Deterrence by denial, then, aims at minimizing the benefits an attacker seeks to gain by improving defensive measures to protect computer systems and networks (Jasper, 2015). It has to do with the persuasion of would-be cybercriminals that the cost of their action is not going to be fruitful and that their aggression is not going to be successful. A number of strategies can be adopted to increase the effectiveness of deterrence by denial: the first strategy is building *redundancy* into the country's infrastructural systems. It is a known fact that redundant systems stop would-be cyberattackers from crippling the entire system (Taipale, 2010). The second strategy is an after-the-fact strategy, which deals with *recovery* (Taipale, 2010). Some theorists refer to this as 'reconstitution' or 'antifragility' (Jensen, 2012). Based on this strategy, it is believed that would-be cyberattackers would be discouraged from launching their attacks if they knew the system was capable of rapidly recovering its capabilities following a cyberattack (Taipale, 2010).

At this point, it is worth noting the value-added of incorporating an active cyber defense strategy into the cybersecurity policy. Active deterrence covers a number of proactive measures. Examining its application to the private sector in the United States, active deterrence refers to cooperation with cybersecurity providers for the detection of cyber interferences (Jasper, 2015). Notwithstanding the importance of active deterrence, a number of theorists and practitioners maintain that active deterrence brings with it a high risk of escalation and might lead to ethical dilemmas caused by its potential impact upon innocent third parties, or what is called collateral damage (Bendiek and Metzger, 2015).

In summary, it is clear that governments can no longer afford to deal with cybersecurity reactively by identifying weaknesses and fixing them. Many countries around the world have realized that being passive in deterring cybercriminal activities and making cybercrimes less attractive is the way to go.

Active Cyber Deterrence/Deterrence by Punishment

When it comes to taking action against attackers, there are many ways to monitor, identify and counter criminally inclined cyberattacks. In the mainstream criminological context, Bentham describes deterrence-by-retaliation, or deterrence-by-punishment, as imposing the 'significant likelihood of any culprit being apprehended, brought to trial, found guilty and then receiving a sentence,' (Bowring, 2013). These active cyber defenses are equivalent to air defense systems that oversee the sky for enemy aircraft and shoot down inbound artilleries. Network monitors that watch for and block ('shoot down') hostile packets are one example, as are honeypots that attract or deflect adversary packets into safe areas. There, they do not harm the targeted network, and can even be studied to reveal attackers' techniques.

Another set of active defenses involves collecting, analyzing and sharing information about potential threats so that network operators can respond to the latest developments. For example, operators could regularly scan their systems looking for devices vulnerable to or compromised by the Mirai botnet or other malware (Bendiek and Metzger, 2015). If they found some, they could disconnect the devices from the network and alert the devices' owners to the danger.

Active cyber defense does more than just deny attackers opportunities. It can often unmask the people behind them, leading to punishment. Non-government attackers can be shut down, arrested and prosecuted, and countries conducting or supporting cyber warfare can be sanctioned by the international community. Currently, however, the private sector is not willing to employ many active defenses because of legal and regulatory uncertainties.

In addition, international standards for cyber space can support deterrence if national governments perceive that they would be named and shamed within the global community for launching a cyberattack or helping to cover up for cybercriminals. As an example, in 2014 the United States brought charges against five Chinese military hackers for launching cyberattacks against American companies. This action led to a positive reaction from the Chinese government: a year after the charges were brought against the Chinese hackers, China and the United States reached an agreement aiming at refraining from stealing and exploiting each other's corporate secrets for commercial advantage. This has led to a noticeable decrease in Chinese cyber espionage against the United States.

In 2015 a group of experts from the United Nations recommended outlawing cyberattacks against critical infrastructure, including a country's computer emergency response teams (CERTs). This was followed by the G20 issuing a statement opposing the theft of intellectual property to benefit commercial entities. It remains to be seen if these actions will deter nation states' cybercriminal activities and minimize governments' willingness to conduct such attacks.

In summary, cyber space will never be immune to attack—any more than our streets will be immune to crime. But with stronger cybersecurity, increased use of active cyber defenses, and international cyber norms, we can hope at least to keep a lid on the problem.

Cyber Deterrence and Cybersecurity Policies

There are a number of characteristics associated with an effective deterrence strategy. Goodman (2010) identified a number of attributes which characterize a successful deterrence strategy. The authors believe the following four characteristics are applicable to cybercriminal activities carried out on developing nations. First is what he calls *deterrent declaration*; this is intended to keep the cybercriminals from launching attacks on the country's infrastructure. Here the country will make a declaration warning the would-be attackers of the consequences of their actions. This might be classified as passive or active deterrence. The second characteristic is what is termed *credibility*; this is defined as the cybercriminal's belief that the attacked country will be able to carry out the *deterrent declaration*, in other words, for the attacked country to respond accordingly. The third characteristic is *denial measures*. These are the defensive aspects of deterrence, which consist of preventive measures (passive measures). In other words, this concerns the belief of the would-be cybercriminal that when an attack is taking place, the defensive measures will minimize the likelihood of success of the attack. The fourth characteristic is *penalty measures*. This is associated with retaliation (active measure). According to the deterrence theory, to be effective, penalty measures have to be immediate, harsh and painful.

Based on the above, it is believed that any successful cybersecurity policy needs to address the four above attributes. It is believed that these attributes constitute a necessary condition for a well written/implemented cybersecurity policy.

How Can Developing Nations Improve Cyber Deterrence?

1. Developing cybersecurity policy with enough teeth to enforce the penalties set forth in the policy;
2. improving active defense of their cyber environment by fortifying protection of their cyber infrastructure; and
3. abiding by international norms set forth for cyber space. This requires cooperation among the various developing nations and the beefing up of capacity building.

The main components of deterrence theory are punishment (of offensive nature), and denial (of defensive nature). Determining the main factors of criminal deterrence depends on a clear understanding of what matters most to offenders and their perception of the costs and benefits associated with a cybercriminal act. It is important to emphasize that deterrence through punishment takes place in response to criminal laws which serve as a system of deterrent threats. Becker (1968) identifies the following ten requirements to deter by punishment: rationality, value system, threat, communication, sanctions, certainty, celerity, severity, proportionality and knowledge.

Through the process of content analysis of cybersecurity policies of a number of developing and emerging countries, the authors will identify and highlight the various constructs of deterrence contained in those policies.

CONCLUSION

This chapter was dedicated to the coverage of deterrence theory, resource-based theory, and other approaches, such as the economic approach and the public goods approach to cybersecurity. A large number of countries in the developing/emerging world have undergone, or are in the process of undergoing, digital transformation in their economic, political and social activities. While this digital transformation wave is up and running, many of those countries have stopped short of developing effective and comprehensive cybersecurity policies and strategies to help guide decision makers, citizens and regulators in what concerns cyber space. They have also failed to revamp their legal systems to deal with the many challenges associated with the information age. In order for developing/emerging countries to take full advantage of the digital transformation and improve their ability to learn, be creative, and create synergy through cooperation, they need to pay attention to how to deal with the new changes brought about by cyber space. Increasing awareness, developing cyber laws and underlining accountability are among the many topics addressed by a comprehensive and effective cybersecurity policy.

As indicated in this chapter, for deterrence to be effective, three conditions have to be met by cybersecurity policies: (1) they must include reference to the ability to attribute; (2) they must have the ability to communicate deterrence capabilities; and (3) they must have a certain level of credibility to act on the stated intentions (Trujillo, 2014). Achieving those three conditions is not as easy as it might sound, and as has been demonstrated over and over again, it is extremely difficult to attribute an attack to a specific actor or nation. As demonstrated empirically, in some cases, forensics can be used to assess attribution but this can be done only on a limited number of cases. While a cybersecurity policy does not help much with the attribution problem, it can signal and communicate a country's intentions to an adversary in case of a cyberattack, and as such deter criminals from engaging in the act.

Developing/emerging countries need to be aware of the fact that cybersecurity is not only the concern of the public sector or government. It is also a big concern of the private sector, and as such any cybersecurity policy should address the role of the private sector in creating a safe and secure cyber space. Unless a country deals with cybersecurity from all its angles, it will not be able to create a safe, trusted cyber environment.

To improve the likelihood of success in this domain, it is extremely important for countries to engage in partnerships of some kind and cooperate with other countries. Needless to say, cyber space is borderless and an attack on one system is an attack on all systems; by the same token, an attack on one country is an attack on all countries. Many countries are taking the role of partnership and cooperation in cyber space very seriously. One example is the Korean Internet Security Agency, which has created a Global Center for Cybersecurity for Development aiming at helping other developing/emerging countries with cybersecurity issues and challenges. Another example is the European Agency for Network Information Security whose main purpose is sharing incidents' data throughout Europe.

For our purpose, resources are based in an environment and, depending on the characteristics of that environment, focusing on one resource or another could create strategic advantage which might lead to positive outcomes. A number of scholars have analyzed the issue of an economic entity's sustainable advantage in terms of resource-based and institutional factors and suggested that entities are able to create or develop institutional capital to enhance optimal use of resources (Oliver, 1997). Consequently, economic entities have to manage the social context of their resources and capabilities in order to be profitable.

Research using resource-based theory and examining macro strategy difference in the social context of developing economies is absent. Similar to most resources that create competitive advantage at the micro level, resources for competitive advantage at the macro level in developing economies are mainly intangible. Although some capabilities are standard across all economies (for example first-mover advantage), others are particularly significant in developing economies (Hoskisson et al., 2000). The economic literature has paid attention to the revenue-generating promises of developing economies, and as such has focused mainly on big developing and emerging economies such as China, India and Russia. Firms that are able to manage the discouraging environments in developing economies grab hold of the benefits of first-mover advantages; few benefit from being fast followers in emerging and developing countries. Regardless of being a first-mover or fast follower, such advantages are very difficult to harness without good institutional infrastructure. Consequently, it is essential to understand the relationship between economic success (failure) and the changing nature of the institutional environment.

Achieving effective cybersecurity is not easy, and United States policymakers—as well as leaders of other countries—face critical issues, including the cyber activities of both China and the United States, that must be addressed if that goal is to be reached. At present the strategic understating of cybersecurity suffers from a 'tragedy of the commons' phenomenon by which many influential actors presume that someone else is providing for security. This phenomenon is especially highly diffused in developing and emerging countries given the level of despair about the size and complexity of the cybersecurity challenges. While this is the reality, it should not be tolerated; cyber space has no borders and the issues associated with cybersecurity are everyone's problems. Developed countries bear the moral responsibility in helping and supporting developing and emerging economies in this respect (Kleiner et al., 2013).

REFERENCES

Ali, M., Khan, S.U. and Vasilakos, A.V. (2015). Security in cloud computing: Opportunities and challenges, *Information Sciences*, **305**: 357–83.

Anderson, R., Barton, C., Bohme, R., Clayton, R., Van Eeten, M., Levi, M., Moore, T. and Savage, S. (2012). Measuring the cost of cybercrime, in *Proceedings of the 11th Annual Workshop on the Economics of Information Security*, 25–26 June, Berlin: Springer.

Asllani, A., White, C.S. and Ettkin, L. (2013). Viewing cybersecurity as a public good: The role of governments, businesses, and individuals, *Journal of Legal, Ethical and Regulatory Issues*, **16**(1): 7–14.

Bahl, S. and Wali, O.P. (2014). Perceived significance of information security governance to predict the information security service quality in software service industry: An empirical analysis, *Information Management & Computer Security*, **22**: 2–23.

Barney, J.B. (1986). Strategic factor market: Expectation, luck and business strategy, *Management Science*, **32**(10): 1231–41.

Barney, J.B. (1991). Firm resources and sustained competitive advantage, *Journal of Management*, **17**(1): 99–120.

Barney, J.B. (2001). Is the resource-based 'view' a useful perspective for strategic management research? Yes, *Academy of Management Review*, **26**(1): 41–56.

Barney, J. and Hesterly, W. (2012). *Strategic Management and Competitive Advantage*, 4th edn, Harlow: Pearson Education.

Becker, G.S. (1968). Crime and punishment: An economic approach, *Journal of Political Economy*, **76**(2): 169–217.

Bendiek, A. and Metzger, M. (2015). Deterrence theory in the cyber-century: Lessons from a state-of-the-art literature review, Working Paper, accessed 16 January 2019 at https://www.swp-berlin.org/fileadmin/contents/products/arbeitspapiere/Bendiek-Metzger_WP-Cyberdeterrence.pdf.

Biener, C., Eling, M. and Wirfs, J.H. (2015). Insurability of cyber risk: An empirical analysis, *Geneva Papers on Risk & Insurance*, **40**(1): 131–58.

Borst, R.T. and Lako, C.J. (2017). Proud to be a public servant, *International Journal of Public Administration*, **40**(10): 875–87.

Bowman, C. and Ambrosini, V. (2000). Value creation versus value capture: Towards a coherent definition of value in strategy, *British Journal of Management*, **11**: 1–15.

Bowring, J. (ed.) (2013). *The Works of Jeremy Bentham*, 11 vols, 1838–1843, Edinburgh: William Tait.

Brumagin, A.L. (1994). A hierarchy of corporate resources, in P. Shrivastava and A. Huff (eds), *Advances in Strategic Management*, vol. 10A, Greenwich, CT: JAI Press, pp. 81–112.

Burton, J. (2015). Small states and cyber security: The case of New Zealand, *Political Science*, **65**: 216–38.

Cable, J. and Dirrheimer, M. (1983). Hierarchies and markets: An empirical test of the multidivisional hypothesis in West Germany, *International Journal of Industrial Organization*, **1**(1): 43–62.

Charney, S. (2012). Collective defense: Applying the public-health model to the Internet, *IEEE Security & Privacy*, **10**(2): 54–9.

Child, J. and Lu, Y. (1996). Institutional constraints on economic reform: The case of investment decisions in China, *Organization Science*, **7**: 60–67.

Coase, R.H. (1937). The nature of the firm, *Economica*, **4**: 386–405.

Conner, Kathleen (1991). A historical comparison of resource-based theory and five schools of thought within industrial organization economics: Do we have a new theory of the firm?, *Journal of Management*, **17**(1) (March): 121–54.

Demsetz, H. and Lehn, K. (1985), The structure of ownership: Causes and consequences, *Journal of Political Economy*, **93**: 1155–77.

Eyring, M., Johnson, M.W. and Nair, H. (2011). New business models in emerging markets, *Harvard Business Review*, January–February, pp. 11–14.

Franco, M. and Haase, H. (2013). Firm resources and entrepreneurial orientation as determinants for collaborative entrepreneurship, *Management Decision*, **51**, 680–96.

Ganapathy, S. (2018). Singapore and Malaysia are ahead in cybersecurity, but concerns remain, accessed 1 March 2018 at https://www.digitalnewsasia.com/digital-economy/singapore-and-malaysia-ahead-cyber-security-concerns-remain.

Garfinkel, S.L. (2012). The cybersecurity risk, accessed 20 July 2015 at www.csl.sri.com/users/neumann/cacm227.pdf.

Garvey, P., Moynihan, R.A. and Servi, L. (2012). A macro method for measuring economic benefit returns on cybersecurity investments: The table top approach, MITRE Corporation.

Goodman, W. (2010). Cyber deterrence: Tougher in theory than in practice?, *Strategic Studies Quarterly*, Fall: 102–35.

Gordon, L. and Loeb, M. (2007). *Managing Cybersecurity Resources: A Cost-Benefit Analysis*, New York: McGraw-Hill.

Hall, R. (1992). The strategic analysis of intangible resources, *Strategic Management Journal*, **13**: 135–44.

Hall, R. (1993). A framework linking intangible resources and capabilities to sustainable competitive advantage, *Strategic Management Journal*, **14**: 607–18.

Haque, M.S. (2002). Globalization, new political economy, and governance: A third world viewpoint, *Administrative Theory and Praxis*, 24(1): 103–24.

Harris, J., Hunter, J. and Lewis, C.M. (1995). *The New Institutional Economics and Third World Development*, London: Routledge.

Heene, A. and Sanchez, R. (eds) (1997). *Competence Based Strategic Management*, Chichester: Wiley.

Hoskisson, R.E., Eden, L., Lau, C.M. and Wright, M. (2000). Strategy in emerging economies, *Academy of Management Journal*, **43**(3): 249–68.

Jasper, S. (2015). Deterring malicious behavior in cyberspace, *Strategic Studies Quarterly*, **9**(1): 60–85, accessed 12 June 2017 at http://www.airuniversity.af.mil/Portals/10/SSQ/documents/Volume-09_Issue-1/jasper.pdf.

Jefferson, G. and Rawski, W. (1995). How industrial reform worked in China: The role of innovation, competition, and property rights, Washington, DC: The World Bank, accessed 16 May 2016 at http://documents.worldbank.org/curated/en/656451468744004400/How-industrial-reform-worked-in-China-the-role-of-innovation-competition-and-property-rights.

Jensen, E.T. (2012). Cyber deterrence, *Emory International Law Review*, **26**(2): 772–824.

Kabir, N. (2013). Tacit knowledge, its codification and technological advancement, *The Electronic Journal of Knowledge Management*, **11**(3): 235–43.

Karake, Z.A. and Al Qasimi, L. (2003). *The UAE as an Information Society*, Beirut: ESCWA.

Karake, Z.A. and Al Qasimi, L. (2010). *Cyber Law and Cybersecurity in Developing and Emerging Economies*, Cheltenham, UK and Northampton, MA, USA: Edward Elgar Publishing.

Kleiner, A., Nicholas, P. and Sullivan, K. (2013). Linking cybersecurity policy and performance, Microsoft Trustworthy Computing.

Kshetri, N. (2013). *Cybercrime and Cybersecurity in the Global South*, Basingstoke: Palgrave Macmillan.

Lau, C.M. (1998). Strategic orientations of chief executives in state-owned enterprises in transition, in M.A. Hitt, J.E. Ricart, I. Costa and R.D. Nixon (eds), *Managing Strategically in an Interconnected World*, Chichester: Wiley, pp. 101–17.

Lawrence, P. and Lorsch, J. (1967). *Organization and Environment*, Boston, MA: Harvard University Press.

Lee, J. and Miller, D. (1996). Strategy, environment and performance in two technical contexts: Contingency theory in Korea, *Organization Studies*, **17**: 729–50.

Libicki, M. (2009). *Cyber Deterrence and Cyberwar*, Santa Monica, CA: Rand Corporation.

Lippman, S.A. and Rumelt, R.P. (1982). Uncertain irritability: An analysis of interfirm differences in efficiency under competition, *Bell Journal of Economics*, **13**: 418–38.

Luiijf, E., Besseling, K. and De Graaf, P. (2013). Nineteen national cyber security strategies, *International Journal of Critical Infrastructures*, **9**: 3–31.

Mahoney, J.T. and Pandian, J. (1992). The resource-based view within the conversation of strategic management, *Strategic Management Journal*, **13**: 363–80.

Marinelli, S. (2017). The approach of deterrence in the practice of the international criminal law, accessed 2 March 2018 at https://aninternationallaw blog.wordpress.com/2017/04/06/the-approach-to-deterrence-in-the-practice-of-the-international-criminal-court/.

Montgomery, C.A. and Hariharan, S. (1991). Diversified entry by established firms, *Journal of Economic Behavior and Organization*, **15**: 71–89.

Moore, J.E. (2009). *The Death of Competition: Leadership and Strategy in the Age of Business Ecosystems*, New York: HarperCollins.

Mulligan, D. and Schneider, F. (2012). Doctrine for cybersecurity, *Academy of Arts & Sciences*, **140**(4).

North, D. (1990). *Institutions, Institutional Change and Economic Performance*, New York: Cambridge University Press.

Okunoye, A. (2014). Organizational information technology infrastructure in developing countries: A comparative analysis of national vs. international research organizations in two Sub-Saharan African countries, *Journal of Information Technology Case and Application Research*, **5**(2): 8–26.

Oliver, C. (1997). Sustainable competitive advantage: Combining institutional and resource based views, *Strategic Management Journal*, **18**: 697–713.

Oluga, S.O., Ahmad, A.B.H., Alnagrat, A.J.A., Oluwatosin, H.S., Sawad, M.O.A. and Mukta, N.A.B. (2014). An overview of contemporary cyberspace activities and the challenging cyberspace crimes/threats, *International Journal of Computer Science and Information Security*, **12**(3): 62–100.

Pal, R., Golubchik, L., Psounis, K. and Hui, P. (2014). Will cyber-insurance improve network security? A market analysis, in *IEEE International Conference on Computer Communications* (INFOCOM), pp. 235–43.

Palmer, D.A., Jennings, P.D. and Zhou, X. (1993). Late adoption of the multidivisional form by U.S. corporations: Institutional, political, and economic accounts, *Administrative Science Quarterly*, **38**: 100–131.

Peng, M.W. and Heath, P.S. (1996). The growth of the firm in planned economies in transition: Institutions, organizations, and strategic choice, *Academy of Management Review*, **21**: 492–528.

Porter, M.E. (1980). *Competitive Strategy*, New York: Free Press.

Porter, M.E. (1985). *Competitive Advantage*, New York: Free Press.

Prahalad, C.K. and Hamel, G. (1990). The core competence of the corporation, *Harvard Business Review*, **68**(3): 79–91.

Reed, R. and DeFillippi, R.J. (1990). Causal ambiguity, barriers to imitation, and sustainable competitive advantage, *Academy of Management Review*, **15**: 88–102.

Robinson, M., Jones, K. and Janicke, H. (2015). Cyber warfare: Issues and challenges, *Computers & Security*, **49**: 70–94.

Rumelt, R.P. (1987). Theory, strategy, and entrepreneurship, in D.J. Teece (ed.), *The Competitive Challenge: Strategies for Industrial Innovation and Renewal*, Cambridge, MA: Ballinger, pp. 137–58.

Sales, N. (2013). Regulation cyber-security, accessed 20 August 2015 at http://papers.ssrn.com/sol3/papers.cfm?abstract_id=2035069#.

Schiavo-Campo, S. (1998). Government employment and pay: The global and regional evidence, *Public Administration and Development*, **18**: 457–78.

Schneider, F., Sedenberg, E. and Mulligan, K. (2016). Public cybersecurity and rationalizing information sharing. International Risk Governance Center, Lausanne: IRGC.

Schneier, B. (2017). Security and the Internet of Things, accessed 12 January 2018 at https://www.schneier.com/blog/archives/2017/02/security_and_th.html#c6744947.

Soulsby, A. and Clark, E. (1996). The emergence of post-Communist management in the Czech Republic, *Organization Studies*, **17**(2): 227–47.

Stevens, T. (2012). A cyberwar of ideas? Deterrence and norms in cyberspace, *Contemporary Security Policy*, **33**(1): 148–70.

Suhomlinova, O. (1999). Constructive destruction: Transformation of Russian state-owned construction enterprises during market transition, *Organization Studies*, **20**(3): 451–84.

Taipale, K.A. (2010). Cyber-deterrence, in law, policy and technology: Cyberterrorism, information warfare, digital and internet immobilization, Hershey, PA: IGI Global, accessed 11 July 2017 athttp://papers.ssrn.com/sol3/papers.cfm?abstract_id=1336045.

Thompson, J.D. (1967). *Organizations in Action*, New York: McGraw-Hill.

Trujillo, C. (2014). The limits of cyberspace deterrence, *Joint Force Quarterly*, **75**, accessed 12 January 2018 at http://ndupress.ndu.edu/JFQ/Joint-Force-Quarterly-75/Article/577560/the-limits-of-cyberspace-deterrence/.

United Nations Conference on Trade and Development (UNCTAD) (2015). *Information Economy Report 2015: Unlocking the Potential for E-Commerce in Developing Economies*, accessed 3 November 2015 at http://unctad.org/en/ PublicationsLibrary/ier2015_en.pdf.

Wong, J. and Solon, O. (2017). Massive ransomware cyber-attack hits nearly 100 countries around the world, *The Guardian*, 12 May, accessed 12 December 2017 at https://www.theguardian.com/technology/2017/may/12/global-cyber-attack-ransomware-nsa-uk-nhs.

World Bank (2015). *Poverty Overview*, Washington, DC: World Bank, accessed 12 January 2016 at http://www.worldbank.org/en/topic/poverty/overview.

Wu, S.P-J., Straub, D.W. and Liang, T-P. (2015). How information technology governance mechanisms and strategic alignment influence organizational performance: Insights from a matched survey of business and it managers, *MIS Quarterly*, **39**(2): 497–518.

Chapter 4

INTRODUCTION

Development of National Cybersecurity (NCS) strategies, cybersecurity laws and policies falls behind the development in information and communication technology (ICT) innovations. Strategies, policies and legal structures designed to deal with cybersecurity issues and problems, and to create a sense of urgency of building a culture of cybersecurity, cannot be generally adopted and implemented due to a host of structural factors of a country and the number of limitations posed on the country. These might be economic, cultural, social or political constraints and not necessarily technological. Whereas the economics of cybersecurity focuses on the cost–benefit analysis approach, the authors believe that more high-level theoretical approaches, such as economic modeling based on the resource-based theory of an economic entity and the deterrence approach would derive greater benefits.

In the following section we will provide an overview of the economics of security, covering models that helped define economic-based models for the Internet economy from the 1990s, and trying to identify gaps in models' structures and implementation. We then move to formulate the hypotheses dealing with economic variables thought to determine the levels of quality, maturity and compliance of a country's cybersecurity policies with international standards.

The resource-based view (RBV) of the firm argues that the performance of an economic entity is, *inter alia*, a function of the resources and skills that are in place and of those economic entity-specific characteristics which are valuable, rare and difficult to imitate or substitute. This concept is in essence based on Coase's theory of the firm, which maintains that the firm is a combination of alliances that have linked themselves in such a way that reduces the cost of producing goods and services for delivery to the marketplace (Coase, 1937). A variation of this RBV is that an economy can create a sustainable competitive advantage by building resources that work together and create synergy to generate organizational and country-based capabilities (Hitt et al., 2016). These capabilities permit economic entities and countries as a whole to adopt and adapt processes that enable them to realize a greater level of output from a given input or maintain their level of output from a lower quantity of input.

The other basic approach we will cover is based on deterrence theory. Cybersecurity policies based on deterrence are characterized as proactive policies in that they try to deter cybercriminals from engaging in illegal activities, thus moving from an active defense approach to an approach of proactive cybersecurity. Craig et al. (2015) traced the evolution of this approach to cybersecurity from a legal perspective. This larger proactive cybersecurity movement calls for built-in system resilience based on technological best practices (Craig et al., 2015).

Following the coverage of the two theories, we will develop a set of hypotheses with the objective of conducting a systematic cross-country analysis of National Cybersecurity Strategies and Policies in a sample of developing and emerging economies. Based on resource-based theory, the overall premise is that in addition to the physical infrastructure and the level of economic development which explains much of the variation in basic Internet use and country e-readiness, cyber activities, especially e-commerce and e-government, also depend significantly on a supportive institutional environment such as national respect for the 'rule of law', the availability of credible payment channels such as credit cards, the support of top leadership, and the existence of a NCS strategy. On the other hand, deterrence theory looks at the institutional mechanisms and policies included in the cybersecurity strategies and policies aiming at deterring criminals from engaging in cybercriminal activities.

Despite its widely cited potential to transform global economies, the use of cyber space, especially commercially, is as yet predominantly a developed world phenomenon. Estimates vary, but it is generally accepted that more than 50 percent of online transactions are confined within the United States borders. In 2017, global e-retail sales amounted to US$2.304 trillion and projections show a growth of up to US$4.88 trillion by 2021 (Statista, 2017). Generally speaking, e-retail sales are expected to increase, albeit slowly, in developing and emerging econ-omies during the same period. China is an outlier, where in 2016 19 percent of all retail sales in this country occurred via the Internet (Statisca.com, 2017). The slow development of cyber activities in other countries is paradoxical, given the intuitive appeal of the notion that the digital age brings with it the disappearance of borders. We can safely state that we cannot paint all countries with the same wide brush; some developing and emerging countries such as the United Arab Emirates (UAE), Singapore and Bahrain have done much better than others in digitizing their economies. While this puzzle has been the subject of much speculation, systematic analysis is sparse. To our knowledge there has been little empirical analysis of the conditions necessary for the development of viable online markets in developing and emerging countries.

In general, research on information technology (IT) and the impact on the economy of electronic commerce in terms of productivity and business value, can be classified into two categories: (1) the production economics-based approach; and (2) the process-oriented approach (Kvochko, 2013). The production economics-based approach employs production functions to examine the relationship between output events and production inputs such as IT and non-IT classified capital and labor. Notwithstanding the many years of debate on the contested 'productivity paradox', several researchers were able to estimate production functions and to find a somehow positive relationship between investment in information technology, including investment in electronic commerce technology, and productivity. These findings were supported by several studies and prompted a large stream of literature in this area (Brynjolfsson and Yang, 1996). As Hitt and Brynjolfsson (1996) point out, while the theory of production envisages that lower prices for IT will generate benefits in the form of lower production costs for a given level of output, it is unclear on the question of whether economic entities will raise their performance advantages in terms of supra-normal profitability. The predominant model of competition in the Internet economy is more like a web of interactions than the hierarchical command-and-control model of the industrial economy, which is referred to as the Internet Ecosystem. The Internet economy has low barriers to entry, and so it is expanding rapidly due to a number of characteristics including: (1) lower search costs for consumers; (2) quick comparisons of products and service; (3) lower prices; (4) high level of consumer services from raw material to the time the customer disposes of the item; (5) differentiation and customization; and (6) personalization of products and services.

The process-oriented approach, on the other hand, aims at explaining the process through which IT investments improve intermediate operational performance, which in turn may affect higher levels of financial performance. An early study by Mukhopadhyay et al. (1995) assessed the business value of electronic data interchange (EDI) in a manufacturing setting. Their findings indicate that EDI facilitated the effective use of information to systematize material movements between manufacturers and their suppliers, which resulted in considerable cost savings and inventory cutback. As an inter-organizational information system, EDI has some features in common with the Internet-based initiatives, but it also shows signs of important differences as EDI is, by and large, a more expensive, proprietary technology under the control of one large manu-facturer or supplier. In contrast, Internet technologies may induce large-scale variations within an organization as well as in its dealings with customers and suppliers. It is important to note that most of these studies were carried out before the extensive use of the Internet, and as such they logically did not include variables associated with Internet initiatives and e-commerce capabilities.

A promising framework for enhancing the theoretical basis of cyber activity value is the RBV of the economy, which links economic performance to economic and organizational resources and capabilities. Economic entities create performance advantages by assembling resources that work together to create added capabilities. To create sustainable advantages, these resources, or resource combinations, would have to be economically valuable, relatively scarce, difficult to imitate, or imperfectly mobile across economic entities (Matoso and Abib, 2015). Resources can be combined and integrated into unique clusters that enable distinctive abilities within an economic entity firm. In the infor-mation systems literature, the RBV has been used to explain how firms can create competitive value from IT assets, and how sustainability resides more in the available skills to leverage IT than in the technology itself.

IT payoffs depend heavily on how the various IT resources work together in creating synergy. Computers, databases, technical platforms and communication networks form the core of an entity's overall IT infrastructure resources. Although the individual components that go into the IT infrastructure are commodity-like, the process of integrating the components to develop an integrative infrastructure tailored to a firm's strategic context is complex and imperfectly understood (Weill and Broadbent, 1998). The RBV has been extended with the dynamic capabilities perspective (DCP) to tackle the practicality of unstable markets and swift technological changes. DCP refers to the ability of a firm to achieve new forms of competitive advantage by renewing technological, organizational and managerial resources to fit with the changing business environment. In this environment, capabilities that enable rapid and purposeful reconfiguration of a firm's resources are the means through which both industry position and timely unique resources can be obtained. This model implies that dynamic capabilities are essentially change-oriented capabilities that help economic entities recon-figure their resource base to meet growing customer demands and competitor strategies. The ability to anticipate technological change and adopt the appropriate strategies may create a path of growth that would generate a performance advantage. Resources are dynamic because the economic entities are continually building, adapting and reconfiguring internal and external competences to attain congruence with the changing business environment when the rate of technological change is rapid, time-to-market is critical, and the nature of future competition and markets is difficult to determine. Dynamic capabilities create resource configurations that generate value-creating strategies (Eisenhardt and Martin, 2000).

Consistent with DCP, cyber space can be considered to be a dynamic capability. Internet-enhanced organizations continually reconfigure their internal and external resources to employ digital networks to exploit business opportunities. Thus, Internet-enhanced organizations exemplify the characteristics of dynamic capabilities as they engage routines, prior and emergent knowledge, analytic processes, and simple rules to turn IT into customer value (Wheeler, 2002).

Because this book seeks to extend the IT value literature to the domain of Internet-enabled e-commerce and e-government initiatives in developing and emerging countries, it is natural to ask if Internet initiatives are different from pre-Internet technologies (for example PC, mainframe, legacy systems). In fact, the economic characteristics of the Internet are significantly different from those of pre-Internet computer technologies. In this post-PC era, we see more transactions done on the customers' mobile devices and this is where the growth in e-commerce will be centered. The Internet is unique in terms of connectivity, interactivity and open-standard network integration. These characteristics have very different bearings on customer reach and richness of information. Prior to the Internet, firms often used standalone, proprietary technologies to communicate inadequate data at best. It was difficult and/or costly for a firm to relate to its customers, suppliers and business partners. In contrast, the Internet facilitates a two-way, real-time information exchange between a firm and its customers and suppliers.

Given these unique potentials of the Internet, many countries have adopted e-commerce as a strategy for growth and development. Yet the way that e-commerce is ingrained in business processes differs from one country to another. In fact, it is how economic entities leverage their investments to generate unique Internet-enabled resources and entity-specific competence that determines overall effectiveness of online activities. Economic entities, in the public or private sectors, benefit from the Internet when they embed online capability in their fabric in a way that creates sustainable resource synergy. For instance, the integration of online capability and IT infrastructure may improve connectivity, compatibility and responsiveness of an economic unit at the micro level, which results in better efficiency and lower costs at the macro level.

Given the different ways digitization is transforming countries around the world, it is imperative to understand the factors contributing to the diffusion rate of digitization in developing and emerging economies. To get to the bottom of this, one has to examine the socio-cultural-political and economic factors leading to the diffusion of the Internet, the mobile platform, the Internet of Things (IoT), artificial intelligence (AI), cloud computing and social media in the various countries. Diffusion rates differ greatly from country to country and from industry to industry within the same country. The digital divide is more pronounced in the developing countries of Africa and Latin America.

Much of the academic discussion on the connection between the diffusion rate of ICT and development can be classified in one of two categories: techno-optimism and techno pessimism (Hoang, 2017). Proponents of the techno-optimism perspective argue that a high level of ICT diffusion will increase economic growth and improve political and cultural literacy. Back in 2010, Larry Diamond coined the term 'liberation technology', referring to how ICT can result in economic and social freedom and increase political participation by allowing a large number of people to connect and share information around the globe. While he did not refer to the impact of the network effect directly, implicitly his thesis points to the role of ICT in increasing the size and value of the network (Diamond, 2010). Special emphasis is dedicated to the role played by the interactive capabilities of Web 2.0.

The techno-optimistic proponents point to how the new forms of technology can be used to ensure the success of collective actions, such as the Arab Spring movement in the Middle East and North Africa. To this point, researchers at the University of Washington analyzed the content of more than 3 million tweets, hundreds of hours of YouTube videos and gigabytes of blogs and Facebook postings, and concluded that these social media tools played a critical role in organizing, coordinating and managing the Arab Spring social movement in new ways (Couts, 2011). The techno-optimists also see eye to eye with the proponents of modernization theory who argue that in order for developing/emerging economies to advance, they must adopt the technological advancements of more developed economies in order to accelerate the degree of growth and level of development (Jakobi, 2014). The main idea here is that as the high level of diffusion of ICT narrows the digital divide between developed and developing economies, it fast-tracks the degree of growth and development by decreasing information asymmetry, increasing efficiency, stimulating creativity and innovation, and collectively reducing risks associated with political and social unrest.

The second category of experts falls in the techno-pessimist category. Proponents of this perspective, unlike the techno-optimists, argue that there is a positive relationship between the impact of the technology and the socio-economic conditions of the users. To them, a large chunk of the population of developing countries are illiterate and have low levels of education, preventing them from reaping the benefits associated with the technology. In addition, the techno-pessimists argue that in most developing economies, the financial resources needed to invest in digital devices and services are not available. They view the new technology as a factor in increasing the gap between the haves and have nots where the privileged are able to leapfrog through technology adoption while others will be left behind (Hoang, 2017).

Looking at the relationship between techno-pessimists and economic theories, they seem to align well with the proponents of the dependency theory who attribute the slow rate of development to the economic discrepancy between the haves and the have nots, the rich and the poor.

Regardless of which approach and perspective is adopted, the diffusion of ICT and investing in cyber space raise important questions about cybersecurity and the strategies and policies adopted by the various countries to secure their IT infrastructure and their cyber space. Hence, the crucial value of a well developed cybersecurity policy in those countries.

From a trade-related perspective, the Internet's greater connectivity allows more direct interaction with customers and tighter data sharing with suppliers, leading to growth in trade among different countries. Internet-based e-commerce can be adopted to enhance traditional IT systems in many ways, for example using a Web-based, graphical interface to improve the user-friendliness of enterprise resource planning (ERP) systems; implementing Internet-based middleware to make EDI connections more flexible and affordable for smaller businesses; connecting various legacy databases by common Internet protocol and open standard; using eXtensible markup language (XML)-based communication to increase the ability of exchanging invoice and payment documents online between companies; and analyzing online data to better understand customer demand.

Based on the above, it is important to concentrate on resource synergy as a promising path to cyber space effectiveness, and on deterrence as a cybersecurity policy main ingredient. The RBV provides a solid theoretical foundation for studying the contexts and conditions under which cyber, Internet-based economies may result in more productivity and performance improvements in emerging and developing economies. In particular, it directs us toward a well-adjusted and stable position, one that recognizes the commodity view of the technology per se, while permitting the possibility of synergetic associations arising from combining the capabilities of electronic commerce, other IT infrastructure, and other resources.

Unquestionably, the most significant impediment to the development of commerce in cyber space in many developing and emerging countries is the lack of necessary physical infrastructure, particularly household access to personal computers and a cost-effective telecommunications system. However, indications from New Institutional Economics (NIE) support the notion that we should look beyond these immediate indicators to examine how the institutional environment, including a well-articulated cybersecurity policy and a set of cyber strategies, in a country contributes to (or undermines) confidence in a new market such as e-commerce/e-government and supports private investment in this specific medium. Empirical evidence has revealed that the integrity of the institutional environment, particularly with respect to the 'rule of law' supported by a clear cybersecurity policy and strategy is important for the development of e-commerce and e-government. Only in such an environment can participants in cyber space have confidence in a satisfactory performance or adequate legal recourse should the transaction break down.

To summarize, ICT capability is classified as comprising: (1) a physical IT infrastructure; (2) human IT resources (including technical IT skills, and managerial IT skills); and (3) intangible IT-enabled resources (such as customer orientation, knowledge assets and synergy), including the set of policies and strategies governing the use of cyber space.

TYPES OF RESOURCES

Based on the RBV literature, resources can be classified as either (1) property-based or (2) knowledge-based resources. Property-based resources are tangible, such as equipment, machinery, land and so on, while knowledge-based resources are intangible, including skills, competences, experience, relationships, cooperation and intra-organizational structures and systems.

As stated above, a crucial criterion in resource-based theory is the availability of barriers to prevent the imitation of resources. Not all resources can be imitated with the same degree of ease. Protecting a resource by property rights creates a barrier to prevent others from imitating it. Some examples include contracts, deeds of ownership or patents. Other resources are protected by knowledge barriers preventing competitors from imitating an entity's processes or skills; this has to do with the non-resident memory of the organization.

Research has started recently to utilize and develop both classical and modern property rights theory. However, there is an agreement that this theory is crucial for understanding economic value generated by a multifaceted network of contractual associates. Under a scenario where the contract is incomplete and implicit, the effects on value created are very difficult to determine (Klein et al., 2012).

Scarce resources monopolizing scarce factors of production which are enforceable by long-term contracts embodying exclusive rights to a valuable technology or tying up channels of distribution are examples of property-based resources. Such resources protect an economic entity from competition by creating and protecting assets that are not available to competitors or would-be competitors. Although IT infrastructure itself will seldom create a sustainable advantage, it can definitely lead to the creation, assimilation and distribution of critical knowledge needed to foster creativity and innovation among economic actors (Popa et al., 2016).

Even if competitors have the necessary knowledge to imitate and replicate the resource, they cannot do so because they do not have the legal right to imitate the resource successfully. In fact, one might make the case that in order for property-based resources to generate unusual economic returns they require protection from exclusionary legal contracts, trade restrictions, or first-mover pre-emption (Jurevicius, 2013).

Knowledge-based resources allow entities to flourish not by preventing competition, but by providing said entities with the skills to adapt their products to market needs and to deal with competitive challenges. It is important to point out here that the protection of knowledge barriers is not absolute; it may be possible for others to develop similar knowledge and talent, but this usually takes time, and by then a firm may have gone on to develop its skills further and to learn to use them in distinct ways (Geroski et al., 2013).

In addition to property-based and knowledge-based resources, insights from the New Institutional Economics theory suggest that we should look beyond these direct indicators into how the institutional environment in a country contributes to (or hinders) confidence in a new market and supports private investment in the new technology. Not only institutional physical resources, but also knowledge-based resources are important determinants of how successful Internet-based initiatives can be applied in a developing/emerging country.

The NIE theory is an attempt to integrate a theory of institutions into economics. Cybersecurity policy and the institution in charge of putting teeth into the enforcement of the policy fall under the aegis of this theory. The NIE theory builds on, transforms and extends neoclassical theory to allow it to deal with a host of issues beyond its knowledge. What it maintains and builds on is the basic assumption of scarcity. What it discards is instrumental rationality. NIE views economics as a theory of choice subject to constraints; they make use of price theory as a crucial part of the analysis of institutions.

COUNTRIES' ECOSYSTEMS

Developing and emerging countries will place lots of faith in cyber space for their development journeys. Cyber space is a fundamental transmission mechanism through which technology-induced changes will spread across many layers of a developing country's hierarchy. Two sectors are singled out for their importance of growth and development: health and education. The application of ICT to those sectors can certainly contribute to the achievement of basic development objectives and can, in the long term, lead to increases in efficiency and effectiveness, in addition to leading creativity and innovation in a society. However, the upward movement of economic growth that the Internet and cyber activities can bring about would probably, and more importantly, result in a more immediate and sustainable contribution to the reduction of poverty and increase in economic progress, one of the Millennium Goals specified by the United Nations.

Addressing the comparatively low levels of productivity in a large number of developing countries, the adoption of e-commerce in these countries can lead particularly to large relative improvements in productivity. In most cases, these gains are not derived directly from the technology itself but through incremental improvements resulting from organizational changes in the production process that are made possible (or indispensable) by the technology. An encouraging factor is that e-commerce seems to be spreading in a number of developing countries faster than was the case in previous technological revolutions, and this will increase the relevance and applicability of a well designed cyber-security policy and strategy. To grease the wheels of e-commerce and e-government and facilitate their fast diffusion, the institutional environment in developing and emerging economies has to be favorable.

An important question that needs to be addressed, however, is what aspects of the institutional environment are most important for promoting transactional integrity in cyber space and hence in supporting investment in these new markets? Based on an institutional perspective, this question can be analyzed from the following key feature: the overall integrity of the nation's cyber cultural system, related to the degree to which the economy is guided by a National Cybersecurity strategy. This is motivated by the credibility of payment channels available to cyber activity participants, which in turn is a function of the country's financial institutions and regulations and the existence of a law that governs electronic commerce transactions, that is, cyber law that is guided by a clear and well-structured national cybersecurity strategy.

Developing and emerging countries can profit from the opportunities provided by e-commerce for exploiting competitive advantages not achievable in the 'old economy'. E-commerce gives small and medium sized enterprises (SMEs) the ability to access international markets that used to be difficult to enter due to high transaction costs and other market access barriers. Labor-intensive services can now be delivered using cyber space as a medium, providing new opportunities for developing countries with relatively cheap labor. The emergence of successful industries such as software development or tele-service and tele-medicine in several countries are examples of this. Thanks to e-commerce, entrepreneurs in developing countries can also access cheaper, better-quality trade-related services, such as finance and/or business information.

Finally, cyber activities can stimulate growth in developing countries by helping to improve the transparency of the operation of markets and public institutions. For instance, by simplifying business procedures, cyber activities not only reduce the cost for businesses of complying with domestic and international trade-related regulations, but also reduce the cost of corruption, a burden that often most severely affects SMEs and other weaker players in the economy (Brangetto and Aubyn, 2015).

For all these above-stated promising benefits to materialize, a number of institutional measures and mechanisms are required in order to create an enabling environment for e-commerce, and to address areas such as infrastructure, applications, payments systems, human resources, the legal framework and taxation. The following analysis of national cybersecurity strategies and policies in a cross-section of developing countries should prove that not only are physical infrastructure measures important in explaining variations in basic cyber activity adoption and Internet use, but also intangible institutional measures are critical to the success of online business, specifically the existence of a comprehensive National Cybersecurity strategy which guides and coordinates those institutional measures. As stated earlier, in addition to addressing the issue at hand from a deterrence theory perspective, this book will also examine the quality and comprehensiveness of National Cybersecurity strategies in a number of developing countries from an institutional, resource-based perspective.

EMPIRICAL ASSESSMENT

Countries and economies are interconnected. If information systems in one economy are not protected effectively, then the underlying infrastructures of all the interconnected economies are threatened. Thus, the fight against cyberattacks is primarily dependent on a national cybersecurity strategy and policies of every country. Specifically, cybersecurity is contingent upon every economy having (1) sound laws that criminalize attacks on systems and networks and ensure that law enforcement officials have the authority to investigate and prosecute crimes made possible by technology; and (2) strategies and policies that permit international collaboration with other parties in the fight against computer-related crime. In addition, for these policies to be effective given the nature of cybercrimes, they have to be coordinated and harmonized across borders. In order to reach a global harmonization of cyber legislation, and a common understanding of cybersecurity and cybercrime among countries, a culture of safe cyber space is to be created within and among countries. A National Cybersecurity strategy is the tool that coordinates the work of all agents at the national and international levels, and harmonizes the work of all institutions inside and outside the borders of a country. At the international level, a convention is generally a more airtight arrangement, where parties may be held legally responsible for violations under international law. The most active United Nations (UN) entity in leading the development of comprehensive and global cybercrime legislation is the International Telecommunications Union (ITU). This institution is exceptionally positioned to develop a global agreement on cybercrime and has been working steadfastly in advancing this cause.

In 2001, the UN initiated the World Summit on the Information Society (WSIS) and put the ITU in charge to lead and coordinate the multi-phased activities of WSIS. The work of WSIS got off the ground with Phase one in Geneva in December 2003; Phase two took place in Tunisia in 2005. The latest WSIS summit took place in March 2018 in Geneva, Switzerland. In addition to bridging the digital divide and outlining the 2030 agenda of the information society, the main emphasis was on creating enabling environments and building confidence and security in the use of ICTs (WSIS, 2018). The summit identified a number of challenges facing countries around the world, especially developing and emerging countries. Among those universally applicable challenges identified due to the vulnerabilities in the current IT infrastructure are data breaches, phishing attacks, ransomware, the challenges associated with attribution of the perpetrator of attacks, Distributed Denial of Service attacks (DDoS), and other challenges associated with the IoT, cloud computing, and the mobile platform (WSIS, 2018).

Following these summits, the ITU took on the central role in coordination and harmonization of the activities among UN member countries in order to build confidence in information security in cyber space. The responsibility of the ITU is to seek agreement on a framework for international cooperation in cybersecurity in order to reach a common understanding of cybersecurity threats among countries at all stages of economic development (that includes developing and emerging economies) and put into action solutions aimed at addressing the global challenges to cybersecurity and cybercrime.

In May 2007, a Global Cybersecurity Agenda (GCA) was launched by the United Nations Secretary-General, as a global framework for dialogue and international cooperation aimed at proposing strategies for solutions to enhance security in the information society. The main goal of the GCA is the elaboration of strategies for the development of a 'model of cybercrime legislation' that is globally applicable and interoperable with existing national and regional legislative measures. In order to support the ITU's Secretary-General in developing strategic proposals to Member States, a High-Level Experts Group (HLEG) was set up in October 2007. In June 2008, the HLEG of more than 100 international experts provided its recommendations on strategies in the following five work areas: legal measures; technical and procedural measures; organizational structures; capacity building; and international cooperation. These recommendations are being adapted by a large number of developing and emerging economies in their effort to devise their cybersecurity agendas. As of the writing of this book, 72 out of 193 ITU Member States currently have a publicly available NCS. Forty-nine of those countries are developing or emerging economies (ITU, 2015).

The Council of Europe/Budapest Convention

An important international convention dealing with cyber space and cybersecurity is the 2001 Council of Europe's Convention on Cybercrime, also known as the Budapest convention. The Council of Europe Convention was a recognition by member states that the cybersecurity issue has become so important that it deserves an international treaty. Since 2001, ICT has played a major role in transforming societies and has made them highly exposed to cybersecurity risks. Seventeen years later, this convention remains the most significant international agreement on cybercrime and electronic activities, in addition to being a significant achievement in combating cybercrime. It was signed on 8 November 2001 and entered into force on 1 July 2004, and by November 2016 50 countries were parties (European countries, plus Australia, Canada, Dominican Republic, Israel, Japan, Mauritius, Panama, Sri Lanka and the USA). In addition, 17 countries have signed the convention or have been invited to accede to it. The convention sets forth a comprehensive framework for international cooperation against computer crimes and requires member states to outlaw specific activities. These international agreements acknowledge that the boundless nature of many illicit activities compels individual states to cooperate to restrain emerging threats. Since it entered into force, important countries like Brazil and India have declined to approve the convention on the basis that they did not participate in its preparation. Russia is not in support of the convention, stating that adoption would violate Russian sovereignty, and has usually refused to cooperate in law enforcement investigations relating to cybercrime.

The Budapest Convention on Cybercrime is perceived to be the best legislation to deal with what are referred to as cybercrime havens. It is based on the principle that harmonizing national laws will facilitate cooperation between law enforcement officers investigating crimes in cyber space and eliminate the haven scenario by ensuring that cybercriminals can be prosecuted and extradited for prosecution. Countries are called on to sign and ratify the convention to outlaw cybercrime offenses, to ensure that their laws provide the facility to help officers from other countries investigating cybercrimes, and to ensure they have jurisdiction to prosecute such crimes. The convention acts as a preventive measure by criminalizing actions that endanger the confidentiality, integrity and availability of computer systems, networks and computer information/data.

By ratifying or acceding to the convention, countries agree to ensure that their domestic laws criminalize the conducts described in the section on substantive criminal law and establish the procedural tools necessary to investigate and prosecute such crimes.

As of the writing of this book (April 2018), 16 countries from our sample (Bulgaria, Czech Republic, Estonia, Georgia, Hungary, Israel, Latvia, Lithuania, Mauritius, Poland, Romania, Serbia, Slovakia, South Africa, Turkey and Ukraine) have signed, ratified and/or brought the convention into force. Russia has refused to sign the Convention on Cybercrime because it did not manage to agree upon appropriate terms for cross-border access to data processing networks.

In addition to calling for capacity building and raising awareness, the year 2013 raised the issue to a higher level whereby the UN and EU called for a broader agreement on cybersecurity capacity building. This main issue was the focus of the Global Cyber Space Conference in Seoul, which culminated in a joint project between the UN and the EU, the Global Action on Cybercrime (GLACY). In addition, the EU decided to create a central office for cybersecurity capacity building, Cybercrime Programme Office (C-PROC). In 2016 the C-PROC office was engaged in a series of projects in Eastern and South-Eastern Europe. The GLACY plan implemented projects in a number of developing countries including Morocco, Senegal, South Africa and Sri Lanka. The GLACY project ended in October 2016, to be followed by the GLACY+ Project, which aims to share the experiences of those countries that participated in GLACY 1 and share their knowledge with other countries of their respective regions (EC, 2017). The GLACY+ will extend its services to countries in Latin America and is expected to end in February 2020.

The United Nations Resolutions

The UN has been very active in combating cybercriminal activities. Two resolutions are worth mentioning here: UN Resolution 57/239 (2002), and UN Resolution 58/199 (2004). The first resolution deals with the creation of a global culture of cybersecurity; in doing so, it identifies the following nine criteria:

1. Awareness: participants should be aware of the need for security of information systems and networks and what they can do to enhance security.
2. Responsibility: participants are responsible for the security of information systems and networks in a manner appropriate to their individual roles. They should review their own policies, practices, measures and procedures regularly, and should assess whether they are appropriate to their environment.
3. Response: participants should act in a timely and cooperative manner to prevent, detect and respond to security incidents. They should share information about threats and vulnerabilities, as appropriate, and implement procedures for rapid and effective cooperation to prevent, detect and respond to security incidents. This may involve cross-border information sharing and cooperation.
4. Ethics: given the pervasiveness of information systems and networks in modern societies, participants need to respect the legitimate

interests of others and recognize that their action or inaction may harm others.

5. Democracy: security should be implemented in a manner consistent with the values recognized by democratic societies, including the freedom to exchange thoughts and ideas, the free flow of information, the confidentiality of information and communication, the appropriate protection of personal information, openness, and transparency.

6. Risk assessment: all participants should conduct periodic risk assessments that identify threats and vulnerabilities; that are sufficiently broad based to encompass key internal and external factors, such as technology, physical and human factors, policies, and third-party services with security implications; that allow determination of the acceptable level of risk; and that assist in the selection of appropriate controls to manage the risk of potential harm to information systems and networks in the light of the nature and importance of the information to be protected.

7. Security design and implementation: participants should incorporate security as an essential element in the planning and design, operation and use of information systems and networks.

8. Security management: participants should adopt a comprehensive approach to security management based on risk assessment that is dynamic, encompassing all levels of participants' activities and all aspects of their operations.

9. Reassessment: participants should review and reassess the security of information systems and networks and should make appropriate modifications to security policies, practices, measures and procedures that include addressing new and changing threats and vulnerabilities.

UN Resolution 58/199 (2004) further emphasizes the 'promotion of a global culture of cybersecurity and protection of critical information infrastructures'. Specifically, it recognizes the growing importance of information technologies for the promotion of socioeconomic development and the provision of essential goods and services. It also addresses the increasing links among most countries' critical infrastructures and that these are exposed to a growing number and a wider variety of threats and vulnerabilities that raise new security concerns. It encourages member states and relevant regional and international organizations that have developed strategies to deal with cybersecurity and the protection of critical information infrastructures to share their best practices and measures that could assist other member states in their efforts to facilitate the achievement of cybersecurity. Among others, these two resolutions act as guiding principles to countries around the world and place the issue of cybersecurity in the limelight.

Association of Southeast Asian Nations

The Association of Southeast Asian Nations (ASEAN) is the first regional organization to adopt a harmonized cyber space legal framework consistent across jurisdictions. By mid-2010, all ASEAN member countries had enacted consistent national e-commerce legislation. Part of the success of the ASEAN e-Commerce Project is due to its focus on global harmonization and international interoperability, rather than merely on regional harmonization. This focus on international interoperability included the selection of international models and templates, particularly the UN Convention on Electronic Contracting, for the implementation of domestic e-commerce law in ASEAN member countries. This ensured that ASEAN's e-commerce legal infrastructure would also be compatible with international developments, providing greater certainty for consumers and greater consistency for businesses. ASEAN has close to 150 million digitally active consumers but it is deemed that e-commerce in the ASEAN countries lags because of logistics and payments infrastructure shortfalls (Tao, 2016).

In dealing with cybercrime legislation, ASEAN member states have established the high-level ASEAN Ministerial Meeting on Transnational Crime (AMMTC). Of the ten member countries of the ASEAN Group, five are part of our sample; these are Indonesia, Malaysia, the Philippines, Singapore and Thailand. The ASEAN countries have been pioneers in the fight against cybercrime, with the e-ASEAN Reference Framework for Electronic Commerce Legal Infrastructure as a good starting point for such development. However, the e-ASEAN reference framework is strictly limited to basic e-commerce laws. Despite recognizing the need for implementation, the laws do not provide any guidelines for adopting legislation or codes of practice to address data and privacy protection, consumer protection, cybercrime, intellectual property, admissibility of computer outputs as evidence in court, or Internet content. The e-ASEAN reference framework also excludes issues of cross-border e-commerce such as conflicts of laws or taxation. The ASEAN states pledged to act to develop, enact and implement cybercrime and cybersecurity laws well suited to their national conditions by relying on relevant international guidelines for the detection, prevention, combat and mitigation of cyber-attacks. They further recognized the added-value of a national framework for cooperation and partnership in dealing with criminality in cyber space, and advanced the creation of such a framework.

In November 2007 ASEAN member states realized the value of wider cooperation in this area from China and South Korea. A joint APEC–ASEAN workshop on network security was held in the Philippines in 2007 to share knowledge and experience in capacity building in cyber-security and cybercrime. The Convention on Cybercrime developed by the ITU was introduced as a reference legal model for Asian Pacific Economic Cooperation (APEC) and ASEAN members. Discussions were also held on legislation and building technical expertise in digital forensics. More recently, in May 2008, member states adopted a set of resolutions on cybercrime. At present, seven out of the ten ASEAN countries have cybercrime laws in place, and Indonesia has a draft law. Legislations contain similar offenses, but vary slightly.

Offenses covered concentrate on unauthorized access, unauthorized access with the intent of committing an offense, and unauthorized modification of computer material. The legislation also contains provisions that make it a crime to disclose computer access codes without authorization.

Two ASEAN countries shine in their effort to fight cybercrime; these are Singapore and Malaysia. Malaysia was a pioneer in this respect by enacting the Cybercrime Act early in 1997, followed by the Digital Signatures Regulations in 1998. Singapore followed suit by enacting its Electronic Transactions Act 1998. The e-transaction laws in Malaysia and Singapore follow international conventions and those in European countries.

Further, the Singaporean Electronic Transactions Act of 1998 has elaborate articles concerning, among others, the recognition of foreign certification authorities, revocation of certificates, and revocation without the consent of subscribers (MarketResearch.com, 2001). ASEAN member states had committed to the establishment of an integrated ASEAN Economic Community (AEC) by 2015 (though it seems many ASEAN countries are still struggling to achieve the goals of the AEC (Yue Chia and Plummer, 2016)). A significant target within this commitment is the development of a harmonized legal infrastructure for e-commerce, as set out in the Roadmap for Integration of e-ASEAN Sector. This roadmap calls for ASEAN countries to adopt the best practices and guidelines on cyber law issues (that is, data protection, consumer protection, intellectual property, internet service provider (ISP) liability, and so on) in order to support regional e-commerce activities.

On another related topic and in a recent development, there is a clear and strong trend in the ASEAN region to protect privacy through comprehensive legislation that is closely aligned with the European Union approach.

Asian Pacific Economic Cooperation

At a meeting in Mexico in 2002, the countries of APEC pledged to fight cybercrime. Member countries declared their intention to make an effort to enact a comprehensive set of laws dealing with cybersecurity and cybercrime. In 2005, this pledge was renewed by encouraging all APEC countries to consider the European Convention on Cybercrime as a model, and to attempt to develop and pass cyber laws compatible with international legal instruments, including the Convention on Cybercrime. As for individual countries, China, the Philippines and South Korea have specifically addressed certain aspects of cybercrime in their criminal codes, e-commerce enabling laws, other legislative instruments, and in case law. With respect to copyright offenses, penalties are imposed for online copyright infringement in the countries that have copyright protection laws explicitly extending to the online environment.

In response to this call from leaders, the Security and Prosperity Steering Group (SPSG) was formed with the mandate of focusing on capacity building and legislative drafting of comprehensive cybercrime laws. Further assistance was provided to individual countries to tackle their specific requirements and needs in developing wide-ranging legal frameworks and forming effective law enforcement and cybercrime investigative units.

A Judge and Prosecutor Cybercrime Enforcement Capacity Building Project was completed in 2008 for APEC countries to help with capacity building in legal expertise on cybercrime. The project calls for the development of training material for judges and prosecutors to train the trainers; material was translated into local languages to help with the understanding and implementation of the rules (APEC, 2008).

As for individual countries, in December 2008 India passed the Information Technology (Amendment) Bill that provides for imprisonment, which could extend to a life term, for those indulging in cyber-crimes and cyber terrorism and a jail term of up to five years for publishing or transmitting obscene material in electronic form. The bill seeks addition of provisions to deal with cybercrimes such as transmitting sexually explicit materials in electronic form, breach of confidentiality, disclosure of data by an intermediary, and e-commerce fraud. It also addresses issues related to stolen computer resources, identity theft, violation of privacy, and transmitting sexually explicit materials. The bill also proposed the establishment of a special body, the Cyber Appellate Tribunal, to deal with cybercrime (*The Hindu*, 2008). The Department of Electronics and Information Technology (DeitY) promotes e-governance, the electronics and IT industry, and India's role in internet governance

(Vision and Mission). It works to develop human resources, promote research and development, improve digital services, and strengthen cyber space security. The 2013 National Cybersecurity Policy, India's first ever cybersecurity strategy, determined by DeitY, is implemented through a number of initiatives that aim to safeguard information and IT, fight cyber threats, and decrease adversity caused by cybersecurity incidents. However, the strategies addressed in the policy neglect the individual's right to privacy, allowing the government to obtain any information it deems fit to protect the sovereignty and security of the state by infiltrating systems to gather personal, private data. The strategy also fails to elaborate on how the various teams and organizations mentioned will work together and function to improve India's cybersecurity (Siboni, 2014).

Organization of American States

In 1999, member countries of the Organization of American States (OAS) approved the setting up of a group of governmental experts on cyber-crime. The following countries in our sample are members of the OAS: Argentina, Bolivia, Brazil, Chile, Columbia, Ecuador, Mexico, Peru, Uruguay and Venezuela. Brazil boasts the most advanced Internet and e-commerce industry in Latin America and the fifth largest telecom infrastructure worldwide. This is due to privatization of Brazilian telecom services and associated advancements (IBLS, 2009). In his 2014 work, Angarita found that 70 percent of Latin American countries have some type of data protection within their constitutions. Moreover, different countries (for example, Argentina, Antigua and Barbuda, Colombia, Costa Rica, Mexico, Peru and Uruguay) have already enacted or are currently drafting data protection laws.

One of the leading fears raised in Latin America has been defining and penalizing cybercrimes, and dealing with those by either creating new laws or amending existing ones. Brazil proposed a bill containing cybercrime provisions and presented it to Congress, where it met strong opposition from civil society. The bill itself aimed at defining the rights and responsibilities of Internet users rather than enacting a criminal law. This ended up with the approval of the Civil Rights Framework for the Internet (Marco Civil), relating to issues such as the protection of fundamental rights online, network neutrality, intermediary liability, responsibilities of the public sector and data retention (Cybersecurity in Latin America and the Caribbean, 2016). Most of the laws, however, have been enacted without a comprehensive umbrella of national cybersecurity strategy or policies.

Another trend in the Latin American region is a mounting concern about the protection of personal data and online privacy. After the Snowden disclosures in 2013, people have become more aware of their personal data and privacy issues. The concern for privacy will be magnified given the role that the increased diffusion of Internet penetration plays in the countries of Latin America, and the increased realization and understanding of the role that the Internet and online commerce play in economic growth and development.

It is fair to state that in the Latin American region, cybersecurity has not been a topic of importance for individuals and/or governments. Much of the concern for cybersecurity in the region is oriented toward (and somehow concentrated in) the defense and military establishment, paying little or no attention to human rights. Having said that, many countries have jumped on the bandwagon to develop cybersecurity policies in multi-stakeholder platforms, including different governmental branches, academia, the technical community, civil society, and the private sector.

Some countries in Latin America have started to adapt their legal and economic systems to address e-commerce and cybercrime in order to take full advantage of the role ICT can play in development. Internet use in the Latin American region has been climbing steadily since 2002. The impact of the development and application of laws on the development of e-commerce activities is reported by many countries to be encouraging, leading to an increase in ICT-related business opportunities and a greater level of foreign direct investment. This applies especially to Argentina, Brazil and Chile (the ABC countries). Since 2002, these countries have developed and implemented laws on such issues as digital signatures, privacy, e-contracts, consumer protection and intellectual property rights (IPRs).

These actions are directed at removing barriers to the progress and growth of e-commerce, e-government, and the use of ICT by raising the level of trust among users of e-platforms. The adaptation of national legal structures is an important development in ICT-related policies and procedures that the various governments should establish to promote e-commerce.

Brazil's financial sector is the regional leader in adopting information technologies; the country is widely considered the regional leader of Internet marketing and online sales, service and support. It appears that the Brazilian financial sector has capitalized on its IT experience to adopt e-commerce technologies and integrate them with existing information systems. Brazil is considered the largest networked economy in Latin America. In 2015 it was ranked sixth highest in world market cellular phone users and seventh in world market software; the Brazilian cellular phone market is estimated to be US$9 billion annually, with an average consistent annual growth of 10 percent (Eurobrasil, 2015). In addition, Brazil is among global leaders in the development of e-government applications, such as e-learning, e-procurement, online tax applications, and the national election system. Given the foregoing facts, one expects cyber laws in Brazil to be well ahead of other emerging economies; this is not the case, however. The only development that has come out of the industry is self-regulation. In 2007, the Brazilian Association of Internet Service Providers (ABRANET) published a self-regulatory code for ISPs describing the roles of ISPs in terms of facilitating communications and protecting users.

As for Argentina, in mid-2008 it approved law 26388, which updates its criminal code and sanctions against cybercrime. On 4 June 2008 and after numerous debates, the Argentinean 'Camara de Diputados' characterized as crimes the following conducts: (a) distribution and possession with the intent to distribute child pornography; (b) email violations; (c) illegal access to information systems; (d) distribution of virus and damage to information systems; (e) aggravated crimes against information systems; and (f) interruption of communications. According to these updates, it is now a crime in Argentina to access emails without authorization; the new law also makes illegal the deletion of electronic communications by persons other than their addressee. The law also criminalizes the interception or capture of private electronic communications (this may cover Voice over Internet Protocol (VoIP) communications). In addition, unauthorized access to private or public databases and information systems became a new type of crime in Argentina, punishable by a prison term. Breach of data and information, including revealing information to third parties, is now punishable under the new law. Further, the new law criminalizes those who change, damage, or improperly use information systems, including documents, or infect systems with viruses.

Notwithstanding the comprehensiveness of the provisions of the Argentinean cyber law, the sentences are not harsh enough to deter persistent cybercriminals. In other words, the law does not have enough teeth to make it successful in combating cybercrime.

Argentina defines their cybersecurity strategy as the 'National Program for Critical Information, Infrastructure, and Cybersecurity (ICIC)'. The National Office of Information Technology (ONTI) published the second draft of the National Cybersecurity and Critical Infrastructure Protection Plan 2013–2015. This plan is based on four pillars: raising awareness; securing digital assets; promoting judicial and academic understanding of information security; and critical information infrastructure. In July of

2011, the ICIC was established under the ONTI by the cabinet administrators, who were dependent on the presidency of the nation. The ICIC is comprised of four individual groups, which are in charge of various aspects of issues related to their cybersecurity strategy. The first group is the Critical Infrastructure Group (GICI), which aims to survey, identify and classify strategic infrastructure and crucial information. It is also responsible for developing policies and strategies aimed at the protection of critical information infrastructure. The second group, the Preventive Action Group (GAP), conducts research and preventative actions to reduce security incidents. The third group, the Computer Emergency Response Team (CERT), manages information security incident reports and provides possible solutions to the security incidents in an organized and unified fashion. Lastly, Healthy Internet was launched to raise awareness about the associated risk in the use of digital media.

The National Program for Critical Information, Infrastructure, and Cybersecurity, created by Resolution No. 580/2011 JGM, aims to promote the creation and adoption of a specific regulatory framework that promotes the identification and protection of strategic infrastructure and critical institutions. The collaboration of the public and private sectors has helped develop appropriate strategies for a coordinated approach to the implementation of relevant technologies. ONTI is the main agency that is responsible for implementing a national cybersecurity strategy. ONTI's main objective is to implement the innovations in public administration. ONTI develops systems that are used in management procedures and sets security standards for the incorporation of new technologies. It also ensures information security through the National Public Administration, in response to computer network attacks. ONTI is involved in implementing and monitoring the digital certificates, which allows electronic records to be processed safely and efficiently. In short, ONTI aims to promote the integration of new technologies, compatibility and interoperability, while promoting technological standardization.

The Cybercrime Act is Argentina's only regulation to control the actions that have occurred on the Internet. The act is used to incorporate new computer-related offenses in current types of crimes. This way Argentina does not have to create a law for the new types of crimes. The ONTI also coordinates with the private and public sector to adhere to the ICIC (2015).

In September 2013 the defense ministers of Argentina and Brazil agreed to work together to improve their cyber defense strategies following the knowledge that the United States was spying on their countries. In an attempt to improve literacy rates and 'close the social and educational gaps across the country' Argentina installed a program called Connect Equality. The program has already sent out 4 million netbooks to students across the country to incorporate ICTs in its technologies (ICIC, 2015).

Argentina's cybersecurity is still a work in progress and in the coming years more programs and laws will be enacted to further Argentina's understanding and incorporation of their ICTs in everyday life.

More recently, in 2017, Justice 2020, a governmental initiative for the development of public policies sponsored by the Ministry of Justice and the Data Protection Agency, recommended amendments to the Argentinean Data Protection Law. This led to a bill being drafted in September 2017, which has yet to be submitted for a vote by the legislative branch of government (LawReviews, 2017). However, Argentina has been moving steadfastly on the road of revamping its legal structure to cover cybercrimes, raising cybersecurity awareness, and taking a leadership role in regional cooperation in this domain.

The development of National Cybersecurity Strategy and Policies is becoming a necessary condition with the increased diffusion of e-commerce in the economy; this is the case for many of the Latin American countries. According to a study by Visa Incorporated, business-to-consumer (B2C) e-commerce in Latin America, including retail, travel and tourism, rose to nearly US$11 billion in 2007, up from about US$5 billion in 2005 and US$7.78 billion in 2006. Sales in 2013 topped US$69.9 million and are expected to grow at a rate of 9 percent up until 2018 (Statista, 2015).

Countries of the Middle East

Countries in the Middle East, except Israel and to a lesser extent the United Arab Emirates (UAE) and Saudi Arabia, are still struggling to understand the value of cybersecurity. Officially, the UAE was the first country in the region to adopt cybercrime legislation, with its Cybercrime Law No. 2. This law was followed by the 2012 Federal Law No. 5, which classifies a range of online activities as crimes and empowers the newly created cybercrime police unit to monitor online activities and try to identify cybercrimes and criminals (Ali Khasawneh and Ahern, 2012). In 2014 the UAE established a cyber command integrated within the General Headquarters of the national armed forces (Bindiya, 2014). In 2017 the UAE government published its strategy on cybersecurity, which aspires to boost cyber resilience and create both local and global partnerships in order to better deal with cyber threats.

In January 2008 Saudi Arabia unveiled 16 articles for prosecuting technology-assisted crimes, specifically mentioning identity theft and running extremist websites. Under the new law, people found guilty of using computers to commit crimes could face up to ten years in prison and fines of up to 5 million Saudi riyals. The law establishes that website defacement is a crime worthy of punishment, while data theft could carry a significant fine of more than US$130 000 or even a maximum one-year prison sentence. The same punishment could apply to those found guilty of defamation using electronic means or those who unlawfully break into private electronic networks. Users spreading malware could find themselves paying US$800 000 and spending up to four years in a Saudi jail, less than those found guilty of spreading immorality. People setting up websites with pornographic content or content that defames humanity, or sites with information promoting drug use, may be punished with fines of up to US$1.3 million and five years of jail time. More recently, in November 2017, Saudi Arabia set up a new authority for cybersecurity, the National Authority for Cyber Security, which is made up of the head of state security, the head of intelligence, the deputy interior minister and assistant to the minister of defense (Reuters, 2017). The authority will report directly to the Palace and its major objective is to increase cybersecurity and protect the country's infrastructure and its vital interests.

Although the Gulf Cooperation Council (GCC) (which includes Bahrain, Kuwait, Oman, Qatar, Saudi Arabia and the UAE) is not party to any global anti-cybercrime agreement, the Arab Convention on Combating Information Technology Offences exists at the regional level and forms the basis for cooperation in cybersecurity (Taher, 2015).

In recent years, there have been a number of initiatives aimed at improving the status of cyber societies in the Middle East region. The most recent are: (1) the electronic transactions law issued by Qatar (2010); (2) the cybercrime law in the Kingdom of Jordan (2010); (3) the e-Signature and network services law (2011) as well as the law to cover cybercrime issues in Syria (2012).

Some countries such as Algeria and Morocco took the approach of introducing laws to protect intellectual property by modifying and updating their existing intellectual property laws (ESCWA, 2015).

Countries of Africa

According to the United Nations, the continent of Africa is composed of 54 states, all of which come under the umbrella of the African Union (AU). The following countries in our sample are members of that union: Algeria, Egypt, Nigeria, South Africa and Tunisia. Currently, there are eight regional economic communities (RECs) within the union, each established under a separate regional treaty. One REC, the Southern African Development Community (SADC), including Zambia, Zimbabwe, South Africa, Malawi and Mozambique, initiated efforts to enact compatible cybercrime laws in 2005 (ITU, 2008).

The 2017 Internet diffusion rate in Africa is close to 35 percent, a great increase of 9 percent on 2010. In spite of the high level of increase in digitization, the development of cybersecurity policies and strategies has been very slow in the continent. Even though progress on this front has been very slow, some individual African countries have taken the initiative and moved ahead with legislation to address cybercrime; South Africa is the most advanced in this respect and its cybercrime legislation is regarded as a model law for the region.

Chapter XIII of the Electronic Communications and Transactions Act of South Africa, passed in 2002, defined cybercrime to include, among other things: (1) unauthorized access to, interception of, and interference with data; (2) computer-related fraud, extortion and forgery; and (3) aiding or abetting a cybercriminal. In addition, the act specifies the penalties associated with these crimes to include a jail sentence and fines. According to the act, the Director-General can appoint a cyber inspector who will have the power to inspect any website or activity on any information system in the public domain and report any unlawful activity to the appropriate authority. The inspector has the power to investigate the activities of a cryptography service or authenticating service provider to see if they are compliant with the act. The inspector may also demand the production and inspection of relevant licenses and registration certificates as provided for in any law.

To achieve its cybersecurity goals, South Africa established the National Cybersecurity Policy Framework (NCPF) 'to create a secure, dependable, reliable and trustworthy cyber environment that facilitates the protection of critical information infrastructure' (enisa.europa, 2015). The NCPF listed a simple strategy that any country should follow to develop its cybersecurity infrastructure; this includes improving the country's infrastructure; devising a cyber law to deal with cybercrimes; enhancing institutional cooperation; raising public awareness and developing training programs. The government agency in charge of overseeing this strategy is the Department of Communication (DOC). The DOC started by creating the legal provisions that they hoped would address the many cybersecurity issues at hand. However, the country understands that the implementation of a strict and secure cybersecurity policy will require more authority and resources than merely those enacted by the DOC.

South Africa's strategy references both national security strategies and critical infrastructure strategies. A key part of the framework recognizes the need for a mechanism to ensure that the infrastructure is protected against cyber-related crimes. The framework also points out that securing South Africa's critical infrastructure will support national security, economic prosperity and social wellbeing. The framework also recognizes that most of South Africa's critical infrastructure is privately owned or operated on a commercial basis. The NCPF uses this as justification for its stance that the government and private sector must work together to implement South Africa's critical infrastructure strategy. The strategy focuses on regulating the areas of information classification, information security procedures, access to critical information, authentication on critical information, storage and archiving of critical databases, incident management, and physical and technical protection of national critical information infrastructure.

The NCPF addresses many different sources of threats. A dedicated Cybersecurity Response Committee is purposed to investigate, prosecute and combat various sources of threats, which include cyber espionage, cyber terrorism, cybercrime and cyber warfare. Many of these fall under the category of cyber extremism (cyber terrorism/warfare). For example, cyber espionage groups as well as independent criminals employ phishing as a tactic to invade digital spaces and extract critical information like email account logins and credit card information. According to the most recent report on phishing incidents, South Africa was the most attacked country by cybercriminals in January 2016 (ITnewsafrica, 2016). South Africa is employing several congruent sub-strategies that will make sure threats like phishing are mitigated. For example, through cryptographic technology as well as National Critical Information Infrastructure regulations, information classification and digital capital can be verified more quickly and at a higher level than before. The NCII regulations also allow for safe storage and archiving of critical databases.

South Africa's cybersecurity strategy is also heavily dependent on collaboration from other countries. In terms of globalization, the NCPF recognizes the international cooperation that must take place in order for a critical infrastructure strategy to be effective. Because of the borderless nature of the Internet, South Africa's National Cybersecurity Framework recognizes the need to collaborate with other countries to fight cybercrime. In South Africa's cybersecurity plan, the nation is to become a member and participate in two particular international organizations: Forum of Incident Response and Security Teams (FIRST) and International Multilateral Partnership Against Cyber-Terrorism (IMPACT). FIRST consists of organizations within a multitude of countries including the UN, who assist in preventing and handling computer security-related incidents. IMPACT is the first UN-backed cybersecurity alliance. South Africa is willing to make necessary international alliances as long as they are subject to existing international agreements and their constitution.

This work will necessitate reviewing existing national cybersecurity strategies and documents that deal with cybercrimes. Internet-based attacks and crimes are increasing in Nigeria as cybercriminals continue to steal data from businesses and individuals. Cybercriminals are becoming more and more sophisticated, which has led cyber experts to issue a warning that if the government fails to do something to stop them, many Nigerians may be in danger of fresh attacks. This is because cybercriminals are now discovering new ways to exploit people, networks and the Internet and many people are very vulnerable to such attacks. Nigeria is third in the top ten countries that are highly susceptible to fraudulent attacks through electronic mail and webpages. Statistics from the Internet Crime Complaint Center highlight an ever-increasing concern around the nature and dynamics of the fraudulent attacks taking place. Thirty of the 54 African countries have cybersecurity laws on their books.

Two other African countries that have made strides as far as cybersecurity policies and strategies are concerned are Mauritius and Rwanda. As far as cybersecurity maturity is concerned, Mauritius was ranked first in Africa and has already developed legislation addressing cybercrime, e-commerce, data protection and privacy as well as an established Computer Emergency Response Team (CERT). Compared to other African countries, Mauritius is a distant outlier (ITU, 2017). The 2017 report *Global Cybersecurity Index* (GCI) by the ITU ranked Rwanda as the second country in Africa as far as commitment to cybersecurity is concerned; in addition, Rwanda was ranked 36th worldwide (ITU, 2017).

The fast diffusion of ICT across the African continent over the past 15 years has led to improved economic conditions, more utilization of the mobile platform and increased susceptibility to cybercrime and cyberattack. Notwithstanding the increased level of digitization in the continent, legislation has not been symmetrical with technological innovation.

The absence of regulation and legislation addressing cybersecurity in most of the African countries has made the world more vulnerable to substantial cybersecurity risks.

CONTENT ANALYSIS OF CYBERSECURITY POLICIES

The following section covers the content analysis of the cybersecurity policies of the countries in our sample. The analysis is performed based on five constructs covering: economic; technical/technological; policy;

political; and social aspects of the policies of the countries in question (see Tables A4.1–A4.5 in the Appendix). Table A4.1 represents the economic construct of the cybersecurity policy. This is assessed based on the existence of three determinants in the policy; these are: (1) a reference to economic prosperity; (2) a reference to globalization; and (3) a reference to international and regional cooperation. Table A4.2 represents the social construct of the cybersecurity policy; this is identified by the following variables: (1) confidence in ICT; (2) improving social life; (3) reference to protecting children; (4) (h)activism; and (5) protecting human rights. In Table A4.3, the third construct, technical, is determined by the description of how the country is to protect its technological infrastructure through policies and laws. Table A4.4 defines the determinants of the policy construct. These are: (1) reference to protecting national security; (2) controlling organized crimes; (3) dealing with espionage; (4) application of the rule of law; (5) emphasis on public/private sector cooperation; and (6) a provision to raising awareness in the country. Lastly, Table A4.5 represents the political construct of the cybersecurity policy; this is determined by the following: (1) reference to a country's defense; (2) ways to deal with cyberwars raged by nation states; and (3) approaches to deal with (cyber)terrorism.

The results of the content analysis outlined in these five tables will be used to calculate the level of quality and comprehensiveness of a country's cybersecurity policy and strategies. This will be presented in Chapter 5 of this book.

FORMULATION OF HYPOTHESES

The set of hypotheses in the current research addresses the determinants of the quality and comprehensiveness of National Cybersecurity strategies in developing and emerging economies. The following section will identify economic resources and constraints that might support (undermine) the development of an effective National Cybersecurity strategy in those countries. Chapter 5 will cover the sample of countries, methodology and operational variables that will be included in the analysis.

Soft Side Infrastructure

The soft side infrastructure is mainly concentrated in the human resources of a country and the development of its technical skill-sets (in addition to other soft factors) capable of dealing with protecting a country from cybercriminal activities. These soft side resources constitute a key and a shield in protecting a country's hard infrastructure. Added to the technical skill-set, other soft side components include: (1) the response in a timely manner to cybercriminal attacks; and (2) the attribution of the attacks to specific people/nations/territories.

The challenges faced by any emerging or developing country are the quantity and quality of the repository of human technical knowledge available to society. Since financial resources are only a means to acquire productive assets, resources critical to cyber activities are primarily embedded in technical infrastructure and human skill-sets. Most policy makers agree that unless technology users in a country are educated about the opportunities and benefits offered by ICT and unless they are trained to use the Internet, creating economic and social value from cyber activities will not be successful. Some go further to argue that training and education are the main challenges for most developing and emerging countries looking at participating in the digital economy (GlobalHR, 2016). Training and education are fundamental to the effective use of the Internet as a medium, and consequently to regulating activities in cyber space. In a networked society, many of the benefits relate directly to the capability to use data and information to create new knowledge. Therefore, IT skills of the human resource component are considered to be a core component of a successful information society strategy. In many developing countries, as compared to the developed world, the literacy rate is generally low and the level of education is insufficient for full implementation of the changes required to move into a full-fledged information society. In addition, given the fast technological change related to ICT, continuous learning is required; this means employees and citizens of any country need to improve their existing skills or acquire new ones on a continuous basis. In this domain, governments can play an important role in enhancing information and technological literacy through the country's education system. Training teachers in the use of the Internet and communications technologies in the classroom will lead to a new generation of IT-literate children. Making cybersecurity education an integral component of the K-12 education systems and university levels is vital in creating informed citizens capable of protecting their cyber space and defending their critical infrastructure, both hard and soft. As an example, the country of Estonia is avant-garde in this domain. Following the Russian attack on the country's critical infrastructure in 2007, Estonia created an army of technically educated citizens, called *cyber militias*, whose main purpose is the protection of Estonia's critical infrastructure from cyberattacks (Sterling, 2018).

The quantity and quality of the country's existing technically skilled personnel limit the expansion of its economic base; this is referred to as the 'Penrose effect' (Marris, 1963). Edith Penrose has been credited by several authors adopting a resource-based perspective as having been instrumental in the development of this perspective. Here Penrose's much-cited work on the theory of the growth of the firm provides possibly the most detailed account of an RBV in the economics literature. She notes that a firm is more than an administrative unit; it is also a collection of productive resources, the disposal of which, between different users and over time, is determined by administrative decision. When we regard the function of the private business firm from this point of view, the size of the firm is best gauged by some measure of the productive resources it employs (Penrose, 1959).

The Penrose effect is more pronounced in an emerging or developing economy than it is in a developed one. In the former, the new staff, be they nationals or expatriates, have to go through a time-consuming integration process before they become efficient, productive team players. The constraint is a result of the intimate relationship between two resources: (1) human (especially managerial at the executive level); and (2) organizational resources. The two types of resource have to be well balanced in order that successful measures by local and federal governments can be taken. Hence the first hypothesis:

Hypothesis 1: The quality and comprehensiveness of a country's National Cybersecurity policy is positively correlated with the repository of technically skilled people in a country.

The Economic/Financial Base

While financial resources are not a sufficient condition for a country to equip itself with the required ammunition to protect its critical infrastructure, they are a necessary condition. The RBV of the firm regards the economic unit of analysis as a collection of resources and capabilities that are derived internally by factors such as its assets, skills, knowledge or culture. The RBV has been used by several authors in their research as a mechanism for understanding the manner in which firms operate. From the RBV perspective, resources are often copied by competitors, although cost, patent or exclusive access to certain resources/markets may be a barrier to imitation. This research will use the country's economy as a unit of analysis from a resource-based perspective instead of a firm. In addition, the country's capabilities, which may be defined as complex interactions and coordination of people and other resources, are the means by which an economy reaches a competitive advantage. However, in order to achieve a sustainable competitive advantage, economic actors must enable it to perform value-creating and value-adding activities, which are determined by market forces, that are better than its competitors. For cyber space utilization to be effective, there needs to be an appropriate infrastructure in place.

Even though the domestic financial sector and the capital account in developing and emerging countries were heavily regulated for a long time in the past, recent research has shown how the restrictions have been lifted over time (Klomp and De Haan, 2015). Research has examined financial liberalization that takes into account restrictions on the domestic financial system, the stock market and capital accounts; research also showed that developed countries have tended to use more liberal policies than developing and emerging countries. Although there has been a gradual lifting of restrictions over time, there were periods of reversals in which restrictions were re-imposed. The most substantial reversals took place in the aftermath of the 1982 debt crisis, in the mid-1990s, and after the Argentine crisis in Latin America. Under the current financial conditions and the aftermath of the 2007–2008 sub-prime crisis and the meltdown of financial systems around the world, we see more restrictions and regulations being introduced in the various economic sectors, mainly the financial sector. Just as an example, in response to the 2007–2008 sub-prime crisis, President Obama signed the Dodd–Frank Act of 2010. The US Government response was then reacting to the recent financial crisis to deal with the banks that are deemed too-big-to-fail (Aronsohn, 2016).

In developing countries, liberalization of the regulatory systems has opened the door for international firms to participate in local markets. The privatization of public financial institutions has provided foreign banks an opportunity to enter local financial markets. Macroeconomic stabilization, a better business environment, and stronger fundamentals in emerging markets have ensured a more attractive climate for foreign investment.

In recent years, then, there has been a revival of interest in the role played by financial development in long-term economic growth. A host of studies carried out over the past decade, beginning with King and Levine (1993), have found evidence in favor of the Schumpeterian view that a well-developed financial system promotes growth by channeling credit to its most productive uses. This has now become the conventional wisdom. Further, in the Information Age, the most productive use of finances is investment in cyber space and Internet-based technologies. This will ultimately lead to the development of a well designed National Cybersecurity strategy in an effort to ensure international participants in online trade that cybersecurity is at the top of the agenda of the local government. Hence, the second hypothesis:

Hypothesis 2: The quality and comprehensiveness of a country's National Cybersecurity policy is positively correlated with the level of maturity of the country's financial base.

Access, Technical Capabilities and Internet Penetration

Another related factor is the indigenous technical capability of the developing or emerging country, which is indicated by a number of variables such as national R&D expenditure, the rate of capital formation, and national investment in education. Technology is driving growth at every level of any economy. For example, economists agree that three ingredients are essential to economic growth: capital, labor and technology. Of these three components, technology is probably the most important. Eminent economists estimate that technical growth and technological maturity have accounted for the bulk of economic growth in the largest chunk of developed countries over the past 50 years. Of course, technology improves the productivity of labor. But leading economists who have analyzed the role of technical progress in the postwar period found a greater influence on the productivity of capital.

The fact that more and more people are using the Internet, which is the conduit for the growth of cyber space activities and e-commerce, is not necessarily a sign of the survival of such expansion or of its speed. Some estimates of the numbers of Internet users count anyone (including, for instance, children) who has had access to the Internet in the previous 30 days. A much higher frequency of access is necessary in order to acquire the familiarity and generate the confidence that is needed in order to become a cyber space economic consumer. Particularly in the case of those engaged in business-to-business (B2B) activities, the order of magnitude of their use of the Internet cannot be of some hours per month but must be of hours per day. Indeed, when asked about the use they make of the Internet, people in developing and emerging countries rarely mention e-commerce as a frequent online activity. Email is the most popular use of the Internet in developing countries. It is safe to assume that in developing countries the proportion of Internet users who engage in online activities is lower than average, owing of course to lower per capita incomes but also to other well-known factors such as low credit card usage, lack of relevant products or services, and poor logistics and fulfillment services.

Without an appropriate technological infrastructure, there will be little use of electronic commerce and electronic means by the business community. The network infrastructure needs to be accessible, affordable and of good quality. The telecommunications sector in many developing countries is run by the public sector, where the scope and modalities of privatization and liberalization pose difficult problems. It is worth noting here that countries that have carried out telecommunications sector reforms have experienced significant improvements in their move towards information societies. For example, since adopting a new national ICT plan in 1999, Egypt has successfully increased telephone capacity and teledensity, the capacity of international links to the numbers of mobile phone subscribers and international circuits, and the Internet, while reducing access costs (OECD, 2007).

Developing and emerging countries need to take into consideration that establishing telecommunications infrastructure is costly, and that they might need inflows of foreign direct investment. In general, technological development and technical growth in a developing economy can take place through the transfer of technology and expertise from more advanced and developed countries. A study of 33 countries using American technology showed that there was a positive relationship between rate of development (that is, as measured by the indigenous technical capability) and the proportion of licensing arrangements that were used as the means of technology absorption (Contractor, 1980). Furthermore, in transitional economies such as China, successful transfer of hard technology often has to be accompanied by the transfer of soft technologies such as management know-how (Hendryx, 1986). Overall, we see the growth-inducing power of technology at the industry level in developed countries. In the United States, for instance, research-intensive industries—aerospace, chemicals, communications, computers, pharmaceuticals, scientific instruments, semiconductors and software—have been growing at about twice the rate of the economy as a whole in the past two decades. In developed countries, we also see technology's growth-inducing power at the level of the individual firm. Recent studies show that firms with access to advanced technologies are more productive and profitable, pay higher wages, and increase employment more rapidly than firms that do not. The evidence is mounting. At the macroeconomic level, the industry level and the firm level, access to technical resources constitutes the engine of economic growth.

In the realm of technology, the so-called enabling technologies are the most important factors in this economic growth equation. Throughout the twentieth century, enabling technologies—such as mass production, machine numerical control, and the transistor—were powerful engines of growth. The integrated circuit was, perhaps, the defining enabling technology of the twentieth century. Since its invention more than 40 years ago, it has enabled a whole range of new products and industries—from the computer to satellite communications—and it has had a profound impact on existing products and processes from automobiles, consumer electronics and home appliances, to a broad range of advanced industrial systems.

The integrated circuit sowed the seeds for the knowledge-based economy and the Information Age that are rapidly growing. Without access to personal computers and Internet connections at a reasonable cost, consumers in developing economies are unable to migrate from traditional markets to electronic markets, and, hence, the need for a law to regulate these cyber activities would be much less imperative. However, even with access to the necessary equipment, people will not become active e-participants unless they have reasonable confidence in the truthfulness of transactions undertaken online. Thus, the presence of an adequate Internet infrastructure is a necessary but not sufficient condition for the development of e-economies; and the development of an e-economy is to be guided by a National Cybersecurity strategy:

Hypothesis 3: The quality and comprehensiveness of a country's National Cybersecurity policy is positively correlated with its indigenous technical capability.

Maturity of Cyber Law

Social theorists, legal scholars and historians concur that law has played a central role in the transformation and industrialization of the West over the past 200 years. The mounting complexity of formal legal systems and the development of constitutionalism and the rule of law during this period are thought to have been key determinants of economic growth and prosperity. Max Weber went as far as affirming that a well-developed legal system was a prerequisite for the development of capitalism (Weber, 1981). Kinship relations, reputation bonds enforced by relatively closely united communities, and a multitude of self-enforcing mechanisms form the most important governance and enforcement mechanisms.

For developing and emerging countries, providing an enabling legal framework is a determining factor to developing a successful cyber space as an economic and social engine, as it affects the ability to conduct transactions online. The main legal challenge of cyber activities is the dematerialization problem, that is, the lack of tangible information. Because of this and other unique characteristics of using cyber space to conduct business, national legal frameworks need to be adapted to enable the development and success of cyber space use. It is important to remember, though, that adjusting the legislative framework to cover activities in cyber space will not solve fundamental problems inherent in the existing legal system of a country. Although it is known that commerce and technology often advance ahead of the law needed to regulate them, it is equally true that technology needs to take into account relevant legal requirements. Furthermore, efficient regulation of cyber space issues such as spam and digital rights management requires that legislative solutions go hand in hand with technical solutions (UNCTAD, 2015).

It has been argued that an institutional and legal perspective would offer researchers a vantage point for conceptualizing the digital economy as an emergent, evolving, embedded, fragmented and provisional social production that is shaped as much by cultural and structural forces as by technical and economic ones. Faced with new forms of electronic exchange, distribution and interaction, ICT researchers cannot reasonably confine their interests to the problems of developing and implementing technologies or even to studying a technology's impact on local contexts. A world of global networking (both technological and organizational) raises issues of institutional interdependence whose understanding requires an appreciation for how prior assumptions, norms, values, choices and interactions create conditions for action and how subsequent action produces unintended and wide-reaching consequences (Orlikowski and Barley, 2001). Recognition of the institutional implications of electronic commerce would focus attention on such complex issues as the blurring of corporate boundaries, national sovereignty, organizational control, intellectual property, individual privacy, and internetworking protocols. Without an institutional structure, electronic commerce and electronic government research might focus more narrowly on technological designs, economic imperatives, or psychological impacts, thus missing important social, cultural and political aspects of technology diffusion.

Wherever the rule of law is weak, that ability to strengthen doing business in cyber space is undermined. It is important to underscore the fact that a strong rule of law influences people's general attitudes, increasing the level of trust in markets and contracting. Given information asymmetries in conducting business online, this trust is particularly important. To illustrate the importance of these features of a strong rule of law, consider countries where citizens grant little legitimacy to legal contracts, relying on more informal approaches when conducting business. Here, personal relationships are important, and people are likely to be leery of any business dealings with faceless strangers (and, conversely, may not hesitate to cheat a stranger with whom they do trade). What is meant by rule of law, then, is the presence of a clear governance arrangement that respects individual and commercial rights and which is enforced consistently and fairly as an important prerequisite for promoting effective use of technology and knowledge. If commercial contracts are not respected, and if businesses can be arbitrarily seized and/or if bureaucratic red tape stifles creative energy, any incubation project will be doomed to failure. The issue of the effect of cyber law on the economy and growth has become the topic of hot discussion over the last several decades among policy makers, practitioners and researchers, especially in economic development circles. For policy makers, this interest grew out of disappointment in the 1980s over the role structural adjustment policies played in growth and development, which has necessitated the need to reform institutions, especially the legal ones. In the late 1990s, a number of researchers linked the legal framework to the development of financial markets and, through finance, to growth and development. La Porta et al. (1998) started an effort to determine whether there was a correlation between the legal framework of a country and the development of its financial system, with the following underlying assumptions: (a) that there is a benchmark for 'good' financial markets (the US model); and (b) that extensive financial markets command growth (La Porta et al., 1998: supra note 7, at 1117–26). The model was gradually transformed into a broad theory about the development of markets, culminating in a so-called 'New Comparative Economics'. Karake and Al Qasimi (2010) studied the resource-based determinants of cyber laws in developing and emerging economies.

The World Bank, among other multinational institutions, jumped on the bandwagon of these ideas and turned them into normative guidelines for development (World Bank, 2015). The pervasive growth in electronic commerce in recent years has raised concerns that existing legal and regulatory regimes are too inconsistent or inadequate in dealing with the issues that electronic commerce raises. Most commentators have, however, noted that ironically it is the lack of substantial legal or regulatory infrastructure that has made the unbridled growth of electronic commerce possible and this has caused some to worry that the application of too much traditional regulation will stifle growth. Some other commentators have taken the point further and argue that modern information markets should largely be defined by agreements and other manifestations of market choice rather than by regulation. At various stages during the development of the Internet, several observers have also expressed disappointment with the inadequacy of domestic legal systems in dealing with issues in cyber space. This is hardly surprising as the principles developed to deal with legal issues in the physical world are sometimes inadequate in dealing with the emerging legal challenge thrown up by the Internet.

The fast growth of the Internet and consequently cyber space activities greatly increases the ease of accessing, reproducing and transmitting information. This ease raises a host of legal issues including the risk of copyright infringement, the protection of patent rights, and the preservation of trade secrets. The Internet also raises privacy concerns and issues pertaining to the validity and enforcement of agreements entered into via the medium of the Internet. Conflict of law issues takes on an added dimension of complexity and confusion due to the inherently fluid nature of the Internet. Users habitually trigger the application of the laws of multiple jurisdictions in a matter of seconds. It is becoming increasingly evident that the process of mapping existing legal concepts and tools into this new domain is not straightforward, and that a number of familiar legal concepts will need to be rethought and, perhaps, re-engineered before they can be applied efficiently in the new environment. Most governments act reactively and amend or create regulations after industry acceptance of these technologies has taken place. This gives rise to the maddening and steadily widening gap between new technologies and adequate government regulation. The existing body of law is, however, not entirely helpless and often the law is able to adapt and tackle some of the emerging legal issues thrown up by online activities. This is done through the process of drawing from precedents and on reasoning by analogy. There is, unfortunately and perhaps understandably, a limit to the ability of the law to adapt itself to emerging technologies: timely legislative intervention to supplant the existing law and to fill in the existing lacunae is often needed to ensure that the law remains current and relevant.

Many governments and regulatory bodies in developing and emerging countries are starting to recognize the economic potential of electronic commerce and electronic government and are considering a number of policy initiatives designed to encourage further development and application of this technology. These initiatives include attempts to overhaul or effect amendments to existing laws to deal with the emerging legal issues that electronic commerce raises. In Singapore, for instance, various amendments to existing legislation and subsidiary legislation have been put in place rationalizing the existing law to cope with moves in various industries toward the electronic framework. The amendments have collectively dealt with computer and electronic evidence, copyright, income tax concessions for cyber trading, electronic dealings in securities and futures, electronic prospectuses, and deregulation of the telecommunications industry.

In Malaysia, the Multimedia Development Corporation has been working on a National Electronic Commerce Master Plan that is designed to facilitate the creation of a favorable environment for the development of electronic commerce. The four key elements in this Master Plan are to boost confidence in online trading, prepare a regulatory framework, build a critical mass of Internet users, and introduce an electronic payments system.

In the Philippines, the passage of the Electronic Commerce Act underpins the government's resolve to create an environment of trust, predictability and certainty in the Philippine system so as to enable electronic commerce to flourish. In India, there have been feverish attempts to update the legal and regulatory framework to make it more relevant in the face of rapid developments in information technology and communications. The Internet service provider and gateway markets have been liberalized and the national long-distance sector has been opened up. In addition, discussions are ongoing for the liberalization of the international long-distance sector and India's up-linking policies are slated to become more liberal. A closer examination of the legislative activity in this area, however, leaves one with the uncomfortable feeling that what is taking place across a large part of the developing world is probably a reaction to perceived legal problems presented by electronic commerce rather than a careful and considered response to the actual issues that this new method of doing business raises.

Most countries have sought to respond to the novel legal problems that crop up in cyber space by enacting new legislation while others have sought to extend the ambit of their current laws to cover the novel scenarios occurring in cyber space. In this flurry of activity, it is not surprising that most countries have not addressed the fundamental issue of whether it would be wise or desirable to apply existing national laws, which have evolved mainly to deal with 'territorially based' concepts and rights, to the realm of cyber space. Accordingly, there have been calls to treat cyber space as a separate jurisdiction for the purposes of legal analysis. Some analysts have suggested that a separate law of cyber space, similar to the law of the high seas, should be formulated. Others have proposed that the norms and practices of the users of the Internet could be relied upon in determining the applicable and appropriate legal principles that should apply to transactions conducted via the medium of the Internet. This would include 'netiquette', which has the potential to constitute the foundation pillars of a workable uniform cyber space law. Based on the above, it is reasonable to assume that cyber laws contribute to better diffusion of digitization and the use of cyber space, and hence incentivize governments to develop a well designed National Cyber-security strategy in an effort to guide the country's e-economy:

Hypothesis 4: The quality and comprehensiveness of a National Cyber-security policy is positively correlated with the level of maturity of a country's cyber law.

Degree of Government Digitization

In the past few years, governments in developed and developing economies have learned from the benefits that the private sector earned from using cyber space and have engaged in the development of their e-government initiatives. Some of these initiatives are still budding, such as those in Oman and Saudi Arabia; others have reached maturity, such as the e-government initiative in the UAE and Singapore. A mound of literature and case studies exists demonstrating the rise and growth of e-government initiatives all around the world (ARMA, 2016). Unlike conventional bricks-and-mortar-based activities, digital delivery procedures are non-hierarchical, non-linear, interactive, and available 24/7. The non-hierarchical nature of Internet delivery allows people to look for information at their own ease. The interactive features of e-government provide both citizens and policy makers with the capability to send as well as receive information. Developments and progress of digitization initiatives in more than 200 countries around the world have attracted an increasing level of interest from academics, researchers, practitioners and policy makers. Developing metrics to measure the diffusion, progress and success of e-governments has been dominated by multilateral institutions such as the World Bank and the UN, consulting companies such as Accenture, and academic institutions such as Brown University and INSEAD (Accenture, 2005). These organizations have independently created and outlined different metrics to measure the diffusion of e-government. However, a common denominator has emerged among the various attempts and that is the preponderance of nations with high gross national products in the top echelons (Singh et al., 2007); this might explain the leadership of developed economies in the development, implementation and success of e-government. It is expected that we will find a strong link between leadership or maturity of e-government and the inclination for countries to develop quality and comprehensive National Cybersecurity strategies. The development of a high quality and widely comprehensive National Cybersecurity strategy is an indication of commitment of the leadership of a country to ensuring the success of its e-government initiatives.

In 2017, Gartner developed a five-level e-government maturity model to help organizations and countries plot their digital business strategy and communicate it to key policy makers and stakeholders (Gartner, 2017). Maturity Level 1 deals with entities where the focus is on moving services online to save costs and to ensure user convenience, but the use of data here is extremely limited. Level 2 is characterized by Open Government where the objective is more on promoting transparency and citizen engagements. Level 3 is data-centric where there is a move from listening to citizens' needs to using data proactively to design projects and processes helpful to citizens. Level 4 is based on open data whereby the government makes whatever data are collected available to citizens and businesses to use and develop analytical models. Data here flow two ways between government and businesses, organizations and other organizations, leading to easier interaction and better services. The last level, 5, called the smart stage, involves adopting a process of digital innovation using open data and embedding this across the entire government. Here innovation is predictable and recurrent, regardless of unforeseen disruptions or anomalies (Gartner, 2017).

Based on the above, it is expected that the link between the dedication of a country's leadership and the quality of governance, on the one hand, and the maturity of e-government initiatives on the other, would lead to the development of a high quality National Cybersecurity strategy as part of a broader roadmap toward better online governance:

Hypothesis 5: There is a positive relationship between the level of a country's digitization maturity and the level of quality and comprehensiveness of a country's National Cybersecurity policy.

CONCLUSION

This chapter has covered the nature of resources and the foundation of institutional environment theory. A number of hypotheses dealing with what is believed to lead to the development of a high quality and comprehensive National Cybersecurity strategy aimed at protecting cyberspace in a country were then developed. The first had to do with the quantity and quality of human resources available to society. It is believed that training and education are fundamental to the effective use of the Internet and hence to the success of electronic commerce. Since the quantity and quality of a country's existing skilled personnel limit the expansion of its economic base (the Penrose effect), it is hypothesized that a country's success in cyber space and its effort in developing a comprehensive National Cybersecurity strategy are positively related to the level of skills of its human resources. The second hypothesis has to do with the financial resources available to a country. In recent years, a host of studies have found evidence of a positive relationship between the strength of the financial base of a country and its economic growth. It is hypothesized that, in the information age, financial investment in Internet-based technologies is positively correlated with economic growth.

Access to Internet-based resources and technical capabilities constitutes the basis of the third hypothesis. Without access to computers and Internet connections at a reasonable cost, citizens in developing economies will be unable to migrate from traditional markets to electronic markets. The fourth hypothesis deals with the role that cyber law plays in facilitating the use of Internet-based technologies in a developing country. Scholars from all professional backgrounds agree that law plays a vital role in the transformation and development of societies. It is believed that, in the developed world, the development of constitutionalism and the rule of law have been the major drivers of economic growth and progress. A number of reasons have been advanced in the resource-based literature to highlight the role a strong rule of law plays in economic growth and development. The argument goes that a strong rule of cyber law affects transactional integrity in an Internet-based society, and thus investment in such markets. Cyber law is hailed to be one of the major drivers of cyber activities and Internet-based business. Because of the unique nature of the Internet, its use creates legal issues and questions, especially in areas related to intellectual property rights and cybercrime. Few countries in the developing world have drafted cyber law, and those that have are still struggling to perfect its implementation. In this study, the authors argue that the existence of cyber law leads to better diffusion of electronic commerce, and subsequently to economic growth and development. Hence, the fifth hypothesis was formulated to state that success in electronic commerce is positively related to the existence of cyber law. The next chapter will cover the formulation of methodology, collection of data, and the testing of the five hypotheses formulated in this chapter.

REFERENCES

Accenture Consulting (2005). E-government leadership: High performance, maximum value, accessed 11 December 2016 at www.accenture.com/NR/rdonlyres/D7206199-C3D4-4CB4-A7D8-846C94287890/0/gove_egov_value.pdf.

Ali Khasawneh, N. and Ahern, G. (2012). TMT legal update: Cybercrimes law – United Arab Emirates, accessed 3 October 2017 at https://www.lexology.com/library/detail.aspx?g=62f0c34f-0d12-4bbe-bb93-decfc71d4105.

Angarita, N.R. (2014). Latin America and protection of personal data: Facts and figures, accessed 10 October 2017 at https://www.privaworks.com/Details/AlertReference/PrintPreview.aspx?guid=28008dff-76f7-415f-a696-e28e5bc95c a6&p=1.

ARMA (2016). Report: E-government exacerbates records challenges in developing nations, accessed at http://www.arma.org/r1/news/newswire/2016/02/24/report-e-government-exacerbates-records-challenges-in-developing-nations.

Aronsohn, J. (2016). From too big to fail to too costly to comply, accessed 3 May 2017 at https://spea.indiana.edu/doc/undergraduate/theses/ugrd-thesis 2016-policy-aronsohn.pdf.

Asian Pacific Economic Cooperation (APEC) (2008), 38th APEC telecommunications and working group meeting plenary session, 15–17 October, accessed 5 November 2016 at www.apectewg.org/jsp/download.jsp?seq55096&board.

Bindiya, T. (2014). UAE military to set up cyber command, *Defense World*, 30 September.

Brangetto, P. and Aubyn, M.K. (2015). Economic aspects of national cyber security strategies, accessed at www.ccdcoe.org publications@ccdcoe.org.

Brynjolfsson, E. and Yang, S. (1996). Information technology and productivity: A review of the literature, *Advanced Computing*, **43**: 179–214.

Coase, R.H. (1937). The nature of the firm, *Economica*, **4**: 386–405.

Contractor, F.J. (1980). The composition of licensing fees and arrangements as a function of economic development of technology recipient nations, *Journal of International Business Studies*, Winter: 47–62.

Couts, A. (2011). Study confirms social media's revolutionary in the Arab Spring, accessed 12 June 2016 at https://www.digitaltrends.com/social-media/study-confirms-social-medias-revolutionary-role-in-arab-spring/.

Craig, A., Shackelford, S. and Hiller, J. (2015). Proactive cybersecurity: A comparative industry and regulatory analysis, *American Business Law Journal*, **52**(4): 721–87.

Cybersecurity in Latin America (2016). Cybersecurity Report 2016: Are we ready in Latin America and the Caribbean? Center for Strategic and International Studies, 14 March.

Diamond, L. (2010). Liberation technology, *Journal of Democracy*, **21**(3): 69–83.

Eisenhardt, K. and Martin, J. (2000). Dynamic capabilities: What are they?, *Strategic Management Journal*, **21**: 1105–22.

Enisa.europa (2015). Cybersecurity policy of South Africa, accessed 2 February 2016 at https://www.enisa.europa.eu/topics/national-cyber-security-strategies/ncssmap/cyber-security-policy-of-south-africa/view.

ESCWA (2015). Cyberlaws and regulations for enhancing e-commerce, March, accessed 11 January 2016 at http://unctad.org/meetings/en/Contribution/CIIEM5_ESCWA_en.pdf, 2015.

Eurobrasil (2015). World's seventh market for technology, Brazil has market participation in ICT trade, accessed 21 July 2017 at http://www.eubrasil.eu/en/2015/09/22/worlds-seventh-market-for-technology-brazil-has-marginal-participation-in-ict-trade/.

European Commission (EC) (2017). International cooperation and development, operational guidance for the EU's international cooperation on cyber capacity building, accessed 3 February 2018 at https://www.iss.europa.eu/sites/default/files/EUISSFiles/Operational%20Guidance.pdf.

Gartner (2017). These levels help CIOs improve the quality of digital government service for citizens, accessed 3 December 2017 at https://www.gartner.com/smarterwithgartner/5-levels-of-digital-government-maturity/.

Geroski, P., Gilbert, R. and Jacquemin, A. (2013). *Barriers to Entry and Strategic Competition*, London: Francis & Taylor Group.

GlobalHR (2016). The role of HR in mitigating cybersecurity threats, accessed 12 March 2016 at http://www.ghrr.com/blog/2016/02/24/the-role-of-hr-in-mitigating-cyber-security-threats/.

Hendryx, S.R. (1986). Implementation of a technology transfer joint venture in the People's Republic of China: A management perspective, *Columbia Journal of World Business*, Spring: 57–66.

Hitt, L. and Brynjolfsson, E. (1996). Productivity, business profitability, and consumer surplus: Three different measures of information technology value, *MIS Quarterly*, **20**(2): 121–42.

Hitt, M., Xu, K. and Carnes, C. (2016). Resource based theory in operations management research, *Journal of Operations Management*, **42**: 77–94.

Hoang, P. (2017). Determinants of ICT penetration in the Asia-Pacific. Hong Kong: ISA, accessed 3 January 2018 at http://web.isanet.org/Web/Conferences/HKU2017-s/Archive/3fdb2d05-9fbf-4c45-a6fb-f0207cfd5fab.pdf.

IBLS (2009). The impact of telecom sector privatization on e-Commerce in Brazil, accessed 12 February 2016 at www.ibls.com/members/docview.aspx?doc52343.

ICIC (2015). ICIC Argentina, accessed 13 March 2016 at http://www.icic.gob.ar/.

International Telecommunication Union (ITU) (2008). ITU global cybersecurity agenda: A global strategic report, accessed 3 January 2009 at www.itu.int/osg/csd/cybersecurity/gca/global_strategic_report/index.html.

International Telecommunication Union (ITU) (2015). ITU national cybersecurity strategy guide, accessed 7 June 2016 at http://www.itu.int/ITUD/cyb/cybersecurity/docs/ITUNationalCybersecurityStrategyGuide.pdf.

International Telecommunication Union (ITU) (2017). *ICT 2017: Facts and Figures*, Geneva: ITU.

ITnewsafrica (2016). South Africa: The most attacked by cybercriminals, accessed 27 February 2016 at http://www.itnewsafrica.com/2016/02/south-africa-most-attacked-by-cybercriminals/.

Jakobi, A. (2014). Determining geographical inequalities of information accessibility and usage: The case of Hungary, *European Journal of Geography*, **5**(1): 48–61.

Jurevicius, O. (2013). Resource based view, accessed 29 June 2016 at https://www.strategicmanagementinsight.com/topics/resource-based-view.html.

Karake, Z. and Al Qasimi, L. (2010). *Cyber Law and Cyber Security in Developing and Emerging Economies*, Cheltenham, UK and Northampton, MA, USA: Edward Elgar Publishing.

King, R. and Levine, R. (1993). Finance and growth: Schumpeter might be right, *Quarterly Journal of Economics*, **108**(3): 681–737.

Klein, P., Mahoney, J., McGahan, A. and Petelis, C. (2012). Who is in charge? A property rights perspective on stakeholder governance, *Strategic Organization*, **10**(3): 304–15.

Klomp, J. and De Haan, J. (2015). Bank regulation and financial fragility on developing countries: Does bank structure matter? *Review of Development Finance*, **5**(2): 82–90.

Kvochko, E. (2013). Five ways technology can help the economy, *The World Economic Forum*, accessed 12 May 2017 at https://www.weforum.org/agenda/2013/04/five-ways-technology-can-help-the-economy/.

La Porta, R., Lopez-de-Silanes, F., Shleifer, A. and Vishny, R. (1998). Law and finance, *Journal of Political Economy*, **106**(6): 1113–55.

LawReviews (2017). The privacy, data protection and cybersecurity law review – Edition 4: Argentina, accessed 2 February 2018 at https://thelawreviews.co.uk/edition/the-privacy-data-protection-and-cybersecurity-law-review-edition-4/115 1243/argentina.

MarketResearch.com (2001). Cybercrime and business security in Malaysia and Singapore, accessed at MarketResearch.com.

Marris, R.L. (1963). A model of the 'Managerial' enterprise, *Quarterly Journal of Economics*, **77**: 185–209.

Matoso, J. and Abib, G. (2015). Competitive advantage of a franchise in the software market: The case of TOTVS. *Journal of Information Systems and Technology Management*, **12**(3): 627–46.

Mukhopadhyay, T., Kekre, S. and Kalathur, S. (1995). Business value of information technology: A study of electronic data interchange, *MIS Quarterly*, **19**(2): 137–56.

Organisation for Economic Co-operation and Development (OECD) (2007). *Communications Outlook*, Paris: OECD.

Orlikowski, W. and Barley, S. (2001). Technology and institutions: What can research on information technology and research on organizations learn from each other?, *MIS Quarterly*, **25**(2): 145–65.

Penrose, E.T. (1959). *The Theory of the Growth of the Firm*, New York: Wiley.

Popa, S., Soto-Acosta, P. and Loukis, E. (2016). Analyzing the complementarity of web infrastructure and e-innovation for business value generation, *Program*, **50**(1): 118–34.

Reuters (2017). Saudi Arabia sets up new authority for cyber security, 1 November, accessed 11 March 2018 at https://uk.reuters.com/article/saudi-cyber-security/saudi-arabia-sets-up-new-authority-for-cyber-security-idUKL8N 1N68EP.

Siboni, G. (2014). Cybersecurity: Build-up of India's national force, in *Digital Debates: CyFy Journal 2015*.

Singh, H., Das, A. and Joseph, D. (2007). Country-level determinants of e-government maturity, *Communications of the Association for Information Systems*, **20**(40): 632–48.

Statista (2015). Online shopping, accessed 19 July 2016 at http://www.statista.com/topics/871/online-shopping/.

Statista (2017). Retail e-commerce sales worldwide from 2014 to 2021, accessed 11 January 2018 at https://www.statista.com/statistics/379046/worldwide-retail-e-commerce-sales/.

Sterling, B. (2018). Estonia cyber security, *Wired*, accessed 1 February 2018 at https://www.wired.com/beyond-the-beyond/2018/01/estonian-cyber-security/.

Taher, M. (2015). Commentary on the Arab Convention for Combating Information Technology Offences, Association for Freedom of Thought and Expression (AFTE), accessed 19 April 2017 at https://afteegypt.org/digital_freedoms/2015/03/11/9770-afteegypt.html.

Tao, A.L. (2016). E-commerce struggles for growth in ASEAN countries, *ComputerWeekly.com*, accessed 28 May 2016 at http://www.computerweekly.com/news/450281370/ECommerce-in-Asean-still-a-tough-sell.

The Hindu (2008). Parliament approves Cybercrime Bill, 24 December, accessed 11 June 2017 at www.thehindu.com/2008/12/24/stories/2008122456021400.htm.

United Nations Conference on Trade and Development (UNCTAD) (2015). *Information Economy Report 2015*, New York, USA and Geneva, Switzerland: United Nations.

Weber, Max (1981). *General Economic History*, New Brunswick, NJ: Transaction Books.

Weill, P. and Broadbent, M. (1998). *Leveraging the New Infrastructure: How Market Leaders Capitalize on Information Technology*, Boston, MA: Harvard Business School Press.

Wheeler, B.C. (2002). NEBIC: A dynamic capabilities theory for assessing Net-enablement, *Information Systems Research*, **13**(2): 125–46.

World Bank (2015). Justice and the rule of law, accessed 11 August 2017 at http://www.worldbank.org/en/topic/governance/brief/justice-rights-and-public-safety.

WSIS (2018). *High-Level Track Outcomes and Executive Brief*, Geneva: UN Publication.

Yue Chia, S. and Plummer, M.G. (2016). *ASEAN Economic Cooperation and Integration: Progress, Challenges and Future Directions*, Cambridge: Cambridge University Press.

APPENDIX

Table A4.1   Economic construct

Country	Economic Prosperity	Globalization	International Cooperation
Argentina	No	No	Yes
Bahrain	Yes	No	No
Brazil	Yes	Yes	Yes
Bulgaria	No	No	Yes
Chile	Yes	Yes	Yes
China	Yes	Yes	Yes
Columbia	No	Yes	Yes
Czech Republic	No	Yes	Yes
Ecuador	No	No	Yes
Egypt	Yes	No	Yes
Estonia	Yes	Yes	Yes
Georgia	Yes	Yes	Yes
Hong Kong	Yes	No	No
Hungary	Yes	Yes	Yes
India	Yes	Not clear[1]	Yes
Indonesia	No	No	Yes
Iran	No	No	Yes
Israel	Yes	No	Not clear
Ivory Coast	No	No	Yes
Jordan	Yes	No	Yes
Kazakhstan	No	No	Some[2]
Kenya	Yes	No	Yes
Latvia	Yes	Yes	Yes
Lithuania	Yes	Yes	Yes
Malaysia	Not clear	Yes	Yes
Mauritania	No	Yes	No
Mauritius	Yes	Yes	Yes
Mexico	Yes	Yes	Yes
Morocco	Not clear	Yes	Yes
Nicaragua	No	No	No
Nigeria	Yes	Yes	Yes

Country	Economic Prosperity	Globalization	International Cooperation
Oman	No	Not clear	Yes
Peru	No	No	Yes
Philippines	Yes	Yes	Yes
Poland	Yes	Yes	Yes
Qatar	Yes	Yes	Yes
Romania	Not clear	Yes	Yes
Russia	Yes	No	Yes
Rwanda	Yes	Yes	Yes
Saudi Arabia	Yes	Yes	Yes
Serbia	Yes	Yes	Yes
Singapore	Yes	Yes	Yes
Slovakia	Yes	Yes	Yes
South Africa	Yes	Yes	Yes
South Korea	No	No	Yes
Taiwan	Yes	Yes	Yes
Thailand	No	No	Yes
Turkey	Yes	Not clear	Yes
UAE	Yes	Yes	Yes
Uganda	No	Yes	No
Ukraine	No	Yes	Yes
Uruguay	No	No	Not clear
Venezuela	No	No	Not clear
Zimbabwe	Yes	No	Not clear

Notes:
1.   'Not clear' indicates that the policy does not explicitly state the existence of a specific determinant but the authors determined that there is an implicit implication in the content.
2.   Mainly with Russia.

Table A4.2   Social construct

Country	Confi-dence in ICT	Social Life	Protecting Children	(H)Activ-ism	Year CERT Estab-lished	Protecting Human Rights
Argentina	No	No	Not in policy[1]	Not in policy[2]	2013	Yes
Bahrain	Yes	No	No	Yes	2013	No
Brazil	No	Some	Not in policy[3]	Not in policy[4]	1997	No
Bulgaria	No	Some	No	No	2008	No
Chile	Yes	Yes	Yes	Not in policy[4]	2001	Yes
China	No	No	No	No	2002	Yes
Columbia	No	No	Not in policy[5]	Yes	2009	No
Czech Republic	Yes	No	No	Yes	2011	Yes
Ecuador	No	No	Not in policy[6]	No	2013	No
Egypt	Yes	Yes	Yes	No	2009	No
Estonia	Yes	Yes	Yes	No	2008	Yes
Georgia	Yes	No	No	No	2011	No
Hong Kong	Yes	No	No	No	2015	No
Hungary	No	No	Yes	No	2013	No
India	Yes	Yes	Not in policy[7]	Yes	2004	No
Indonesia	No	No	Not clear	No	2007	No
Iran	No	No	Not clear	No	2008	No
Israel	No	Yes	Yes	No	2006	Yes
Ivory Coast	No	No	Yes	No	2009	No
Jordan	Yes	No	No	No	2017	No
Kazakhstan	No	No	Yes	No	2009	No
Kenya	Yes	Yes	No	Yes	2012	No
Latvia	Yes	No	Yes	No	2006	Not in policy[8]

Country	Confi-dence in ICT	Social Life	Protecting Children	(H)Activ-ism	Year CERT Estab-lished	Protecting Human Rights
Lithuania	Not clear	No	Not in policy[9]	No	2006	No
Malaysia	Not clear	No	Not in policy[10]	No	1997	No
Mauritania	Yes	No	No	No	No CERT	Yes
Mauritius	Yes	No	Yes	No	2008	No
Mexico	Yes	Not clear	No	Yes	2010	Yes
Morocco	Yes	Not clear	Not in policy[11]	No	2011	No
Nicaragua	No	No	No	No	No CERT	No
Nigeria	Yes	Yes	Yes	Yes	2015	implicit
Oman	Yes	No	Yes	No	2010	No
Peru	No	No	Yes	Yes	2009	No
Philippines	Yes	Yes	No	Yes	2016	Yes
Poland	Yes	Some	Yes	No	2008	Not in policy
Qatar	Yes	Yes	No	Yes	2005	Yes
Romania	Yes	No	Not in policy[12]	No	2011	Yes
Russia	No	Implicit	Not in policy[13]	Yes	2001	Implicit
Rwanda	Yes	No	Not in policy[14]	Yes	2014	No
Saudi Arabia	Yes	Yes	Not clear	No	2006	No
Serbia	Yes	No	Not clear	No	2017	No
Singapore	Yes	No	No	No	1997	No
Slovakia	Yes	Not clear	Implicit	No	2009	Implicit
South Africa	Yes	No	Yes	No	2003	No
South Korea	Yes	No	Not in policy[15]	No	2004	Yes
Taiwan	Yes	No	No	No	1998	Yes
Thailand	No	No	Yes	No	2000	No

Country	Confi-dence in ICT	Social Life	Protecting Children	(H)Activ-ism	Year CERT Estab-lished	Protecting Human Rights
Turkey	No	No	Not in policy[16]	No	2013	Implicit
UAE	Yes	Not clear	Not in policy[17]	Yes	2008	No
Uganda	No	Not clear	No	No	2013	No
Ukraine	Yes	No	Not in policy[18]	No	2007	Yes
Uruguay	No	No	Not in policy[19]	No	2008	Not in policy[20]
Venezuela	No	No	Implicit	Not in policy[21]	2008	No
Zimbabwe	Yes	Not clear	Yes	Not clear	No CERT	Yes

Notes:
1. https://fosigrid.org/argentina. In 2008 Argentina passed a comprehensive cybercrime law, specifying penalties for online crimes like hacking, distributing child pornography, and illicit data interception.
2. https://adcdigital.org.ar/wp-content/uploads/2016/09/Cybersecurity-Argentina-ADC.pdf.
3. Child and Adolescent Act (Law 8,069/1990) provides for the crime of handling child pornographic materials.
4. http://www.coha.org/cyber-security-and-hacktivism-in-latin-america-past-and-future/. Latin Americans are also some of the most avid users of social media, which can pose many threats. Applications such as Facebook and Twitter have become outlets that can be used to set up illegal meetings, as well as to buy and transfer malware, phishing/pharming techniques, and similar malicious software. To combat this increasing trend, many countries in Central and South America have passed cybercrime legislation and created cyber defense systems. Foremost among them are Argentina, Brazil, Chile, Colombia, Mexico, Panama, Peru, and Venezuela.
5. https://www.itu.int/en/ITU-D/Cybersecurity/Documents/Country_Profiles/Colombia.pdf. Specific legislation on child online protection has been enacted through the following instruments: (a) The Criminal Code (Article 218 and 219A); (b) Law no. 679*.
6. https://www.itu.int/en/ITU-D/Cybersecurity/Documents/Country_Profiles/Ecuador.pdf. Article 528.6* of the Criminal Code; Articles 52, 69* and 72* of the Childhood and Adolescence Code, January 2003.
7. Section 20 of the Protection of Children from Sexual Offences Bill.
8. Latvia is taking part in international processes, including the work of NATO, the EU, OSCE and UN, to promote the improvement of a secure, free and accessible cyber space. Latvia supports the first comprehensive resolution of the United Nations Human Rights Council on human rights in the virtual space and will continue to participate and strengthen such initiatives as the Freedom Online Coalition, which focuses on observing human rights and basic freedoms in cyber space, especially the freedom of speech.
9. Article 309 of the Criminal Code.

10. Specific legislation on child online protection has been enacted through the following instruments: (a) Child Act 2001 (Act 611); (b) Section 293, Penal Code (Act 574); and (c) Sections 211 and 233, Communications and Multimedia Act 1998.
11. Specific legislation on child online protection has been enacted through the following instruments: the Criminal Code (Articles 483, 497 and 503).
12. Specific legislation on child online protection has been enacted through the following instruments: (a) Articles 374 and 375* of the Criminal Code; (b) Articles 7, 11, 13 and 14* of the Law on Preventing and Combating Pornography; and (c) Article 51* of the Anticorruption Law.
13. Specific legislation on child online protection has been enacted through the following instruments: (a) Federal Law of the Russian Federation No. 436-FZ on Protection of Children from Information Harmful to their Health and Development; (b) Presidential Decree No. 761 of 1 June 2012, on the National Strategy of Action for Children for 2012–2017.
14. Specific legislation on child online protection has been enacted through the following instruments: Articles 211, 229 and 230 of the Organic Law Instituting the Penal Code.
15. Specific legislation on child online protection has been enacted through the following instruments: (a) Articles 243–245 of the Criminal Code; and (b) Article 8 of the Act on the Protection of Children and Juveniles from Sexual Abuse.
16. Specific legislation on child online protection has been enacted through the following instruments: (a) The Criminal Code (Article 26); (b) Law on Regulation of Publications on the Internet and Combating against Committed Crimes by the Publications of Article 8.
17. Specific legislation on child online protection has been enacted through the following instrument: Article 12 of the prevention of Information Technology Crimes.
18. Specific legislation on child online protection has been enacted through the following instruments: Article 301 of the Criminal Code which does not explicitly mention child pornography but pornographic items in general.
19. Covered by the Child Pornography Act 17.815 (2004).
20. https://www.itu.int/en/ITU-D/Cybersecurity/Documents/Country_Profiles/Uruguay.pdf. Specific legislation on child online protection has been enacted through the following instruments: (a) Article 274* from the Criminal Code, modified by the Law no. 16.707* from July 1995; (b) Law no. 17.815*, 'Commercial or noncommercial sexual violence committed against children, teenagers or mental unable [*sic*.]', August 2004.
21. http://www.coha.org/cyber-security-and-hacktivism-in-latin-america-past-and-future/. Latin Americans are also some of the most avid users of social media, which can pose many threats. Applications such as Facebook and Twitter have become outlets that can be used to set up illegal meetings, as well as buy and transfer malware, phishing/pharming techniques, and similar malicious software.

Table A4.3   Technical construct

Country	Critical infrastructure
Argentina	Yes
Bahrain	Yes
Brazil	Yes
Bulgaria	Yes
Chile	Yes
China	Yes
Columbia	Yes

Country	Critical infrastructure
Czech Republic	Yes
Ecuador	No
Egypt	Yes
Estonia	Yes
Georgia	Yes
Hong Kong	Yes
Hungary	Yes
India	Yes
Indonesia	No
Iran	No
Israel	Yes
Ivory Coast	No
Jordan	Yes
Kazakhstan	No
Kenya	Yes
Latvia	Yes
Lithuania	Yes
Malaysia	Yes
Mauritania	No
Mauritius	Yes
Mexico	Yes
Morocco	Yes
Nicaragua	No
Nigeria	Yes
Oman	No
Peru	No
Philippines	Yes
Poland	Yes
Qatar	Yes
Romania	Yes
Russia	Yes
Rwanda	Yes
Saudi Arabia	Yes
Serbia	Yes
Singapore	Yes
Slovakia	Yes

Country	Critical infrastructure
South Africa	Yes
South Korea	Yes
Taiwan	Yes
Thailand	Yes
Turkey	Yes
UAE	Yes
Uganda	Yes
Ukraine	Yes
Uruguay	No
Venezuela	No
Zimbabwe	Yes

Table A4.4   Policy construct

Country	National Security	Organized Crimes	Espionage	Rule of Law	Public/ Private Cooperation	Awareness
Argentina	Yes	Not in policy	No	Yes	Yes	Yes
Bahrain	Yes	Yes	Yes	Partial	No	Yes
Brazil	Yes	Yes	Yes	Yes	Yes	Yes
Bulgaria	Yes	Yes		Partial	Yes	In progress
Chile	Yes	Yes	Yes	Yes	Yes	Yes
China	Yes	Yes	Yes	Law enacted	No	No
Columbia	Yes	Yes	Some	Law enacted	Yes	Yes
Czech Republic	Yes	Yes	Yes	Yes	No	No
Ecuador	Yes	Yes	No	Law enacted	Minimal	Minimal
Egypt	Yes	No	No	Enacted	Yes	Yes
Estonia	Yes	Yes	Yes	Yes	Yes	Yes
Georgia	Yes	Yes	No	Law enacted	Yes	Yes
Hong Kong	No	No	No	Law enacted	Not in policy	Yes

Country	National Security	Organized Crimes	Espionage	Rule of Law	Public/ Private Cooperation	Awareness
Hungary	Yes	No	No	Yes	Yes	Yes
India	Yes	Yes	No	Yes	Yes	Yes
Indonesia	Minimal	Minimal	No	Yes	No	Minimal
Iran	No	No	No	Yes	No	Yes
Israel	implicit	Yes	Not clear	Yes	Yes	Yes
Ivory Coast	No	Yes	No	Law enacted	Yes	Minimal
Jordan	Yes	Yes	No	Minimal	Yes	Yes
Kazakhstan	Yes	Yes	No	Minimal	Some	Yes
Kenya	Yes	Yes	Partially	Minimal	Yes	Yes
Latvia	Minimal	No	No	Yes	Not clear	Yes
Lithuania	Yes	Not clear	No	Yes	No	No
Malaysia	Yes	No	No	Yes	Not clear	Yes
Mauritania	implicit	No	No	Yes	Yes	Yes
Mauritius	Yes	implicit	No	Yes	Yes	Yes
Mexico	Yes	Yes	No	Law enacted	Yes	Yes
Morocco	No	No	No	Enacted	Yes	Yes
Nicaragua	Not in policy	No	No	Law enacted	No	No
Nigeria	Yes	Yes	Yes	Yes	Yes	Yes
Oman	Minimal	Minimal	No	Yes	Yes	Yes
Peru	Yes	Some	Law	Yes	Minimal	Minimal
Philippines	Yes	Yes	Yes	Law enacted	Yes	Yes
Poland	Yes	Yes	Yes	Law enacted	Yes	Yes
Qatar	Yes	Yes	No	Yes	Yes	Yes
Romania	Yes	Yes	No	Yes	Yes	Yes
Russia	Yes	Minimal	No	Yes	Yes	No
Rwanda	Yes	Yes	No	Law enacted	Yes	Yes
Saudi Arabia	Yes	Yes	Minimal	Law enacted	Yes	Yes
Serbia	Yes	Yes	No	Law enacted	Yes	Yes

Country	National Security	Organized Crimes	Espionage	Rule of Law	Public/ Private Cooperation	Awareness
Singapore	Yes	Yes	Yes	Yes	Yes	Yes
Slovakia	Yes	No	No	Yes	Yes	Yes
South Africa	Yes	No	Yes	Minimal	Yes	Minimal
South Korea	Some	Some	Some	Yes	Yes	Yes
Taiwan	Yes	Yes	No	Yes	Yes	Yes
Thailand	Minimal	Minimal	No	Yes	No	Yes
Turkey	Yes	Minimal	No	Yes	Yes	Yes
UAE	Yes	No	No	Yes	Yes	Yes
Uganda	Yes	No	Yes	Yes	No	Minimal
Ukraine	Yes	Yes	Yes	Minimal	Yes	Yes
Uruguay	No	Not in policy	No	Yes	No	Not in policy
Venezuela	No	Not in policy	Not in policy	Law enacted	ITU	Not in policy
Zimbabwe	Yes	No	No	Partial	No	Yes

Table A4.5 Political construct

	Defense	Cyberwar/ Nation State	Terrorism	Protecting Human Rights
Argentina	Yes	No	Not in policy	Yes
Bahrain	No	Yes	No	No
Brazil	Yes	Yes	Not in policy	Not clear
Bulgaria	Yes	No	Not in policy	No
Chile	Yes	Implicit	No	Yes
China	Yes	No	Yes	Yes
Columbia	Yes	No	Yes	No
Czech Republic	Yes	No	Yes	Yes
Ecuador	Not in policy	No	No	No
Egypt	Yes	No	No	No

	Defense	Cyberwar/ Nation State	Terrorism	Protecting Human Rights
Estonia	Yes	No	No	Not clear
Georgia	Yes	Yes	Yes	No
Hong Kong	No	No	No	No
Hungary	Implicit	Yes	No	No
India	Yes	No	Yes	No
Indonesia	Yes	No	No	No
Iran	Implicit	Minimal	No	No
Israel	Yes	Minimal	Yes	Yes
Ivory Coast	No	No	No	No
Jordan	Yes	Yes	No	No
Kazakhstan	No	No	No	No
Kenya	No	Yes	Yes	No
Latvia	Yes	No	No	Not clear
Lithuania	Yes	No	No	No
Malaysia	Implicit	No	No	No
Mauritania	Implicit	No	No	Yes
Mauritius	Implicit	Yes	Minimal	No
Mexico	No	No	No	Yes
Morocco	No	No	No	No
Nicaragua	No	No	No	No
Nigeria	Yes	Yes	Yes	Implicit
Oman	No	No	Yes	No
Peru	Implicit	No	Implicit	No
Philippines	Yes	No	Yes	Yes
Poland	Yes	No	Yes	Not clear
Qatar	Implicit	No	No	Yes
Romania	Yes	Minimal	Yes	Yes
Russia	Yes	No	Yes	Not clear
Rwanda	Implicit	Yes	Yes	No
Saudi Arabia	Yes	Minimal	Yes	No
Serbia	Implicit	No	Minimal	No
Singapore	Yes	No	No	No
Slovakia	No	No	Yes	Not clear
South Africa	No	No	Minimal	No

	Defense	Cyberwar/ Nation State	Terrorism	Protecting Human Rights
South Korea	Yes	Yes	Minimal	Yes
Taiwan	Yes	Yes	No	Yes
Thailand	Minimal	No	No	No
Turkey	Implicit	No	No	Not clear
UAE	Implicit	No	Partial	No
Uganda	Yes	No	Yes	No
Ukraine	Yes	Yes	Yes	Yes
Uruguay	Implicit	No	No	Not in policy
Venezuela	No	No	No	No
Zimbabwe	Yes	No	Yes	Yes

Chapter 5

INTRODUCTION

National economies around the world have become increasingly dependent on technology-driven infrastructures. Over the past 10 years, developing and emerging countries have seen a surge in investments in information and communication technologies (ICT). However, in addition to the legal systems, strategies and policies dealing with cybersecurity have lagged behind. A number of theorists and practitioners have evaluated the economic, political and social impact of this phenomenon; some have pointed to the limiting nature of the absence of well articulated cybersecurity policies while others have considered the lack of cybersecurity strategies and policies devastating.

Cyber space is chaotic, but its imperatives are becoming more vigorous every day. Since cyber space is not confined or restricted by geographic boundaries, it makes it difficult to regulate it successfully by geographically defined legislative systems at the national or even regional level. The increased speed of information generation and electronic media is making information resources generated anywhere in the world available to all global citizens. Emerging and developing countries are the foremost beneficiaries of the recent revolution in communication and information technology. This revolution serves, and is able to serve, all sectors and segments of society: the areas of education, healthcare, social policy, commerce and trade, government, agriculture, communications, and research and development all are prime winners.

The correlation between information, communication, and economic growth is well documented, making the usefulness of networks nearly self-evident. Electronic networking is a strong, speedy and economical way to communicate and to exchange information. When networks are available, collaboration among various entities and individuals, as well as countries, seems to come into being almost spontaneously. The growth of the online economy has been overwhelming. In recent days, the sharing economy or the phenomenon of collaborative consumption has been gaining momentum not only in developed but in developing countries also, especially the newly industrialized ones. In many countries, government and business entities have depended on the Internet to, among other things, decrease transaction costs, reach a wider audience, and improve profitability. In the world of the Internet, consumers seem to be the main beneficiaries: they use the Internet as a way to gather information and increase the efficiency and effectiveness of their search and to reduce their transaction and total costs. However, more reliance on the Internet would make it a necessity to develop laws to tackle cyber-related attacks and cybercrimes. Unfortunately, not many emerging and developing countries have jumped on the bandwagon of developing comprehensive cyber laws, which has led to a widening *legislative digital divide*[1] in the world.

The digital divide is a very serious matter for those who are currently behind in Internet access, for they are not able to enjoy many benefits of being wired and are handicapped in participating fully in society's economic, political and social life. These benefits include finding lower prices for goods and services, working from home, acquiring new skills using distance learning, making better-informed decisions about healthcare needs, and getting more involved in the education of their children. These are only some of the myriad benefits provided by having access to the Internet. Thus, for citizens of developing countries, lagging behind in Internet access entails further lagging behind in economic progress and the quality of life. Emerging and developing countries lagging behind in making use of cyber space find themselves in an increasingly difficult position as they attempt to promote their exports, attract capital investment and jobs, and transform their economies. A variety of reasons have been suggested for the digital and legislative divide, from lack of telecommunications infrastructure, dearth of computer skills on the part of business and consumers, failure of regulatory reform and establishment of standards, to the poor state of physical infrastructure, such as roads and rail.

The fastest growing emerging and developing countries are those with the highest degree of openness to imports and exports, according to the IMF's latest World Economic Outlook (IMF, 2016). The Internet facilitates a country's integration in the global economy and helps increase its import/export of goods and services. Political and economic reforms support economic growth of those countries; in addition, the economies are boosted by increased investor confidence, ease of doing business, and rising exports. Cyber space is a medium that increases a country's openness. A symmetry exists between trade liberalization and high levels of Internet adoption.

The majority of the countries cited as failing to liberalize trade are found to have very low Internet penetration rates, mainly as a result of poor investment in their telecommunications and other critical infrastructure, and the low diffusion rate of computer use. The International Telecommunication Union (ITU) reports that within the Western hemisphere and some emerging countries, Internet use is highest in those countries where density of telephone use is greater, where the provision of telecommunications services is more competitive, and where the combined costs required to access and use the Internet are lower than other parts of the world (ITU, 2015).

The literature on Internet diffusion and cyber activity adoption in emerging and developing countries is growing slowly, and some evidence exists describing the impediments to Internet diffusion (Safeena and Date, 2015). A survey by the International Trade Center (ITC) discovered that businesses in developing countries view their Internet connectivity as a valuable communications tool, but fail to incorporate the technology as an aspect of their competitive strategy or sustainable competitive advantage. Knowing the value of a specific resource is a totally different matter from making use of it to gain and sustain competitive advantage. Business perception contributes to the fact that less than a third of the surveyed countries included electronic trade as a component of their national export development strategies, an excellent indicator of the need for close cooperation between government and business during this technology adoption phase.

To facilitate the introduction of the Internet and eventually electronic commerce/services, the necessary condition is the creation of telecommunications infrastructure, or the backbone of cyber activities. For developing countries, financial resources needed to invest in telecommunication infrastructure are one of the major barriers since most countries are cash starved and rely mainly on foreign aid. A number of initiatives undertaken by developed countries are helping to narrow the digital divide, though these are limited in terms of scope and depth. As an example, Internet penetration levels in Africa are about 30 percent; mobile diffusion rate is close to 70 percent and broadband access accounts for more than 90 percent of Internet subscriptions. In terms of equity and distribution among African countries, we still see a huge digital divide. At the high end of the continuum, countries such as Morocco have penetration rates above 50 percent, and we still see other countries like Zimbabwe with single-digit rates (Nyirenda-Jere and Biru, 2015).

As far as cost is involved, great initiatives are taken to improve and reduce the cost structure of access to the Internet in Africa, which currently stands at 30 or 40 times the cost in developed countries. One initiative is the establishment of Internet exchange points (IXPs) at the local level. The continent of Africa now has more than 30 IXPs and is well on the way to reaching at least one IXP per country, leading to increased connection speed and decreased cost of communications (Nyirenda-Jere and Biru, 2015).

While developing the ICT infrastructure is a necessary condition for economies to jump on the bandwagon of making use of cyber space, the sufficient condition to encourage people to venture into cyber space is increased trust in the cyber world by developing policies governing this new world and enacting a legislative environment that will protect users on the cyber highways.

Cybersecurity policies serve as a compass when people use cyber space, and cyber laws act as an insurance policy for those who dare to venture into it. A number of multilateral entities, such as the ITU and the European Union, have developed what is referred to as a 'model' set of laws for cyber space, and are providing the necessary support to emerging and developing countries to draft their own cyber laws. However, many of these emerging and developing countries still lag behind in this area. While cyber laws act as an insurance policy for users in order to encourage them to venture into cyber space, the development of policies and strategies to help them navigate their journey into this somehow new environment is instrumental.

The remainder of this chapter deals with data collection on the various variables identified in the previous chapter, the proposed operational measurements of the independent variables and the dependent variable, discussion of methodology, and analysis of the empirical results.

DATA COLLECTION

In order to assess the significance of the various economic resources (both hard and soft) in explaining the development of a quality and comprehensive cybersecurity policy and strategy in emerging and developing countries, the authors assembled cross-sectional data for 63 emerging and developing economies that are considered highly involved in the information/knowledge society, and which have implemented electronic commerce/e-government initiatives. Data on Internet usage and other indicators of electronic commerce activities were collected from the Internet World Stats website (Table 5.1). This measure accounts for the broad spectrum of users who access the Internet in various ways. As indicated by the ITU, the global proportion of Internet use has been rapidly shifting towards developing countries (ITU, 2017).

Table 5.2 shows the sample countries listed according to the World Bank's classification in terms of development. In this classification, economies are divided according to their 2017 gross national income (GNI), formerly referred to as gross national product (GNP) per capita. Each year on 1 July, the World Bank revises its analytical classification of the world's economies based on estimates of GNI per capita for the previous year. As of 1 July 2017, low-income economies are defined as those with a GNI per capita of US$1005 or less in 2017; lower middle-income economies are those with a GNI per capita between US$1006 and US$3955; upper middle-income economies are those with a GNI per capita between US$3956 and US$12 235; and high-income economies are those with a GNI per capita of US$12 236 or more. The updated GNI per capita estimates are also used as input to the World Bank's operational guidelines that determine lending eligibility. The purpose of this conversion factor is to reduce the impact of exchange rate fluctuations in the cross-country comparison of national incomes. The Atlas conversion factor, for any year, is the average of a country's exchange rate (or alternative conversion factor) for that year and its exchange rates for the two preceding years adjusted for the difference between the rate of inflation in the country and that in the G-5 countries (France, Germany, Japan, the United Kingdom and the United States). A country's inflation rate is measured by the change in its gross domestic product (GDP) deflator.

Table 5.1   2017 Internet usage in sample countries

Country	Number of Internet users (millions)	Internet penetration rate
Afghanistan	5.70	15.7
Albania	1.93	97.9
Algeria	18.58	44.2
Argentina	34.79	78.6
Bahrain	1.28	91.5
Bangladesh	80.50	46.4
Bolivia	4.87	44.1
Brazil	139.11	66.9
Bulgaria	4.21	59.8
Cambodia	5.00	31.8

Country	Number of Internet users (millions)	Internet penetration rate
Chile	14.11	77.0
China	772.00	54.6
Columbia	28.53	58.1
Czech Republic	9.32	88.4
Ecuador	13.47	81.0
Egypt	48.22	48.5
Estonia	1.20	91.6
Georgia	2.66	68.0
Hong Kong	6.46	87.0
Hungary	7.88	80.5
India	462.12	34.1
Indonesia	143.26	34.1
Iran	56.70	69.1
Israel	5.94	74.7
Ivory Coast	6.32	26.3
Jordan	5.70	84.1
Kazakhstan	9.97	54.9
Kenya	43.44	85.0
Latvia	1.66	85.6
Lebanon	3.34	75.9
Lithuania	2.34	84.8
Malaysia	25.08	78.3
Mauritania	0.81	17.8
Mauritius	0.80	63.4
Mexico	85.00	65.3
Morocco	22.60	62.4
Nicaragua	1.90	3.8
Nigeria	98.40	50.2
Oman	2.59	78.6
Pakistan	44.61	22.2
Peru	18.00	56.0
Philippines	67.00	62.9
Poland	28.27	73.3
Qatar	2.11	92.0
Romania	12.08	62.8

Table 5.1 (continued)

Country	Number of Internet users (millions)	Internet penetration rate
Russia	109.55	76.4
Rwanda	3.72	29.8
Saudi Arabia	18.30	65.9
Serbia	5.89	67.1
Singapore	4.84	83.6
Slovakia	4.63	85.2
South Africa	30.82	53.7
South Korea	47.35	92.6
Taiwan	20.82	87.9
Thailand	57.00	82.4
Turkey	56.00	59.6
UAE	8.81	93.2
Uganda	19.00	42.9
Ukraine	23.30	52.5
Uruguay	2.40	69.4
Venezuela	19.12	60.0
Vietnam	64.00	66.3
Zimbabwe	6.80	40.2

Source: 2017 Internet World Stats, www.internetworldstats.com.

Table 5.2   World Bank classifications of countries

Country	Classification
Afghanistan	Low income
Albania	Upper middle income
Algeria	Upper middle income
Argentina	Upper middle income
Bahrain	High income
Bangladesh	Lower middle income
Bolivia	Lower middle income
Brazil	Upper middle income
Bulgaria	Upper middle income
Cambodia	Lower middle income

Country	Classification
Chile	High income
China	Upper middle income
Columbia	Upper middle income
Czech Republic	High income
Ecuador	Upper middle income
Egypt	Lower middle income
Estonia	High income
Georgia	Upper middle income
Hong Kong	High income
Hungary	High income
India	Lower middle income
Indonesia	Lower middle income
Iran	Upper middle income
Israel	High income
Ivory Coast	Lower middle income
Jordan	Upper middle income
Kazakhstan	Upper middle income
Kenya	Lower middle income
Latvia	High income
Lebanon	Upper middle income
Lithuania	High income
Malaysia	Upper middle income
Mauritania	Lower middle income
Mauritius	Upper middle income
Mexico	Upper middle income
Morocco	Lower middle income
Nicaragua	Lower middle income
Nigeria	Lower middle income
Oman	High income
Pakistan	Lower middle income
Peru	Upper middle income
Philippines	Lower middle income
Poland	High income
Qatar	High income
Romania	Upper middle income
Russia	Upper middle income

Table 5.2 (continued)

Country	Classification
Rwanda	Low income
Saudi Arabia	High income
Serbia	Upper middle income
Singapore	High income
Slovakia	High income
South Africa	Upper middle income
South Korea	High income
Taiwan	High income
Thailand	Upper middle income
Turkey	Upper middle income
UAE	High income
Uganda	Low income
Ukraine	Lower middle income
Uruguay	High income
Venezuela	Upper middle income
Vietnam	Lower middle income
Zimbabwe	Low income

Source: World Bank classification (2017).

It is expected that countries that are more advanced as measured by the GNI will have a higher quality National Cybersecurity strategy.

MODEL DEVELOPMENT

In the current research, the quality and comprehensiveness of a country's National Cybersecurity policy and strategy (QCNCS) is defined as the dependent variable. The QCNCS is developed and measured by completing a content analysis of the cybersecurity policies and strategies of the countries in our sample using the following determinants:

A National Cybersecurity Strategy is defined as the coordinated policy document that a government uses to express its vision on how it seeks to safeguard its systems, critical infrastructure and citizens in cyber space. The strategy details the ends, ways and means of securing cyber space as far as possible. The strategy may be included in the broader national security strategy, or it may be a standalone document (ITU, 2017).

The Dependent Variable

Chaotic activities in the past few years have ensured that lawyers and policy makers specializing in information technology policy and strategy have been kept busy monitoring developments taking place in many parts of the world. Broadly speaking, cyber space symbolizes a conceptual distinction between activities that take place in the physical or real world and those that occur online or in virtual environments. Beyond conceptual distinctions, we might say that the infrastructure of cyber space is basically digital code, and that this aspect of cyber space makes the virtual landscape unique.

Cybersecurity policies and strategies are not one-size-fits-all and so they must be tailored for each country because each country has unique attributes, tangible and intangible resources and characteristics. Developing and emerging economies are in dire need of guidance on how to develop and implement an effective set of cybersecurity policies and strategies because they are becoming heavy users of the Internet at a time when securing cyber space is becoming a more complicated and difficult task. In researching existing documents of national cybersecurity strategies and policies, and other documents dealing with cyber space, and as recommended by Luiijf et al. (2013), content analysis was performed to identify the following content factors and answer the associated questions:

1. Is there a clear definition of cybersecurity strategy in the published document(s)? This is an extremely important reference point since the existence of a clear and concise definition indicates a strong commitment of the country to securing its cyber space.
2. Is there a specific government agency in charge of drafting the strategy and implementing the policy (military, communication, finance, etc.)? This is another important indicator since the presence of a specific government agency in charge of cybersecurity is a sign of allocating accountability in this specific domain.
3. Does the cybersecurity policy highlight the impact on economic, political, military and social constructs of the country? Following on from this, does the policy define proactive measures to address the safety and security of those constructs? Having said that, and on the proactive side of the spectrum, the quality and comprehensiveness of the policy document will also be partly measured by identifying references to the following:
    3a Is there a reference to national security strategies?
    3b Is there a reference to critical infrastructure strategies?

3c Is there a reference to national defense strategies?

3d Is there a reference to economic prosperity and its relationship to cyberspace?

3e Does the document address globalization issues and highlight the importance of collaboration with other countries in this domain?

3f Does the document address public confidence in Information Communication Technology (ICT)?

3g Does the document address the social life of citizens and how cyber space can improve this construct?

4. On the reactive side of the spectrum, the quality and comprehensiveness of a policy document is also measured by addressing responses to cyber threats from internal and external agents; as such, the content of a country's cybersecurity document is assessed by identifying references to the following:

4a Reference to activisms/extremisms;

4b Reference to criminals/organized crimes;

4c Reference to espionage both by internal and external agents;

4d Reference to foreign nations/cyberwar;

4e Reference to terrorism.

5. It is a known fact that the growth and development of emerging and developing countries are positively related to the increased role of the private sector's contribution to the economic base. Any cybersecurity policy document will fall short if it does not address the role of the private sector in securing cyber space. Government programs are undeniably important, and cybersecurity initiatives are valuable in creating a set of standards, but they will be incomplete if they do not proactively and preventively integrate the role of the private sector. Cooperation between the public and private sectors is instrumental to the defense of a country from cyberattacks; cooperation with the private sector also increases the effectiveness of implementing any cybersecurity policy. As such, the policy document will be evaluated to assess the depth and breadth of the role of the private sector in cooperating with the government and the public sector in order to ensure a safe cyber space.

6. Challenges associated with cybersecurity can only be suitably dealt with through a set of policies and strategies that takes into account the participation of all major stakeholders, and by packaging countries' initiatives in a framework of international cooperation. The call for a multi-stakeholder approach to cybersecurity across borders is not new, but has been slow to gain solid footing. Given

the importance of international cooperation, the quality and comprehensiveness of the NCS policy document is evaluated in terms of its call for a strategy of cooperation with other countries and membership in and cooperation with international organizations such as the ITU and the United Nations (UN).

Given the above specific factors, the quality and comprehensiveness of a country's National Cyber Security Policy (QCNCS) will be rated from 0 to 6. All of the factors (1–6) will be weighed equally; while one can argue that some factors are more influential than others, we do not have enough empirical data to justify the different weighting of the various factors. This will be deferred for later research whereby a sensitivity analysis is performed with respect to the weights of the determinants of the policy content. The maximum score for a country's QCNCS will be 6.

Table 5.3 lists the sample countries that have developed a NCS policy document along with their QCNCS index. These are the countries that will be evaluated in this study.

Just as an example, China's cybersecurity policy is controlled by the Central Cybersecurity and Informatization Leading Group, and is led by President Xi Jinping. Its policy revolves around economic, political and military drivers and addresses cyber threats from criminal, cyberwar and terrorism perspectives. The policy mainly focuses on protecting the power of the Chinese State. Explicit goals include increasing China's broadband expansion, developing security technology for defense against threats, increasing control of the Internet in order to 'uphold good morals in the Net', exploring upcoming generations of mobile networks, and furthering the development of e-government services. Furthermore, China's cybersecurity policy details collaboration and cooperation with a number of countries, including countries outside China's immediate geographical neighbors, as well as the UN and non-governmental organizations (NGOs).

China published its first document in 2003; this was initially drafted by the National Coordinating Small Group for Cyber and Information Security. In the Spring of 2014, the Chinese Government formed the Central Cybersecurity and Informatization Leading Group in a move to enhance cybersecurity in China. The Leading Group has a close connection to the State Council Internet Information Office, or the Cyberspace Administration of China, which is expected to enable rapid development and implementation of cyber-related guidelines and laws.

As far as international cooperation is involved, China and the United States have an agreement to cease attacks on either nation's critical infrastructure by agreeing to refrain from supporting the cyber theft of business secrets. Notwithstanding the cooperation agreement between China and the United States, a large chunk of cyberattacks in the United States originates from China. It is thought that in order to support the growth of its national economy, China is involved in cyber economic espionage aiming at collecting useful information to help its domestic industries and its national research and development. China advocates for the peaceful use of cyber space and maintains a position of 'no first use' of cyber weapons, nor will it attack civilian targets. The country emphasizes its right to protect its national security interests in cyber space, in that the country is willing to counterattack if it is attacked. To respond to terrorism, China has passed a new anti-terrorism law that includes new regulations mandating that telephone companies and Internet Service Providers (ISPs) provide technical interfaces, decryption and any technical support for the government when required to do so. However, as expected, this prompted a controversial debate among citizens about consumers' privacy and security (*Wall Street Journal*, 2016).

As far as the private sector is concerned, the implementation of policies between private and public cybersecurity is not completely clear in the Chinese strategy document. In addition, it seems that privately owned businesses' development of security standards has been limited. Based on the content analysis of China's National Cybersecurity document, the value of its QCNCS was determined to be 3 out of 6.

Another example is the country of Singapore. In 2005, the government of Singapore passed the initial Information Communication Security Master Plan, which highlighted Singapore's cybersecurity strategy and policy for the public sector. In 2008, Singapore modified its policy with a second plan that aimed to transform Singapore into a 'Secure and Trusted Hub'. Singapore's aim of combating cyberattacks was implemented through multiple governmental agencies, led by the Info-communications Development Authority (IDA) of Singapore.

The IDA of Singapore works to facilitate the adoption of information technologies mainly to drive economic growth in the country. It engages both business and technology communities to develop effective solutions to address cybersecurity challenges facing Singapore. The IDA created the National Cyber Security Masterplan of 2018, a published document affirming the country's cybersecurity strategy in an effort to enhance cybersecurity competence in the public and private sectors, to increase the security of critical technology infrastructure, to grow Singapore's pool of cybersecurity experts, and to promote the adoption of cyber-security measures. A number of agencies are involved in keeping cyber space protected from internal and external threats. The work of those agencies is coordinated by the Cyber Security Agency (CSA). The CSA is responsible for directly developing and overseeing cybersecurity strategy and policy in the country.

The critical technology infrastructure protection assessment program tracks the security of key technology infrastructures in Singapore and aims at keeping Singapore secure and resilient. The National Cyber Exercise Program promotes the responsiveness to any cyberattack at the national level. It performs cross-sector exercises to make sure that Singapore responds successfully to a national cyber threat. Due to cyber threats becoming increasingly sophisticated, the cyber watch center of Singapore employs several advanced tools to provide the government with security monitoring. The threat analysis center leverages advanced analytical tools to assess large volumes of data in order to identify cyber threats with accuracy and efficiency, thereby providing public agencies with detailed cyber threat recommendations.

Recently, and starting in 2015, the CSA worked with the private sector to support the local IT security ecosystem. Singapore is one of the most technologically connected countries in Asia, and therefore the CSA is designed to provide centralized oversight of national cybersecurity functions. The establishment of the CSA follows a number of cyberattacks in Singapore in recent years, including one on the Prime Minister's office, and a security breach that affected more than 1500 SingPass accounts used to access e-government services. Establishing the CSA is an integral part of the National Cyber Security Masterplan of Singapore. Recently, the CSA set up a Security Operations Center in every sector to ensure a coordinated response in the event of a cyberattack. The aim of the new centers is to raise awareness, build capabilities and safeguard critical infrastructure from cyberattacks.

With regard to training and raising awareness, the IDA's Cyber Security Awareness Campaign reinforces security awareness for the private and public sectors on a national level. The National Info-communications Security Competition (NISEC) aims to educate the public about cybersecurity including simple yet secure online practices. In addition, the IDA focuses on increasing national security and defense against cyberattacks, including phishing and Advanced Persistent Threats (APTs). This includes enhancing the resiliency of the Government and Critical Infocomm Infrastructure (CII) as the government works closely with critical sectors on cybersecurity exercises. They also assess critical infrastructure for vulnerabilities, ensuring security capabilities and measures in order to mitigate cyberattacks.

The Singapore cybersecurity strategy document reinforces the role of cybersecurity by addressing key economic sectors. The IDA has also implemented a multilayered industry structure consisting of a network company, a number of operating companies, and numerous retail service providers to ensure that Singapore will realize significant economic benefits from the Next Generation Nationwide Broadband Network (Next Gen NBN).

Additionally, the document references their security functions, and how short-staffed the Global Information Security Workforce was in 2013. Thus, the Singaporean Government strives to work on their international collaboration with other countries to combat cyber threats. These include the Association of Southeast Asian Nations (ASEAN), and Telecommunications and IT Ministers' Meetings (TELMIN), a regional platform that enhances cooperation among ASEAN members. Singapore is also a key contributor in promoting trade and the use of ICT through the ASEAN Network Security Action Council (ANSAC), and the ASEAN–Japan Information Security Policy. Finally, the IDA focuses on creating a safe and secure online cyber experience for its citizens by leveraging popular social media and promoting safe online practices. The Singapore Government engages many other countries and contributes to the international effort to combat cyber threats, including the ASEAN Telecommunications and IT Ministers' Meeting, the ASEAN–Japan Annual Engagements, the Asia Pacific CERT, and the ASEANCERT Incident Drill. These collaborations have connected cybersecurity experts and created a communal effort to defend against cybersecurity threats effectively.

Although the IDA of Singapore does not explicitly address specific perspectives, it does provide a general plan to prepare for cyber threats. Their strategic plan focuses on APTs. APTs feature highly sophisticated and targeted malware. They can bypass typical cybersecurity measures and have compromised organizations seemingly equipped to defend against them.

Furthermore, in an attempt to mitigate cyberattacks, Singapore works closely with critical sectors on cybersecurity exercises to assess critical infrastructure for vulnerabilities. Recent government measures to accomplish the aforementioned goal include the CII Protection Assessment program, which was implemented to assess the security of Infocomm systems and ensure that CIIs are both secure and resilient. The Critical Infocomm Infrastructure Security Assessment (CII-SA) tests the adequacy of the protection measures within the CII. The IDA issued the Secure and Resilient Internet Infrastructure Code of Practice in order to set certain standards to ensure that security is consistently maintained.

Table 5.3   Countries' QCNCS

Country	QCNCS	Country	QCNCS
Afghanistan	1.20	Mauritania	2.00
Albania	1.50	Mauritius	5.00
Algeria	2.50	Mexico	3.50
Argentina	3.50	Morocco	4.00
Bahrain	4.50	Nicaragua	2.10
Bangladesh	2.30	Nigeria	3.00
Bolivia	2.70	Oman	4.00
Brazil	4.00	Pakistan	2.30
Bulgaria	4.50	Peru	4.00
Cambodia	1.70	Philippines	3.00
Chile	4.50	Poland	5.50
China	3.00	Qatar	4.00
Columbia	3.50	Romania	4.00
Czech Republic	5.50	Russia	4.00
Ecuador	2.80	Rwanda	4.00
Egypt	2.50	Saudi Arabia	2.10
Estonia	6.00	Serbia	3.00
Georgia	4.00	Singapore	5.00
Hong Kong	5.00	Slovakia	5.50
Hungary	5.50	South Africa	4.00
India	3.00	South Korea	6.00
Indonesia	3.00	Taiwan	4.00
Iran	3.00	Thailand	3.00
Israel	5.50	Turkey	3.50
Ivory Coast	1.50	UAE	3.00
Jordan	4.00	Uganda	3.00
Kazakhstan	5.00	Ukraine	3.00
Kenya	3.00	Uruguay	2.10
Latvia	5.00	Venezuela	3.00
Lebanon	1.80	Vietnam	2.90
Lithuania	5.00	Zimbabwe	1.50
Malaysia	4.00		

Source: Developed by the authors.

Along with these implementations, the Singapore Government focuses on proactive defense in an attempt to mitigate cyberattacks. The government has updated detection and analysis capabilities. For example, the Enhanced Cyber Watch Centre (CWC) uses advanced tools and techniques to improve detection and effectiveness of security monitoring in the public sector. On top of this, the Enhanced Threat Analysis Centre (TAC) uses analytical tools to evaluate large amounts of data to provide public agencies with more detailed cyber threat analyses (Singapore National Security Masterplan, 2018).

In recent years the Government of Singapore has called on the private sector to help mitigate cybersecurity risks. The Ministry of Defense has recently prioritized preparation for a wider range of cybersecurity threats and decreasing rates of information theft. As Singapore is famously business-friendly, with a relatively low corporate tax rate and regulatory reforms for tax compliance, the government of Singapore has a close relationship with the private sector. As the nation's businesses control a large share of online activity related to national security, the CSA announced that it is closely working with the private sector to increase the security of cyber space in the financial, utilities and healthcare sectors, as well as through recent national legislation enacting rules governing the cybersecurity of the telecoms services.

Based on the content analysis of the Cybersecurity Strategy of Singapore, the QCNCS index was assessed to be 5 out of 6.

Based on the QCNCS in Table 5.3, the countries were classified into five different categories. These are the *cheetahs*, countries with a QCNCS between 5 and 6 inclusive; the *gazelles*, those with QCNCS less than 5 but more than or equal to 4; the *bears*, countries with QCNCS less than 4 but more than or equal to 3; the *koalas*, with QCNCS less than 3 but more than or equal to 2; and the *tortoises*, those with QCNCS less than 2. The five categories with a list of countries in each are shown in Tables 5.3a to 5.3e.

Table 5.3a   The cheetahs

Country	QCNCS	Country	QCNCS
Hong Kong	5	Hungary	5.5
Kazakhstan	5	Israel	5.5
Latvia	5	Poland	5.5
Lithuania	5	Slovakia	5.5
Mauritius	5	Estonia	6
Singapore	5	South Korea	6
Czech Republic	5.5		

Table 5.3b   *The gazelles*

Country	QCNCS	Country	QCNCS
Brazil	4	Romania	4
Georgia	4	Russia	4
Jordan	4	Rwanda	4
Malaysia	4	South Africa	4
Morocco	4	Taiwan	4
Oman	4	Bahrain	4.5
Peru	4	Bulgaria	4.5
Qatar	4	Chile	4.5

Table 5.3c   *The bears*

Country	QCNCS	Country	QCNCS
China	3	UAE	3
India	3	Uganda	3
Indonesia	3	Ukraine	3
Iran	3	Uruguay	3
Kenya	3	Venezuela	3
Nigeria	3	Argentina	3.5
Philippines	3	Columbia	3.5
Serbia	3	Mexico	3.5
Thailand	3	Turkey	3.5

Table 5.3d   *The koalas*

Country	QCNCS	Country	QCNCS
Mauritania	2	Algeria	2.5
Saudi Arabia	2.1	Egypt	2.5
Nicaragua	2.1	Bolivia	2.7
Bangladesh	2.3	Ecuador	2.8
Pakistan	2.3	Vietnam	2.9

Table 5.3e   The tortoises

Country	QCNCS	Country	QCNCS
Afghanistan	1.2	Zimbabwe	1.5
Albania	1.5	Cambodia	1.7
Ivory Coast	1.5	Lebanon	1.8

As far as the cheetahs are concerned, 13 countries were grouped in this category. Those are the avant-garde where the quality and comprehensiveness of cybersecurity policies and strategies are concerned. Countries in this category have unique structure of their policies, with systems in place that can adapt to changing environmental situations. The gazelles category contains 16 countries. The majority of those countries have policies that we characterize as lean and agile, and given they are latecomers to the development of cybersecurity policies and strategies, with well-designed goals and objectives, are sprinting fast in the direction of catching up with the cheetahs. The bears category, with 18 countries, constitutes the lion's share of our sample. A large number of those countries are very populous (China, India, Indonesia and Nigeria); many of the countries in this category have challenging economic (social and political) problems, but they are steadfastly moving in the direction of becoming more active participants in the digitized/information world economy and beefing up their information/online-based activities.

The koalas category contains 10 countries; apart from Saudi Arabia, all the countries in this category are either low, middle-income or lower middle-income countries as classified by the World Bank. Given this fact, the creation of a cybersecurity policy and development of cyber strategies are considered luxuries for those countries. They are moving slowly in this direction, but before they put cyber space on their priority lists, they need to pull a vast percentage of their people from poverty and improve their economic standing. Any development on the cyber front in those countries has to be pioneered and supported by the developed countries and other NGOs, both from a financial and policy crafting angle. Many of those countries participate, to one degree or another, in international or regional organizations addressing cybersecurity issues. The last category, the tortoises, share a lot of characteristics with the koalas, except to them cyber space is not on the radar screen given their economic, social and political turmoil. Countries in this category are not active participants in cybersecurity international or regional bodies.

Determinants

A number of variables were deemed important/necessary in determining the level of quality and comprehensiveness of national cybersecurity policies. The following section discusses those independent/explanatory variables. As a practical matter, both the increasing importance and the expanding use (increase in range and depth) of the Internet are making distinctions between real space and cyber space less noticeable. This remains true despite the fact that cyber space still presents a remarkable number of novel legal questions involving how computer users carry out various transactions involving cyber activities through the interconnection of computing and communications technologies. Although the lack of reliable or relevant precedence renders legal practice in this area difficult and, quite often, annoying, the challenges are also exciting.

Cyber law
In the developing and emerging countries in our sample, it is observed that while, in general, cyber laws have been enacted in a number of countries, a large number still fall short of what can be considered adequate and/or comprehensive cyber legislation, which we refer to in this book as an early stage of mature cyber law. Generally, the majority of countries have enacted legislation relating to e-commerce/e-government, including e-signature and acceptance of e-documents and e-contracts. In addition, many have tackled intellectual property issues, which are largely addressed under general copyright laws, rather than under specific cyber laws related to intellectual property (Karake and Al Qasimi, 2010). The author addressed this specific issue at length in an earlier publication (Karake and Al Qasimi, 2010).

Not surprisingly, because of the unique nature of the Internet, its use creates unique legal questions, challenges and issues, particularly with respect to intellectual property rights and cybercrime. In addition, e-government requires a regulatory and public policy environment conducive to electronic commerce, protection of rights and an enabling legal framework for the digital transformation of government operations. Policy agendas include issues such as privacy, security, digital signatures, consumer protection, international trade, telecommunications, taxation and the digital divide. Industrial age laws, their interpretation and intent are, in many instances, not applicable or, worse, detrimental to a growing digital economy and society. Investment in the education of legislators around technology issues is a prerequisite to the successful use of cyber space. Without digital signatures, for instance, companies are hard pressed to engage in electronic commerce. Businesses require assurance that an electronically signed document can be enforced against the sender. At present, in most countries, there is no definitive court decision ruling that an electronic document can be 'signed' electronically in legal systems and in circumstances where the signature remains a formal requirement of law. This 'signature' issue is intimately related to a technical, legal issue of proof. In a court case, a party seeking to enforce a contract has the burden of proving that (1) the document was signed by the person who it claims to have come from; and (2) the document presented is, in fact, the one that was signed. In India, for instance, e-signatures are indeed legally binding (Nightingale, 2016).

An example of tough cybersecurity laws is that passed by China in November 2016, which, among other things, bans online service providers from collecting and selling users' personal information and gives users the right to have their information deleted. The law forbids companies from moving data beyond the mainland of China, and requires a security review process for key hardware and software deployed in China. In addition, the new law requires companies to assist authorities conducting security investigations into individuals, companies and other nations (*South China Morning Post*, 2017). China's tough cybersecurity law came into force in May 2017. Egypt has formulated a cyber law which failed to pass a vote in the parliament as of April 2018. This 45-article law includes clear obligations that service providers need to adhere to in order to protect the privacy of users, including providing users and government entities with certain data, such as names of the service providers, their address and contact information (AlBawaba, 2018). The Egyptian Parliament is debating launching a new law to counter cybercrimes.

Table 5.4 shows whether or not the countries in our sample have enacted a separate cyber law, and, if so, the year in which the law was enacted.

As developing and emerging countries join the World Trade Organization (WTO) they have been adapting their legal and regulatory systems to accommodate trademark, patent and intellectual property rights (IPR) protection. Some countries have been part of the early stages of IPR protection; others have retroactively signed agreements and sought membership in the World Intellectual Property Organization (WIPO). As of 2018, only four countries in our sample were not members of the WTO; these are Algeria, Iran, Lebanon and Serbia.

Table 5.4 Cyber law in sample countries

Country	Law (Y/N)	Year enacted
Algeria	No	
Argentina	Yes	2001
Bahrain	Yes	2015
Bolivia	No	
Brazil	Yes	2001
Bulgaria	Yes	1999
Chile	Yes	2000
China	Yes	2017
Colombia	Yes	1999
Czech Republic	Yes	2000
Ecuador	Yes	2002
Egypt	No	
Estonia	Yes	2007
Georgia	Yes	2012
Hong Kong	Yes	2000
Hungary	Yes	2001
India	Yes	2008
Indonesia	No	
Iran	Yes	2012
Israel	Yes	2001
Ivory Coast	Yes	2013
Jordan	Yes	2016
Kazakhstan	Yes	2014
Korea	Yes	2001
Latvia	No	
Lebanon	No	
Lithuania	Yes	2003
Malaysia	Yes	1997
Mauritania	No	
Mauritius	Yes	2002
Mexico	Yes	2000
Morocco	Yes	2003
Nicaragua	Yes	2008
Nigeria	Yes	2015

Table 5.4 (continued)

Country	Law (Y/N)	Year enacted
Oman	Yes	2008
Pakistan	Yes	2008
Peru	Yes	2000
Philippines	Yes	2000
Poland	Yes	2001
Qatar	Yes	2014
Romania	Yes	2001
Russia	Yes	2001
Rwanda	Yes	2018
Saudi Arabia	Yes	2009
Serbia	Yes	2012
Singapore	Yes	1998
Slovakia	Yes	2002
South Africa	Yes	2002
Sri Lanka	Yes	2016
Taiwan	Yes	2001
Thailand	Yes	2000
Turkey	No	
UAE	Yes	2006
Uganda	Yes	2013
Ukraine	Yes	2017
Uruguay	Yes	2000
Venezuela	Yes	2008
Vietnam	Yes	2002

Source: Compiled by the authors from various resources.

Developing and emerging countries' participation in interim treaties is uneven. These include the WIPO Copyright Treaty (WCT), the Trademark Law Treaty (TLT), and the Patent Law Treaty (PLT). As of May 2018, for instance, only 94 states worldwide were members of the WCT. Copyright protection extends to expressions and not to ideas, procedures, methods of operation, or mathematical concepts as such (WIPO, 2016). Forty-three countries in our sample of 63 are members of the WCT, or 68 percent. Algeria was the latest co-signatory, having become a member in November 2014. As of May 2018, only 42 countries worldwide have brought the TLT into force. As Table 5.4 indicates, as of May 2018, only 23 countries, or 37 percent, in our sample have brought this treaty into force and an additional 8 countries have signed the treaty. As of May 2018, 15 countries in our sample have enforced a PLT treaty, that is, 23 percent of the sample countries. Table 5.5 shows the status of countries in our sample on IPR as of 2018.

Table 5.5   Status of countries on IPR (2018)

Country	WTO member since	WCT	TLT	PLT
Afghanistan	2016			
Albania	2000	2005		2010
Algeria		2014		Signed 2000
Argentina	1995	2002		
Bahrain	1995	2005	2007	2005
Bangladesh	1995			
Bolivia	1995	Signed 1996		
Brazil	1995			Signed 2000
Bulgaria	1996	2002		
Cambodia	2004			
Chile	1995	2002	2011	
China	2001	2007	Signed 1994	
Columbia	1995	2002	2012	
Czech Republic	1995	2002	1996	Signed 2000
Ecuador	1996	2002		
Egypt	1995		1999	
Estonia	1999	2010	2003	2005
Georgia	2000	2002		
Hong Kong	1995			
Hungary	1995	2002	1998	2008
India	1995			
Indonesia	1995	2002	1997	
Iran				
Israel	1995	Signed 1997	Signed 1994	Signed 2000
Ivory Coast	1995		Signed 1994	Signed 2000

Table 5.5 (continued)

Country	WTO member since	WCT	TLT	PLT
Jordan	2000	2004		
Kazakhstan	2015	2004	2002	2011
Kenya	1995	Signed 1996	Signed 1994	Signed 2000
Latvia	1999	2002	1999	2010
Lebanon				Signed 2000
Lithuania	2001	2002	1998	2012
Malaysia	1995	2012		
Mauritania	1995			
Mauritius	1995			
Mexico	1995	2002	Signed 1994	
Morocco	1995	2011	2009	
Nicaragua	1995	2003	2009	
Nigeria	1995	Signed 1997		2005
Oman	2000	2005	2007	2007
Pakistan	1995			
Peru	1995	2002	2009	
Philippines	1995	2002		
Poland	1995	2004	Signed 1995	Signed 2000
Qatar	1996	2005		
Romania	1995	2002	1998	2005
Russia	2012	2009	1998	2009
Rwanda	1996			
Saudi Arabia	2005			2013
Serbia		2003	1998	2010
Singapore	1995	2005		
Slovakia	1995	2002	1997	2005
South Africa	1995	Signed 1997	Signed 1994	
South Korea	1995	2004	2003	
Taiwan	2006			
Thailand	1995			
Turkey	1995	2008	2005	Signed 2000

Country	WTO member since	WCT	TLT	PLT
UAE	1996	2004		
Uganda	1995			Signed 2000
Ukraine	2008	2002	1996	2005
Uruguay	1995	2009	Signed 1994	
Venezuela	1995	Signed 1996		
Vietnam	2007			
Zimbabwe	1995			

Source: Collected by the authors from various sources.

Karake and Al Qasimi (2010) developed a Cyber Law Index (CLI) for the countries in our sample. The index was developed using a content analysis of the various laws enacted by the countries in addition to their engagement in a global world and as international actors, indicated by their memberships in the WTO and the various WIPO initiatives such as the WCT, PLT and TLT.

The CLI variable is constructed in its composite form based on:

1. Content analysis of the legal texts of national laws of the sample countries; we strived to isolate those provisions dealing with cyber legislation. We then conducted an analysis of existing cyber laws in the sample countries in terms of whether such laws have covered the following five areas: data protection, e-transactions, e-commerce/e-government, intellectual property, and cybercrime.
2. A country's membership in the WTO.
3. A country's membership in the WCT.
4. A country's membership in the TLT.
5. A country's membership in the PLT.

The above five components are not equally weighted. The authors judged component (1), content of the cyber law, to be the most important; consequently, it is given a 65 percent weight. Next in terms of importance is membership in the WTO, with a weight of 20 percent. The remaining three components (WCT, TLT and PLT) are weighted at 5 percent each. Table 5.6 shows the CLI for the sample countries.

Table 5.6   CLI for sample countries

Country	CLI	Country	CLI
Afghanistan	0.2	Mauritania	0.1
Albania	0.1	Mauritius	0.6
Algeria	0.15	Mexico	0.4
Argentina	0.15	Morocco	0.55
Bahrain	0.8	Nicaragua	0.1
Bangladesh	0.2	Nigeria	0.4
Bolivia	0.15	Oman	0.5
Brazil	0.5	Pakistan	0.15
Bulgaria	0.6	Peru	0.6
Cambodia	0.1	Philippines	0.6
Chile	0.6	Poland	0.9
China	0.3	Qatar	0.6
Columbia	0.7	Romania	0.7
Czech Republic	0.9	Russia	0.4
Ecuador	0.65	Rwanda	0.3
Egypt	0.5	Saudi Arabia	0.2
Estonia	0.85	Serbia	0.2
Georgia	0.4	Singapore	0.8
Hong Kong	0.7	Slovakia	0.9
Hungary	0.85	South Africa	0.5
India	0.7	South Korea	0.9
Indonesia	0.45	Taiwan	0.7
Iran	0.15	Thailand	0.7
Israel	0.9	Turkey	0.4
Ivory Coast	0.2	UAE	0.6
Jordan	0.2	Uganda	0.4
Kazakhstan	0.15	Ukraine	0.3
Kenya	0.3	Uruguay	0.6
Latvia	0.7	Venezuela	0.2
Lebanon	0.1	Vietnam	0.25
Lithuania	0.5	Zimbabwe	0.1
Malaysia	0.85		

Source: Developed by Karake and Al Qasimi (2010).

Countries are usually at very different starting positions in the task of building their digital infrastructure to facilitate the development and diffusion of the Internet and the use of cyber space. ICT infrastructure determines the level of access and technical capabilities of an economy, and is defined as the share of total economic infrastructure used to support electronic business processes and conduct electronic commerce transactions. The innovation of the Internet technology, coupled with different environmental and policy externalities, leads to distinctive arrangements determining specific diffusion paths among individual countries and regions. Identifying unique resources of countries is essential for understanding digital-base diffusion in these countries. Some large developing countries, such as Brazil, are faced with obstacles and opportunities to spread the use of the Internet across their economies and societies. Telecommunication infrastructure is often a stumbling block for developing countries. Based on this statement, countries lagging behind a certain level of communication infrastructure would be severely handicapped for Internet diffusion and the use of cyber space.

Our access and technical capabilities measures focus on a number of indicators describing the availability of reasonably priced access to the Internet. For most current applications, Internet access requires a personal computer, plus a phone connection to the Internet, although access via mobile phone is becoming the overwhelmingly utilized alternative in some applications and in many countries in our sample. For the purpose of our study, we use the ITU's ICT Development Index (IDI) to measure a country's level of technical maturity. This index was developed by the ITU for the purpose of allowing countries to benchmark their information/knowledge development initiatives regionally and globally. The ICT Development Index (IDI) was first developed and presented at the World Summit on the Information Society (WSIS) in 2008, and has been revamped since. The conceptual basis of the IDI index is based on a three-stage model: the first stage deals with measuring ICT readiness, and it reflects the level of networked infrastructure and access to ICT; the second stage measures ICT intensity and it reflects the level of use of ICT in the society; and the third and last stage measures ICT impact and it reflects the result of efficient and effective use of ICT by individuals and entities, both public and private. These three elements combined measure a country's path toward becoming an information/knowledge-based society (ITU, 2015).

Based on the IDI three-stage model, three types of indicators were identified: (1) ICT access indicators, such as mobile phone diffusion rate and rate of computer diffusion; (2) ICT use indicators, such as Internet users per 100 inhabitants, fixed broadband Internet subscribers per 100 inhabitants, and mobile broadband subscriptions per 100 inhabitants; (3) ICT skills indicators, such as adult literacy rate and secondary enrollment ratio.

Table 5.7 lists the countries in our sample along with their 2017 IDI. As stated above, this index represents a benchmark measure that can be used to monitor and compare developments in ICT between countries and over time. The first set of IDIs was developed by ITU in 2008; in this book, we use the 2017 IDIs (that is the latest index available to the author at the time of writing this book).

As stated by the ITU, the main objectives of the IDI are to measure:

- the *level and evolution over time* of ICT developments within countries and the experience of those countries relative to others;
- progress in ICT development *in both developed and developing countries*;
- the *digital divide*, that is, differences between countries in terms of their levels of ICT development; and
- the *development potential* of ICTs and the extent to which countries can make use of them to enhance growth and development in the context of available capabilities and skills (ITU, 2015).

The conceptual framework of the IDI consists of the following three-stage model:

Stage 1: *ICT readiness* – this measures a country's level of networked infrastructure and *access* to ICTs (Access);
Stage 2: *ICT intensity* – this is a measure of the level of *use* of ICTs in a country (Use); and
Stage 3: *ICT impact* – this factor measures the efficiency and effectiveness of ICT use in a country (Skills).

In our sample countries, South Korea (IDI, 8.85) ranked number one on the IDI index followed by Hong Kong (IDI, 8.61), Estonia (IDI, 8.14) and Singapore (IDI, 8.05). Afghanistan (IDI, 1.95), Rwanda (IDI, 2.18), Uganda (2.19) and Mauritania (IDI, 2.26) ranked at the bottom of the list. Based on the ITU report, the IDI results show that all countries show an improvement in their ICT Development Index over the past five years. The 2017 report also shows that South Korea remained at the top of the list and Eritrea remained at the bottom of the list. The average IDI for our sample was 5.54 in 2017, compared to an average of 4.95 for the 176 countries measured by the ITU in the same year.

Table 5.7 2017 IDI Index

Country	Index	Country	Index
Afghanistan	1.95	Mauritania	2.26
Albania	5.14	Mauritius	5.88
Argentina	6.79	Mexico	5.16
Bahrain	7.60	Morocco	4.77
Bangladesh	2.53	Nicaragua	3.27
Bolivia	4.31	Nigeria	2.60
Brazil	6.12	Oman	6.43
Bulgaria	6.86	Pakistan	2.42
Cambodia	3.28	Peru	4.85
Chile	6.57	Philippines	4.67
China	5.60	Poland	6.89
Columbia	5.36	Qatar	7.21
Czech Republic	7.16	Romania	6.48
Ecuador	4.84	Russia	7.07
Egypt	4.63	Rwanda	2.18
Estonia	8.14	Saudi Arabia	6.67
Georgia	5.79	Serbia	6.61
Hong Kong	8.61	Singapore	8.05
Hungary	6.93	Slovakia	7.06
India	3.03	South Africa	4.96
Indonesia	4.33	South Korea	8.85
Iran	5.58	Taiwan	7.80
Israel	7.88	Thailand	5.67
Ivory Coast	3.14	Turkey	6.08
Jordan	6.00	UAE	7.21
Kazakhstan	6.79	Uganda	2.19
Kenya	2.91	Ukraine	5.62
Latvia	7.26	Uruguay	7.16
Lebanon	6.30	Venezuela	5.17
Lithuania	7.19	Vietnam	4.43
Malaysia	6.38	Zimbabwe	2.92

Source: ITU (2017).

The upper quartile of economies in the IDI index, all of which have IDI values of 7.00 and above, includes 15 countries in our sample, that is, close to 24 percent of the sample. Although the IDI index confirms that emerging countries in the Asia/Pacific and Arab States regions are among high performing countries (including South Korea, the overall top performer) in terms of access, use and skills, there are still major differences in ICT development as measured by the IDI index between and within world regions, a true indication of the digital divide. The average regional values for countries in Europe, the Americas and the Arab States all exceed the global average of 4.95. Africa, on the other hand, has by far the lowest average IDI value, at 2.53, almost less than half of that in every other region. The Internet Penetration Rate will be used alongside the IDI index in order to measure the maturity of the IT infrastructure in a country.

Soft-side Resources

Soft-side resources refer to the development of the skill-set of the human wealth available in the developing/emerging part of the world. This resource is extremely vital given the high number of young people in those countries. If one looks at the continent of Africa, with 1.3 billion inhabitants accounting for 17 percent of the world population, one sees a large youth bulge. It is estimated that the median age in this continent is 19.3 years, showing a very fertile area for development and skill building. The Human Development Index (HDI) is a widely discussed measure of the effect of economic development on the wellbeing of the people. The United Nations Development Program (UNDP) developed the HDI during the early 1990s when in the economic literature 'per capita income' was considered as an inadequate measure of development (especially for emerging and developing countries). It was argued then that 'real' gross domestic product per person growth is not necessarily a good guide to growth of living standards in the twentieth century. It is probably a considerable underestimate (Crafts, 1999). The HDI shifted the focus of economic development from (per capita) income to a much broader achievement in human life as a resource base.

The HDI measures the overall achievement of a country in three basic dimensions of human development—longevity, knowledge, and decent standard of living—all of which we consider as indigenous resources. Longevity is measured by life expectancy at birth; knowledge (or educational attainment) is measured by a combination of adult literacy (two-thirds weight) and the combined primary, secondary and tertiary enrollment (one-third weight); and standard of living is measured by real

GDP per capita (US$PPP). To calculate the HDI score, first, for each indicator of human development, a range (a maximum and a minimum) is established; the difference of score of a country on each indicator (actual score minus minimum of the range) is divided by the range itself. The HDI is a simple average of the three indicators so obtained (UNDP, 2015).

Despite its popularity as an index, the HDI is not free of criticism. The concept of human development has a broad meaning and cannot be captured by an index or a set of indicators (Streeten, 1994). The index has also been criticized on other grounds. These include the construction of the scale and measurement, methodology (Srinivasan, 1994), and data quality/limitations issues (McGillivray and White, 1993). Despite its limitations, the index is a useful measure to gauge the status of human development in a country. Economists agree that while there is a strong relationship between development and income, human outcomes do not depend on economic growth and levels of national income alone. They also depend on how these resources are used. For instance, democratic participation in decision-making and equal rights for men and women are two of the most important human development indicators but they do not depend on income or GDP.

The HDI is derived from the United Nations *Human Development Report 2016* (2017). This report presents an extensive set of indicators, including 33 tables and 200 variables, on important human outcomes realized in countries around the world. The report highlights remarkable progress on human development over the past 25+ years. In addition to social, economic and political progress, the report underlines how the digital revolution has connected people across countries and societies.

Table 5.8 shows the values of the HDI for each country in our sample. These figures are compiled from the 2015 *Human Development Report* published by the United Nations. This was the latest report which was released on 21 March 2017 and compiled on the basis of estimates for 2015. The HDI is computed based on three key metrics:

- life expectancy at birth; the objective here is to assess a long and healthy life of citizens in a country;
- expected years of an individual staying in school; the objective here is to assess citizens' access to knowledge;
- gross national income (GNI) per capita; the objective here is to assess the standard of living in a country.

Table 5.8   Human Development Index, 2015

Country	HDI	Country	HDI
Afghanistan	0.2418	Mauritania	0.3581
Albania	0.71	Mauritius	0.6882
Algeria	0.6543	Mexico	0.7445
Argentina	0.8571	Morocco	0.4901
Bahrain	0.784	Nicaragua	0.5639
Bangladesh	0.3866	Nigeria	0.3811
Bolivia	0.7424	Oman	0.6624
Brazil	0.7372	Pakistan	0.3337
Bulgaria	0.796	Peru	0.7289
Cambodia	0.5189	Philippines	0.7051
Chile	0.8236	Poland	0.8396
China	0.6734	Qatar	0.6671
Columbia	0.7348	Romania	0.81
Czech Republic	0.8755	Russia	0.8388
Ecuador	0.7037	Rwanda	0.482
Egypt	0.5912	Saudi Arabia	0.7461
Estonia	0.8889	Serbia	0.7796
Georgia	0.7895	Singapore	0.8515
Hong Kong	0.7981	Slovakia	0.8265
Hungary	0.8668	South Africa	0.7282
India	0.4698	South Korea	0.9273
Indonesia	0.6786	Taiwan	0.6749
Iran	0.6882	Thailand	0.664
Israel	0.8545	Turkey	0.7133
Ivory Coast	0.2992	UAE	0.6667
Jordan	0.7202	Uganda	0.5271
Kazakhstan	0.8619	Ukraine	0.8616
Kenya	0.5552	Uruguay	0.8148
Latvia	0.8288	Venezuela	0.7685
Lebanon	0.7374	Vietnam	0.6148
Lithuania	0.8557	Zimbabwe	0.5445
Malaysia	0.7119		

Source: Human Development Report (2015).

A close examination of Table 5.8 reveals that South Korea is ranked number one in our sample with an HDI value of 0.9273, followed by Estonia (0.8889) and the Czech Republic (0.8755). The country that ranked at the bottom of the list in our sample is Afghanistan with an HDI of 0.2418, followed by the Ivory Coast (0.2992) and Pakistan (0.3337). The average HDI value for all countries in our sample is 0.6894, with a standard deviation of 0.1595. This relatively large standard deviation indicates a relatively wide distribution around the mean. This is a stunning indication of what is referred to as the *human development divide* among the countries in our sample.

In our statistical analysis, the HDI will be used as a proxy to measure the soft-side development in a country.

Financial Resources

As discussed in Chapter 4, information technology has led to the promotion of a more intensive use of international financial institutions and gave rise to global international conglomerates. In addition, previous studies have found evidence that a well-developed, sound financial system promotes growth in the economy by channeling credit to its most productive uses (Karake and Al Qasimi, 2010).

A robust, well-functioning financial sector is vital for economic growth and successful cyber activities, especially for developing and emerging economies. It is critical for vigorous sustained growth. As an economy grows and matures, its financial sector must grow with it. It must be able to fit with the increasingly sophisticated demands that are placed on it. To help in the process of development and changes in the structural underpinning of the economy, financial institutions must adapt as economies mature.

However, as economies grow and become more digitized, their agricultural and manufacturing sectors expand somehow and their service sectors develop and grow, their banking sectors need to keep up. Decisions as to which activities to finance are crucial for rapid growth. Growing economic complexity is, of course, an inevitable consequence of growth. It means that the benefits of efficient credit allocation rise, and that efficient credit allocation is financing investments where the payoff is highest. But it also means that the challenges for those assessing alternative loan applicants mount. They must develop means of allocating credit among competing activities. They must learn to assess business plans and identify and manage risk.

For the purpose of this study, we will use the following to assess the financial strength of an economy: (1) access to sound money, as related to monetary policy; and (2) banking and finance as they relate to credit market regulations. For over two decades the Index of Economic Freedom has measured the impact of free markets around the world. A country's monetary policy that affects the stability of its financial base is taken from the 2018 Heritage Foundation Index of Economic Freedom.

With a stable monetary policy, people can rely on market prices for the foreseeable future. Hence, investments, savings and other longer-term plans are easier to make, and individuals enjoy greater economic freedom. In addition to eating away wealth, inflation distorts pricing, misallocates resources, raises the cost of doing business, and undermines the movement of capital and investment into the society.

In the majority of countries, banks provide the essential financial services that facilitate economic growth: they lend money to start businesses, purchase homes, and secure credit that is used to buy durable consumer goods, in addition to furnishing a safe place in which individuals can store their earnings. The more banks are controlled by the government, the less free they are to engage in these activities. Hence, heavy bank regulation reduces opportunities and restricts economic growth and, therefore, the more a government restricts its banking sector, the lower its level of economic growth and the higher its score.

Table 5.9 shows the sample countries rated on the Economic Freedom Index.

Level of a Country's Risk

A major concern for scholars of development and growth is the 'rule of law', country political, economic and social risks and related concepts from other legal systems. The rule of law is a concept that encompasses a number of consequences flowing from the law being the supreme ruler of a society. There are at least three distinct but connected elements:

1.   all citizens are equal before the law;
2.   the courts, not the state, should interpret and apply the law without fear or favor;
3.   citizens should have absolute respect for and faith in the law.

Economic growth, political adjustment, the protection of human rights, and other admirable objectives are all thought to revolve around the rule of law. Policy makers in developing and emerging economies are thus seeking ways to establish or strengthen the rule of law in their countries. Despite the assortment of definitions of the term 'rule of law', most can be classified according to whether they emphasize formal characteristics,

Table 5.9 2018 Economic Freedom Index

Country	Index	Country	Index
Afghanistan	N/A	Mauritania	54.0
Albania	64.5	Mauritius	75.1
Algeria	44.7	Mexico	64.8
Argentina	52.3	Morocco	61.9
Bahrain	67.7	Nicaragua	58.9
Bangladesh	55.1	Nigeria	58.5
Bolivia	44.1	Oman	61.0
Brazil	51.4	Pakistan	54.4
Bulgaria	68.3	Peru	68.7
Cambodia	58.7	Philippines	65.0
Chile	75.2	Poland	68.5
China	57.8	Qatar	72.6
Columbia	68.9	Romania	69.4
Czech Republic	74.2	Russia	58.2
Ecuador	48.5	Rwanda	69.1
Egypt	53.4	Saudi Arabia	59.6
Estonia	78.8	Serbia	62.5
Georgia	76.2	Singapore	88.8
Hong Kong	90.2	Slovakia	65.3
Hungary	66.7	South Africa	63.0
India	54.5	South Korea	73.8
Indonesia	64.2	Taiwan	76.6
Iran	50.9	Thailand	67.1
Israel	72.2	Turkey	65.4
Ivory Coast	62.0	UAE	77.6
Jordan	64.9	Uganda	62.0
Kazakhstan	69.1	Ukraine	51.9
Kenya	54.7	Uruguay	69.2
Latvia	73.6	Venezuela	25.2
Lebanon	53.2	Vietnam	53.1
Lithuania	75.3	Zimbabwe	44.0
Malaysia	74.5		

Source: The Heritage Foundation (2018).

substantive outcomes, or functional considerations. 'The differences between these three conceptions and the implications of each for efforts to establish, measure or foster the rule of law can be found in Stephenson (2001).

Levy and Spiller (1996) have developed a framework to analyze the interaction of the institutional endowment of a country, the nature of its regulatory institutions and the performance of the various sectors. They emphasize that the integrity and value of a regulatory framework differ with a country's political and social institutions. They also observe that performance can be adequate with a wide range of regulatory measures as soon as three complementary means limiting arbitrary administrative action are all in place: (1) substantive restraints on the discretion of the regulator; (2) formal or informal constraints on changing the regulatory structure; and (3) institutions that implement and enforce the above formal constraints.

The basic political institutions of a country refer to the nature of its judiciary and its legislative and executive institutions. Specifically, a self-governing and professional judiciary is a natural candidate for fulfilling the condition of enforcing formal constraints. A dishonest, politically motivated judiciary will be unlikely to side against the government on sensitive matters. Thus, judicial independence and professionalism imply a more confident framework for enforcing contracts, hence increasing the confidence of customers in the economy. Levy and Spiller (1996) further emphasize the role of the contending social interests within a society and the balance between them. In actuality, the more controversial these social interests are, the higher the potential for a reversal of government policies.

The higher the political instability of a country, the higher the potential for opportunistic behavior by governments, and hence the more inefficient will be the performance of the sector. Finally, Levy and Spiller (1996) stress the importance of administrative capabilities. Practically, the higher the administrative potential of the country, the higher the potential superiority of the regulatory system and, hence, the higher the performance of the sector.

For the sake of our study, we employ the most widely accepted measure of the rule of law, which was developed by the PRS Group, a country risk-rating agency, in its *International Country Risk Guide* (ICRG) (PRS Group, 2015). This measure (*LAW*) takes on a value between 0 and 100; higher values indicate a stronger rule of law in a country.

The ICRG Risk Rating System assigns a numerical value (risk points) to a predetermined range of risk components, according to a predefined scale, for each country covered in the analysis. Each scale is designed to award the highest value to the lowest risk and the lowest value to the highest risk. To allow for comparability, all countries are assessed on the same base scale. The risk components are grouped into three risk categories: economic, financial and political. Each risk category is made up of a number of risk components. The sum of the risk points assigned to each risk component within each risk category determines the overall risk rating for that risk category. The objective of the political risk rating is to provide a means of assessing the political stability of the countries covered on a comparable basis. To produce the political risk ratings, the following risk components are used: government stability, socioeconomic conditions, investment profile, internal conflict, external conflict, corruption, the military in politics, and religion in politics. Each of these components is assessed, evaluated and weighted and then they are all combined to produce the political risk factor.

The prime objective of the economic risk rating is to present a way of measuring a country's economic strengths and weaknesses. In general, if a country's strengths outweigh its weaknesses it will be classified as a low economic risk and if its weaknesses outweigh its strengths it will be classified as a high economic risk. Countries' strengths and weaknesses are evaluated and measured by assigning risk points to a number of economic risk components. The minimum number of points that can be assigned to any component is zero and the maximum number is assessed based on the weight that component is given in the overall economic risk assessment (PRS Group, 2015). In all cases, the lower the number of points, the higher the risk. In addition, and to ensure comparability between countries, the components are based on accepted ratios between measured data within the financial and economic structures of the country.

The financial risk rating provides a means of evaluating a country's ability to pay its way. Consequently, this entails a system of measuring a country's ability to finance its official, commercial and trade debt obligations. The financial risk components identified and weighted by the ICRG are: foreign debt as a percentage of GDP; foreign debt service as a percentage of exports of goods and services; current account as a percentage of exports of goods and services; net international liquidity as months of import cover; and exchange rate stability. The method of calculating the composite index is based on a formula that assigns 50 percent to political risk and 25 percent each to financial and economic ratings. Table 5.10 represents the country risk ranked by composite risk rating for 2015.

Table 5.10   ICRG composite risk rating

Country	Composite risk rating	Risk level
Afghanistan	37.5	very high risk
Albania	65	moderate risk
Algeria	67.3	moderate risk
Argentina	66	moderate risk
Bahrain	70.8	low risk
Bangladesh	64	moderate risk
Bolivia	73.5	low risk
Brazil	68	moderate risk
Bulgaria	68.8	moderate risk
Cambodia	69.3	moderate risk
Chile	76	low risk
China	72	low risk
Columbia	64	moderate risk
Czech Republic	76.8	low risk
Ecuador	64	moderate risk
Egypt	59	high risk
Estonia	67.8	moderate risk
Georgia	57	high risk
Hong Kong	81	very low risk
Hungary	71.3	low risk
India	68.8	moderate risk
Indonesia	67	moderate risk
Iran	61.3	moderate risk
Israel	73	low risk
Ivory Coast	61	moderate risk
Jordan	65	moderate risk
Kazakhstan	71.8	low risk
Kenya	64	moderate risk
Latvia	67.5	moderate risk
Lebanon	62.8	moderate risk
Lithuania	74.5	low risk
Malaysia	78.5	low risk
Mauritania	49	very high risk
Mauritius	56	high risk

Country	Composite risk rating	Risk level
Mexico	68.5	moderate risk
Morocco	66.5	moderate risk
Nicaragua	64.5	moderate risk
Nigeria	62.5	moderate risk
Oman	81	very low risk
Pakistan	58.3	high risk
Peru	71.5	low risk
Philippines	72.3	low risk
Poland	74.5	low risk
Qatar	82.3	very low risk
Romania	70	low risk
Russia	64.5	moderate risk
Rwanda	49	very high risk
Saudi Arabia	78.8	low risk
Serbia	62	moderate risk
Singapore	86.8	very low risk
Slovakia	72.5	low risk
South Africa	67.3	moderate risk
South Korea	81.5	very low risk
Taiwan	83	very low risk
Thailand	67	moderate risk
Turkey	63.4	moderate risk
UAE	82.8	very low risk
Uganda	57.8	high risk
Ukraine	54	high risk
Uruguay	72.8	low risk
Venezuela	54.8	high risk
Vietnam	69	moderate risk
Zimbabwe	54.5	high risk

Source: The PRS Group (2015).

Our sample contains seven countries in the very low risk category, or 11.11 percent. Singapore is the least risky country, with an index of 86.8, followed by Taiwan, the UAE and Qatar. The majority of our countries, or 28 countries, in the sample fall in the moderate risk category; this constitutes 44.44 percent of the countries in the sample. Only three countries, or 4.5 percent, in our sample fall in the very high risk category. These are Afghanistan, Mauritania and Rwanda, with composite risk factors of 37.5, 49 and 49 respectively. Eight countries, or 12.51 percent, fall in the high risk category. We use the composite risk factor as defined by the ICRG to assess the rule of law in a given country. In our sample, this measure (*LAW*) takes on a value between 88.3 and 37.5; higher values indicate a stronger rule of law in a country.

Maturity of E-government

Countries vary enormously in their e-government diffusion; variations are the result of a number of factors, both tangible and intangible. West (2008) reports that the most highly ranked e-governments, in order, are South Korea, Taiwan, the United States, Singapore, Canada, Australia, Germany, Ireland, Dominica, Brazil and Malaysia; at the other end of the spectrum, countries such as Mauritania, Guinea, Congo, Comoros, Macedonia, Kiribati, Samoa and Tanzania hardly have a presence online.

Among the countries in our sample, many governmental departments have welcomed the digital revolution and are incorporating a wide range of information and services online for their citizens. Websites as one-stop shops are being set up to smooth the progress of tourism and citizen complaints, and to improve business investment. Some of these have been very successful; Bulgaria and the Czech Republic, for instance, are attracting foreign direct investments through their websites.

As for the Asia-Pacific region, despite their relatively low national income, both Indonesia and Vietnam have advanced the implementation of e-government initiatives in recent years. At the bottom of this group is Pakistan. The Government of South Korea has been expanding the integration of e-government towards smart e-government, fostering the use of public services in a ubiquitous fashion. Under the slogan of 'Moving toward a smaller and more efficient government', the Ministry of Public Administration and Security (MOPAS) actively supports the local government in terms of local administration, finance and regional development for the promotion of greater local autonomy. Notwithstanding the clear superiority of the e-Government South Korean Strategy, a number of challenges can still be identified, such as the digital divide, Internet addiction and cyber ethic. This latter factor is a major determinant of cybercrimes.

As for e-government ranking in Latin America, Chile, Mexico and Brazil ranked third, fourth and fifth, respectively (after the United States and Canada). Uruguay and Venezuela stood at the bottom of the group. The countries of the European Union have all been encouraged to deploy advanced technologies and institute better governance and e-services, while simultaneously pursuing greater transparency, efficiency and inclusion. Among those countries, Estonia, with an index of 0.818, ranked third after Denmark and the United Kingdom, which ranked first and second respectively. At the bottom of the list in this group was Romania, with an e-government index of 0.5632 (UN, 2016). Romania has passed fundamental ICT-related laws, and planned and implemented the first steps towards an Information Society but the country fell short on the implementation of its policies and strategies; just as an example the e-Romania project has yet to be implemented. Having said that, the country has the advantage of good ICT infrastructure in place and an abundance of IT professionals.

For the Africa, Middle East and CIS region, Israel ranks first in this group, with an e-government index of 0.8162; Israel is followed by UAE and Russia in second and third place respectively. E-government in Israel is well matured and widely used in administration implemented using the five layer model of e-government. The overall e-government strategy places information access and integration as a top priority in the country; further, strategic solutions are put in place enabling the government as a whole to impeccably harness information and knowledge resources in order to increase the effectiveness and efficiency of service delivery. The new trends of e-government in the UAE are interesting for the rest of the region, in that they play a leading, avant-garde role in the Gulf region. In addition, the UAE is seeking to establish itself as a smart government leader in the region. This is done by encouraging UAE citizens to use the latest mobile devices and applications, and by bundling m-government services as preferred channels. It is too early to assess the level of success/failure of these initiatives; having said that, the future is going to be about interconnecting government to government, and more collaboration on the government-to-citizen side. The worst performers in this group are Nigeria and Kenya, with e-government indices of 0.2929 and 0.3805. Kenya is trying to improve its position in the e-government sphere in that it has formulated an e-government agenda with the assistance of other countries and international organizations. The Kenyan e-government master plan was developed by the Kenya ICT Authority, and is incorporated in the constitution of Kenya.

In this book, we will use the 2016 United Nations E-Government Development Index (EGDI) maturity measures; this is deemed the most thorough quantitative indicator. The EGDI is based on a holistic view of e-government development, and its methodological framework has remained consistent since it was introduced in 2001, while at the same time its components are carefully adjusted to reflect evolving knowledge of best practices in e-government and changes in the underlying support-ing ICT infrastructure, human capacity development and online service advancement, among other factors. The EGDI is a composite measure of three important dimensions of e-government, namely: provision of online services, telecommunication connectivity and human capacity. The 2016 EGDI classifies 25 countries worldwide with 'very high EGDI' between 0.75 and 1.0. Five countries in our sample are among this list of very high EGDI, these are South Korea, Singapore, Estonia, Israel and Bahrain, ranked number 1, 3, 15, 17 and 18 respectively. The majority of the countries worldwide fall in the middle range, with 62 countries ranked as high EGDI (between 0.5 and 0.75) and 74 countries ranked as middle EGDI (between 0.25 and 0.5). The lowest performing group, ranked as low EGDI (less than 0.25), comprises 32 countries (17 percent). The overall e-government index runs along a scale from zero (having none of these features and no online services) to 1.

RESULTS OF STATISTICAL ANALYSIS

The main objective here is to conduct an analysis to evaluate the correl-ation of technology, soft-side factors, such as development of human resources and the country's level of risk, on one hand, and the level of quality and comprehensiveness of a country's cybersecurity policy and strategy. The initial analysis was conducted by calculating descriptive statistics including frequencies, mean scores and standard deviations. Pearson's Production Moment Correlation analysis was used to determine the correlation of each of the independent variables with the dependent variable at the 0.05 level of significance. After this, multiple regression analysis was performed to determine the weight of each variable in the prediction of developing a cyber law in a specific country.

Table 5.11 presents the definitions of the operational variables used in the statistical analysis. Table 5.12 presents the descriptive statistics of the operational variables used in the statistical analysis.

The empirical results of the stepwise regression analysis are presented in Table 5.13. These OLS estimations were conducted to explore the relation-ships among the different variables defined in Table 5.13 and to test the hypotheses formulated in Chapter 4. The main objective of our analysis is to identify those resources contributing to the level of quality and comprehen-siveness of a country's National Cybersecurity initiatives in developing and emerging economies. As stated in Chapter 4, the authors hypothesized that in addition to physical infrastructure resources, the success of cybersecurity policies depends on the existence of soft resources such as a well established cyber law and the human resources index in a country.

Stepwise multiple regression analysis is valuable in determining which of the independent variables provide a significant contribution when predicting the dependent variable (Mertler and Vannatta, 2013). In this study, stepwise multiple regression analysis was performed to determine if relationships existed between the dependent variable, quality and comprehensiveness of the National Cybersecurity policy (QCNCS) and the independent variables: Internet Penetration Rate (IPR), Human resources Development Index (HDI) and the level of maturity of the cyber law as measured by the Cyber Law Index.

The researchers used the Statistical Package for the Social Sciences (SPSS) to analyze the appropriate data and build the statistical model. The regression analysis included data on 63 countries. Stepwise multiple regression analysis was performed in SPSS and excluded independent variables that did not have a statistically significant relationship with the dependent variable, QCNCS policy. The SPSS results of the stepwise multiple regression analysis contained data to create an equation for each leadership style that included variables exhibiting a statistically significant impact on the prediction.

Multicollinearity

Multicollinearity occurs when highly related independent variables are included in the same regression model. In cross-sectional research, as is the case in our analysis, serious multicollinearity most commonly occurs when multiple measures of the same or similar constructs (Internet Penetration Rate and the IDI) are used as the independent variables in a regression equation. As with exact collinearity, highly related independent variables can occur in more subtle ways as well. Some measures which purport to measure different constructs are based on overlapping sets of similar items so that they will be highly related.

As such, multicollinearity may lead to unstable regression coefficients that are associated with large standard errors. Multicollinearity can also lead to complexities in interpreting the regression coefficients. To measure multicollinearity we look at the squared correlation between each of the pairs of predictor variables which provides an index of bivariate multicollinearity. As its value increases toward 1.0, the magnitude of potential problems associated with multicollinearity increases correspondingly.

The Variance Inflation Factor (VIF) provides an index of the amount that the variance of each regression coefficient is increased relative to a situation in which all of the predictor variables are uncorrelated. A VIF is calculated for each term in the regression equation, excluding the intercept. A commonly used rule of thumb is that any VIF of 10 or more provides evidence of serious multicollinearity involving the corresponding independent variables. Table 5.13 shows that the VIFs are all much less than 10 (a maximum VIF of a bit more than 2), leading us to believe that there is no problem of multicollinearity between the independent variables in our regression model.

In addition to the VIFs presented in Table 5.13, the tolerance factors are provided as well. Tolerance factors indicate that the variance in one independent variable is not caused by variances in other independent variables in our regression mode. A common rule of thumb for values of tolerance factors is that levels less than 0.1 indicate a serious problem of multicollinearity in the model. Examining the tolerance factor in our model, all are way above 0.1, indicating that multicollinearity is not a problem in our model.

Another measure of multicollinearity examines the correlation matrix of the independent variables and the values of the eigenvalues and the condition numbers associated with them. Table 5.14 is decomposed into a set of orthogonal dimensions. Orthogonal dimensions are completely non-overlapping and share no variance in common. The SPSS program performed this decomposition, which is known as principal components analysis. When this analysis is performed on the correlation matrix of the k independent variables, a set of k *eigenvalues* or characteristic roots of the matrix is produced. The proportion of the variance in the independent variables accounted for by each orthogonal dimension i is A/k, where Ai is the eigenvalue. The eigenvalues are ordered from largest to smallest so that each orthogonal dimension in turn accounts for a smaller proportion of the variance of the independent variables. With two independent variables (IVs), if the two IVs are uncorrelated, each eigenvalue will equal 1.0, so that each *independent* dimension will account for $A/2$, or 50 percent of the variance in the set of independent variables. As the independent variables become increasingly correlated, more and more of the variance in the independent variables is associated with the first dimension, so that the value of the first eigenvalue will become larger and the value of the second eigenvalue will become correspondingly smaller. When the correlation coefficient reaches its maximum, *correlation coefficient* = 1.0, the first dimension will account for 100 percent of the variance in the independent variables, whereas the second dimension will account for no additional variance in the independent variables (Doane and Seward, 2011).

The condition number K (kappa) is defined as the square root of the ratio of the largest eigenvalue to the smallest eigenvalue.

Traditionally, a rule of thumb has been suggested that values of K (kappa) that are 30 or larger indicate highly severe problems of multi-collinearity. However, no strong statistical rationale exists for this choice of 30 as a threshold value above which serious problems of multi-collinearity are indicated.

The results presented in Table 5.13 are quite supportive of the authors' argument. The results of the regression analysis are presented below.

Given the nature of the variables, it is expected that they will be highly correlated. Another problem that presents itself in this case is the size of the sample. Results from multivariate statistical analysis based on a small sample may be questionable. However, it is well known that parameter estimates remain unbiased and consistent in ordinary least squares regression despite the presence of multicollinearity. In addition, as can be seen from Table 5.15, the F-statistics for the regression analysis (presented later) are found to be highly significant.

As can be seen from the results above, there are three variables significant at above the 90 percent confidence level; these are the existence of a strong cybersecurity law (CLI), the existence of a well developed human resource base as measured by the HDI, and the Internet Penetration Rate in a country (IPR).

Table 5.11 Definition of the explanatory variables

	Definition
IPR	Internet penetration rate
IDI	ICT Development Index
ICRG	Composite Risk Index
CLI	Cyber Law Index developed by the authors
EFI	country Economic Freedom Index
HDI	country rating on the Human Development Index
EGDI	E-government Maturity Index

Table 5.12 Descriptive statistics of all variables

	Mean	Std. Deviation	N
QCNCS	3.556	1.2409	63
IPR	62.9240%	30.122%	63
CLI	.464	.262	63
IDI	5.479	1.87	63
HDI	.689	.159	63
EGDI	.551	.213	63
EFI	62.397	13.691	63
ICRG	1.825	.0630	63

Table 5.13 Statistical model coefficients[a]

		Unstandardized Coefficients		Standardized Coefficients	t	Sig.	95.0% Confidence Interval for B		Correlations			Collinearity Statistics	
		B	Std. Error	Beta			Lower Bound	Upper Bound	Zero-order	Partial	Part	Tolerance	VIF
1	(Constant)	1.899	.212		8.963	.000	1.475	2.322					
	CLI	3.569	.398	.754	8.965	.000	2.773	4.365	.754	.754	.754	1.000	1.000
2	(Constant)	.187	.397		.470	.640	-.607	.980					
	CLI	2.666	.388	.563	6.873	.000	1.890	3.442	.754	.664	.494	.769	1.300
	HDI	3.091	.638	.397	4.848	.000	1.816	4.367	.668	.530	.348	.769	1.300
3	(Constant)	.321	.378		.851	.398	-.435	1.078					
	CLI	2.062	.423	.436	4.877	.000	1.216	2.908	.754	.536	.331	.578	1.730
	HDI	2.243	.671	.288	3.341	.001	.899	3.586	.668	.399	.227	.620	1.614
	IPR	.012	.004	.282	2.864	.006	.003	.020	.734	.349	.195	.477	2.097

Note: a. Dependent variable: QCNCS.

216

Table 5.14   Collinearity diagnostics[a]

Model	Dimension	Eigenvalue	Condition Index	(Constant)	CLI	HDI	IPR
				Variance Proportions			
1	1	1.872	1.000	.06	.06		
	2	.128	3.831	.94	.94		
2	1	2.834	1.000	.01	.02	.00	
	2	.143	4.445	.09	.85	.02	
	3	.023	11.194	.91	.13	.97	
3	1	3.757	1.000	.00	.01	.00	.01
	2	.151	4.986	.11	.43	.02	.04
	3	.072	7.236	.05	.56	.00	.78
	4	.020	13.776	.84	.00	.97	.17

Note: a. Dependent variable: QCNCS.

Table 5.15   ANOVA[a]

Model		Sum of Squares	df	Mean Square	F	Sig.
1	Regression	54.279	1	54.279	80.371	.000[b]
	Residual	41.197	61	.675		
	Total	95.476	62			
2	Regression	65.873	2	32.936	66.757	.000[c]
	Residual	29.603	60	.493		
	Total	95.476	62			
3	Regression	69.487	3	23.162	52.583	.000[d]
	Residual	25.989	59	.440		
	Total	95.476	62			

Model	R	R Square	Adjusted R Square	Durbin–Watson
1	.754[a]	.569	.561	
2	.831[b]	.690	.680	
3	.853[c]	.728	.714	2.075

Notes: [a] Dependent Variable: QCNCS; [b] Predictors: (Constant), CLI; [c] Predictors: (Constant), CLI, HDI; [d] Predictors: (Constant), CLI, HDI, IPR.

The coefficient of determination for this model ($R2$) is 72.8 percent, and the value of the F-statistic for the entire model is 52.583, which is significant at the 99 percent level. On the whole, the model is significant at the 99 percent level. In addition, we can see from Table 5.14 that the value of the *Durbin–Watson Statistic* test is 2.075, which is more than the cut-off value of 2, indicates the independence of errors in our model (Doane and Seward, 2011).

Based on the statistical analysis, all statistically significant variables are consistently signed; that is, as hypothesized, the model shows a positive relationship between the quality and comprehensiveness of the country's National Cybersecurity policy and the IPR, the level of maturity of CLI, and the HDI. All variables are significant at the 95 percent level of significance. The model failed to support the hypothesis of a positive relationship between the quality and comprehensiveness of a cybersecurity policy and the IDI, an index developed by the ITU. This is a clear indication that having the financial resources to develop the information infrastructure might be a necessary but not a sufficient condition for a well designed cybersecurity policy. The United Arab Emirates and Qatar, for instance, have built a great physical ICT infrastructure, but they did not follow up on developing the necessary soft constructs to control and govern the safe use of their ICT infrastructures. This is in clear contrast to the situation in Estonia, a country with a much lower per capita income but which has built the necessary ICT infrastructure and has designed what is considered to be one of the best soft structures as far as cybersecurity is concerned.

In addition, our statistical model did not support the hypothesis dealing with e-government. As indicated above, countries can build the physical ICT infrastructure to move their public activities online, but fail to develop the necessary controls to make sure their systems operate in a legal, moral and equitable manner. According to our hypothesis, one expects to have a positive relationship between the level of e-government maturity and the quality and comprehensiveness of a country's National Cybersecurity policy, but the statistical analysis failed to support this hypothesis. One reasonable explanation is that countries with a high level of cybercrime, such as Pakistan, the Philippines, and some Eastern European and Latin American countries, have developed their National Cybersecurity policies in a hurry as a reaction to international pressure due to the high level of cybercriminal activities. In other words, they have developed their policies in an effort to deter cybercriminals and for the purpose of appeasing trading partners and international organizations such as the ITU and other UN agencies, and not as a proactive mechanism aimed at encouraging the safe diffusion of activities in cyber space and the diffusion of electronic government.

CONCLUSION

The literature on cyber space use and adoption in developing countries is somewhat limited, although some evidence exists describing the barriers, which include limited Internet accessibility, a lack of competition in international telephone traffic that makes access to the international network expensive, a lack of intra-regional infrastructure, and a disproportionate penetration of the telephone in the urban areas as opposed to rural, more populated areas. To facilitate the diffusion of the Internet and eventually the efficient and effective use of cyber space, the necessary condition is the creation of a communication infrastructure, or what we refer to as a mature technical base. For developing countries, the financial resources needed to invest in communication infrastructure are one of the major barriers since most countries rely on foreign aid. Our statistical analysis shows that the institutional environment and the quality of intangible resources such as the existence of cyber laws, the availability of an IT skill-set and the level of Internet penetration are necessary determinants of a high quality and comprehensive National Cybersecurity policy.

The chapter dealt with data collection on the various variables identified in the previous chapter, discussed the proposed operational measurements of the independent variables and the dependent variable, laid out the methodology for the analysis, and presented and discussed the empirical results. Our analysis supported the main argument that the quality and comprehensiveness of a National Cybersecurity policy in developing and emerging economies depends mainly on important institutional mechanisms, which we refer to as soft resources. This is of central concern to researchers of New Institutional Economics.

NOTE

1. The term is coined by the authors.

REFERENCES

AlBawaba (2018). Egypt Parliament debates launching new law to counter cybercrimes, accessed 29 April 2018 at https://www.albawaba.com/editor choice/egypt-parliament-debates-launching-new-law-counter-cybercrimes-110 4282.
Crafts, N. (1999). Economic growth in the twentieth century, *Oxford Review of Economic Policy*, **15**(4): 18–36.
Doane, L.E. and Seward, D.P. (2011). *Applied Statistics in Business and Economics*, New York: McGraw-Hill.
International Monetary Fund (2016). *World Economic Outlook*, accessed 12 May 2016 at http://www.imf.org/external/pubs/ft/weo/2016/01/.
International Telecommunication Union (ITU) (2015). *Global IT Development Index*, Geneva: ITU.
International Telecommunication Union (ITU) (2017). *ICT 2017: Facts and Figures*, Geneva: ITU.
Karake, Z. and Al Qasimi, L. (2010). *Cyber Law and Cyber Security in Developing and Emerging Economies*, Cheltenham, UK and Northampton, MA, USA: Edward Elgar Publishing.
Levy, B. and Spiller, P. (eds) (1996). *Regulations, Institutions, and Commitment*, New York: Cambridge University Press.
Luiijf, E., Besseling, K. and De Graaf, P. (2013). Nineteen national cyber security strategies, *International Journal of Critical Infrastructures*, **9**(1/2): 3–31.
McGillivray, M. and White, H. (1993). Measuring development? The UNDP's human development index, *Journal of International Development*, **5**: 183–92.
Mertler, C. and Vannatta, R. (2013). *Advanced and Multivariate Statistical Methods: Practical Application and Interpretation*, 3rd edn, Glendale, CA: Pyrczak Publishing.
Nightingale, R. (2016). Is your e-signature legal around the world?, accessed 20 April 2017 at https://www.makeuseof.com/tag/electronic-signature-legal-around-world/.
Nyirenda-Jere, T. and Biru, T. (2015). Internet development and Internet governance in Africa, accessed 11 January 2016 at http://www.internetsociety.org/sites/default/files/Internet%20development%20and%20Internet%20governance%20in%20Africa.pdf.
PRS Group (2015). *The 2015 International Country Risk Guide*, accessed 4 May 2016 at http://www.prsgroup.com/ICRG.aspx.
Safeena, R. and Date, H. (2015). Impact of ICT tools for combating cyber crime in Nigeria's online banking, *Journal of Research in Social Sciences*, **3**(2): 104–20.
Singapore National Cyber Security Masterplan (2018). Accessed 3 April 2016 at https://www.ida.gov.sg/Programmes-Partnership/Store/National-Cyber-Security-Masterplan-2018.

South China Morning Post (2017). China's tough cybersecurity law to come into force this week, accessed 21 December 2017 at http://www.scmp.com/news/china/policies-politics/article/2096094/chinas-tough-cybersecurity-law-come-force-week.

Srinivasan, T.N. (1994). Human development: A new paradigm or reinvention of the wheel?, *American Economic Review*, **84**(2): 238–43.

Stephenson, M. (2001). The rule of law as a goal of development policy, accessed 23 May 2016 at www.worldbank.org/publicsector/legal/ruleoflaw2.htm.

Streeten, P. (1994). Human development: Means and ends, *American Economic Review*, **84**(2): 232–7.

The Heritage Foundation (2018) *2018 Index of Economic Freedom*, accessed 16 January 2019 at https://www.heritage.org/international-economies/commentary/2018-index-economic-freedom.

United Nations (2016). *UN e-Government Survey*, accessed 5 May 2016 at https://publicadministration.un.org/egovkb/en-us/Reports/UN-E-Government-Survey-2016.

United Nations (2017). *Human Development Report 2016: Human Development for Everyone*, United Nations Publications.

United Nations Human Development Program (UNDP) (2015). *Human Development Report: Work for Human Development*, New York: New York University Press.

Wall Street Journal (2016). Untangling China's cybersecurity laws, 3 June, accessed 11 June 2016 at http://blogs.wsj.com/chinarealtime/2016/06/03/untangling-chinas-cybersecurity-laws/.

West, D.M. (2008). Improving technology utilization in electronic governments around the world, accessed 5 November 2016 at www.brookings.edu/~/media/Files/rc/reports/2008/0817_egovernment_west/0817_egovernmen_west.pdf.

WIPO (2016). Technological and legal developments in intellectual property, accessed 2 January 2018 at http://www.wipo.int/export/sites/www/about-ip/en/iprm/pdf/ch7.pdf.

World Bank (2017). New country classifications by income level, accessed 11 December 2017 at http://blogs.worldbank.org/opendata/new-country-classifications-2017.

Chapter 6

INTRODUCTION

In this book, we have provided a guiding framework for understanding the determinants of the quality and comprehensiveness of National Cybersecurity (QCNCS) policies and associated strategies in a number of developing and emerging economies grounded in resource-based and deterrence theory perspectives. The work performed here and the conclusions reached are unique in nature and have several characteristics, none of which has received attention in the managerial, information technology (IT), or economics literature. The analysis of national cybersecurity (NCS) documents' contents and guidelines in a cross-section of developing and emerging countries conducted in this study demonstrated that mainly soft, intangible resources and infrastructure measures are of great importance in explaining variations in quality and comprehensiveness of NCS policies and strategies governing activities and Internet use in those countries. The book developed an index to examine the levels of QCNCS policies and strategies dependent on the strengths of a number of institutional, knowledge base, and physical resources.

The adaptation and diffusion of the Internet for conducting online commerce has widely stretched its reach globally, making access available to previously restricted, deprived markets. Specifically, developing and emerging countries' access to the Internet has been a source of economic, cultural, social and political value-added. The resulting shift to affordable networked computers and devices and the declining costs of telecommunications have made the Internet available to the masses. Given the growth of cyber activities, the absence of a coordinated, comprehensive control framework or strategies has added to the spread of cybercrime in all sizes, shapes and forms.

Data and information are being transformed into digital format at an exponential rate; the amount of data generated, captured and stored is growing at an increasing rate. Ninety percent of the data in the world today has been produced in the past two years. Today, the best guess suggests that at least 2.5 quintillion bytes of data are produced every day; that's 2.5 followed by a staggering 18 zeros(!) (Price, 2015). To put this into perspective, every minute of the day, more than 15 million texts are sent, more than 103 million spam emails are sent, and more than 3.6 million searches are being conducted on Google (Hale, 2017). This information is being shared and distributed around the world through the use of high-speed Internet technology. The volume of digitized information is expected to increase ten-fold by 2020.

Given the economic value of digital information and the ease of distribution via the Internet, as well as the relative fragile security of this medium, there has been a high level of cybercrime in recent years. Cybercrime is a major challenge not only for developing and emerging countries but for developed ones as well. A Ponemon Institute 2015 report found that the mean annualized cost for 58 benchmarked organizations is US$15 million per year; this number shows an increase of 19 percent on the 2014 figure per organization (Ponemon, 2015). The report shows that the net increase over six years in the cost of cybercrime is 82 percent, and it is expected to keep on the upward trajectory. This high rate of cybercrime is an indication of weak security measures, leading to an increased level of victimization.

Cyber space is a very complex environment and its security is not simply a technological question, but one with economic, social, political and cultural dimensions that involves a number of actors: governments, law-makers, the private sector and citizens. Having said that, it is important to note here that little is known about the holistic picture of cybersecurity, and since the Internet is not localized and confined to a geographic area, control over territorial cyber space cannot be easily enforced.

Information and communication systems are exemplified by increasing digital content, widespread mobility, and a superior capacity to transform and move data from one place to another. Advances in technology have compounded the problem; these include, but are not limited to, increased bandwidth, the move to the mobile platform, the diffusion of cloud computing, the spread of the Internet of Things (IoT), and technology affordability. All of these developments have led to more use of cyber space, which consequently has given users and cybercriminals ample opportunity to cause damage, either intentionally or unintentionally. Incidents of criminal activities in cyber space vary from well-known cyberattacks carried out on a large scale, such as the attempt to shut down the Internet in Estonia in mid-2007, to smaller, less publicized incidents including spamming, pharming, identity theft, and so on. As the magnitude and dimension of criminal activities in cyber space increase, users' trust plunges, and entities and countries, especially those on the growth path of the development curve, will be confronted with growing challenges, as their balance sheets and economies will be negatively impacted.

One of the key success factors for cybersecurity is the development of a coherent cyber culture, with recognized rules of behavior that users adhere to voluntarily. This cyber culture will constitute the *compass* for a country's citizens and help decrease cybercriminals' activities. However, such a cyber culture is not easily grasped but has to be built, encouraged and cultivated, especially in emerging and developing countries. A number of initiatives have taken place to provide some practical guidelines in this area; these include the United Nations Resolution 57/239 on the *Creation of a Global Culture of Cybersecurity* (United Nations, 2008), the OECD's *Guidelines for the Security of Information Systems and Networks* (OECD, 2008), The United Nations Resolution 70/1 *Transforming our World: The 2030 Agenda for Sustainable Development* (2015), and the *National Cybersecurity Strategy (NCS) Toolkit* (ITU, 2015).

Further, it is the role of the legislative branch of states to create legal structures governing their jurisdictions and for their governments to tag on and sign up to international regulatory regimes to help ensure security in cyber space. Understanding that cybersecurity needs the development of a cyber culture, reflecting the new reality of cyber space is a necessary requirement for a safer cyber environment. Creating this culture is also dependent on standards of appropriate behavior and the means and tools to punish cybercriminals and bring them to justice. The starting point here is that the need to deter cybercrime and take legal actions against criminals is global, even for those developing and emerging countries with low Internet diffusion rates.

Unfortunately, currently there is a limited authority to impose laws on the borderless environment of the Internet, so improving security is only possible through collective action, and through capacity and awareness building from both national and international perspectives. It is also imperative to create and cultivate an environment characterized with super national cyber health and cyber culture in order to minimize the number and impact of cybersecurity incidents. In today's environment where the IoT enables everything from smart refrigerators to connected pacemakers, it is imperative to think of cyber health and cyber culture as necessary conditions for a safer cyber environment. The development of a quality and comprehensive National Cybersecurity strategy is the tool which will pave the road for the creation of cyber culture cyber health.

The Internet has led to the revamping of many business processes. Global networking has introduced new methods, generated new channels, and increased the scope and depth of business opportunities. In cyber space, the speed of worldwide transactions has improved, leading to disintermediation in many of the business processes, and magnifying the competition at the national and global levels. Presently, e-commerce accounts for a relatively small percentage of the entire business-to-business (B2B) and business-to-customer (B2C) retail markets, world-wide. The two economies that currently have a substantial majority of the B2B and B2C transactions are the European Union and the United States. Each introduction of new technology generally brings with it new, unanswered legal questions that have to be tackled by decision makers and governments. However, information technology has been developing so rapidly that the laws and regulations cannot keep up with these technological advances. The reactive approach of the legal system as far as technology and cyberspace are concerned has made the development and implementation of a National Cybersecurity policy and strategies a necessity. Regulating the Internet is thorny because the application of existing laws to cyber space is not always possible given the borderless nature of cyber space. To help developing and emerging countries deal with critical economic problems and provide new services by the means of collecting data, turning data into information and turning information into knowledge quickly enough to reflect its value as a service, governments are investing more and more in Internet-based technologies, but are lagging on the policy dimension which will help them plan and implement the security of those technologies and of cyber space. To increase consumers' trust in cyber space and to increase the applications of cyber activities, it is essential that countries develop high quality and comprehensive National Cybersecurity policies and strategies to address possible problems, challenges, issues and crimes related to the use of cyber space. This is now a more pressing issue given the fact that cybercriminals are no longer game-minded hackers working individually, but many are now coordinated in profitable businesses with considerable technological and financial resources. These criminals are rapidly developing new software to attack systems and networks and hence wreak havoc on any country's infrastructure.

Although the role and success of cyber space are viewed and perceived differently by different scholars, the fact that it constitutes a major component of global business is no longer doubted. Practically, many countries have adopted various approaches to and created business models around cyber activities. Many of these models are based on using cyber space and cyber activities strategically, creating and enhancing competitive opportunities, increasing the use of technology more effectively, and reinforcing a more stable connection between information technology investments and strategic goals. Many governments have accepted the notion that cyber space can play (and in fact is playing) a strategic role by creating sustainable competitive advantage rather than simply displacing cost. The adoption and diffusion of cyber space activities have taken place with varying degrees of success among countries, depending on their level of economic and social developments, which has led to what is called the digital divide. Similarly, the level of maturity[1] of National Cybersecurity policy strategies in the various countries, especially the differential between developed and developing economies, has led to what the authors call the *cyber strategic divide.*

The *cyber strategic divide* characterized by highly unequal National Cybersecurity policies and strategies associated with the access and use of information and communication technologies (ICTs) exhibits itself at the international, regional and national levels and therefore needs to be addressed by national policy makers at the highest governmental levels, as well as by non-governmental organizations (NGOs) and the international community. The adoption of ICT by the public and the private sectors requires an environment guided by a high-quality, comprehensive National Cybersecurity policy encouraging open competition, trust and security cultures, interoperability and standardization, and the availability of the financial resources needed for the implementation of strategies associated with the policy itself. This requires the implementation of sustainable measures to improve access to the Internet and telecommunications and increase IT literacy at large, as well as development of local Internet content.

The asymmetrical diffusion of technology among different countries and the disparity in access to technologies in developing and emerging economies are apparent in many ways, with considerable consequences for social, cultural, economic and political maturity levels. These end-results are mirrored in the reality that anxiety over the digital divide is translated into more than the digital divide; it is currently associated with what is referred to as *digital exclusion.* The United Nations' 2015 resolution calls for ending poverty in the world by 2030 and for ending *digital exclusion* by 2020 (United Nations, 2015). As of the writing of this book (May 2018), close to 4 billion people still fall in the digital exclusion category. This fact has led to identifying digital exclusion as one of the main challenges of the 21st century (RGS, 2017). Digital exclusion increases digital divides because a significant proportion of the population lack Internet access and/or have low levels of digital literacy.

The positive impact and significance of technology to economic, social and political developments have long been acknowledged. This is more pronounced for ICTs, which cut across all economic operations and have a wide set of applications. ICTs offer the potential for increased availability of information, new means of communication, reorganization of productive processes, and improved efficiency and effectiveness in many different economic activities.

Despite the potential benefits that can be offered by ICT, developing and emerging countries face significant obstacles associated with ICT connectivity and access. The underlying causes of low levels of penetration of the Internet and low levels of adoption and diffusion of online activities in these countries include: a lack of awareness programs aimed at demonstrating what these technologies can offer; insufficient telecommunications infrastructure; expensive ICT access; absence of adequate legal and regulatory frameworks; shortage of requisite human capacity; failure to develop local content; lack of buy-ins among government officials and decision makers; and a lack of entrepreneurship and business culture open to change, transparency and social equality.

Many of the problems are epitomized by highly disproportionate rates of online/cyber space adoption and diffusion across countries. The obvious digital divide between the information technology-rich and the information technology-deprived countries is of mounting concern. A major challenge for policy makers at the national and international levels, therefore, lies in tackling the problem of the digital divide and digital exclusion: between rich and poor countries; rural and urban areas; men and women; skilled and unskilled citizens; young and older users; and large and small enterprises.

For any country, moving forward on the e-world map cannot take place without comprehensive, well-devised e-policies and e-strategies at the highest level of government. In developing and emerging economies, one observes a lack of such strategic orientation, in general, and e-strategic inclination, in particular. E-strategies should be better integrated into the overall policy frameworks and strategies of countries. The inflow of foreign investments and international support through development cooperation measures in the area of cyber space and cyber activities is equally important.

Strategies to improve access to the Internet, and consequently to increase cyber space adoption and diffusion, include opening up local telecommunications markets to promote competition and creating supportive legal and institutional environments to encourage investment in ICT. The objective should be to decrease the cost of Internet access for private sector entities and individuals, as well as for governmental entities. Guaranteeing the availability of a minimum supply of information technology infrastructure for remote and rural areas should be considered an important part of those strategies in developing and emerging economies.

The development of a National Cybersecurity policy and associated strategies would help and complement the Information Security Governance (ISG), both in the private and the public sectors. ISG is an indispensable building block of enterprise governance and involves the leadership, organizational structures, and processes dealing with the protection of informational assets (IT Governance Institute, 2006). At the firm level and in terms of strategic alignment, ISG enables firms to align security with business strategy to support organizational objectives. Firms are also likely to carry out proper measures to decrease risks and possible impacts to a manageable level and incorporate all applicable actors to make certain processes function as planned from end to end (Johnson and Hall, 2009). We can extrapolate this to the country level by stating that a strategically aligned national Cybersecurity Policy will lead to better protection of a country's infrastructure and informational assets. It is argued that having the willingness and ability to regularly assess information security governance from a policy perspective and associated processes provides the best approach of governance performance (Ula and Fuadi, 2017). Further, empirical assessment of information security processes is considered to be the most useful of all security measures.

In addition, to ensure the success of any initiative, human resources development should be at the center of any National Cybersecurity policy and associated strategies; this necessitates including ICT and the protection of cyber space in the curricula of educational institutions, especially in public ones, and providing training in the workplace to increase information technology literacy. To help accomplish some of the objectives of e-strategies, electronic government could be used as a means, including online services offered by governments and e-business and e-payment operations undertaken through the public procurement process.

This concluding chapter outlines the flow of research that was undertaken during the study that formed the basis for this book. The purpose of the chapter is, first, to review and restate the research objectives of the study; second, to discuss briefly the methods employed in the research; and, third, to summarize the empirical findings and sum up the answers to the research questions outlined in the first chapter. This is to be followed by the major conclusions and implications drawn from the analysis. Finally, a number of recommendations are set forth along with suggestions for future research.

UNDERLYING THEORIES

In completing this work, the authors were guided by a number of studies from various disciplines. The IT and Internet diffusion literature helped our understanding of the technological, organizational and institutional factors that affect the dissemination of innovations. In particular, frameworks focusing on country-level Internet diffusion are very strong in including dimensions that are especially pertinent to developing and emerging countries. These include both factors describing the organizational context and factors that specifically reflect a view of technological diffusion. Without a specific focus on institutional factors, it is an anemic and insufficient process for studying the diffusion of cyber activities around the world.

The authors were also guided by research on IT and Internet diffusion in developing and emerging economies; this line of research considers the many issues that these countries face, mainly factors that are often taken for granted in the developed countries in which most theories of Internet and IT diffusion are set. Just as an example is the issue of creating programs to raise awareness of the importance of cyber space and the significance of protecting it from cybercriminals.

The main theme of this research was to take a step forward toward understanding the level of quality and comprehensiveness of countries' National Cybersecurity policy and associated strategies, their determinants and their impact on increasing the understanding and boosting the culture of cybersecurity in developing and emerging countries. In doing so, a framework that is grounded in strong economic theory was developed. The framework used fundamental concepts central to resource-based, deterrence and technology diffusion literature and provided a straightforward understanding of cyber space adoption and Internet diffusion processes by public and private sector entities in developing and emerging countries.

So far, little research using a resource-based view framework and deterrence theory has examined policy and strategy differences in the social, cultural and political contexts of developing and emerging economies. As with most resources that create sustainable competitive advantage, many of those resources in developing and emerging countries are intangible. In developing and emerging economies, however, such advantages are difficult to institute and measure without good relationships with national governments and consequently a comprehensive national policy.

From a macroeconomic perspective, the resource-based view perceives an economy as a bundle of synergetic resources and capabilities. Resources are economy-specific assets and competences controlled and used by countries to develop and implement their policies and strategies. Resources can be either tangible (for example, financial assets, technology hardware and software) or intangible (for example, managerial skills, cultural awareness, reputation, education); they can be heterogeneous across economic sectors, and some resources are valuable yet rare, difficult to imitate, or non-substitutable, giving the economy some distinctive core capabilities, and providing the country with a stable base for sustainable competitive advantage.

Many of the resources that provide sustainable competitive advantage tend to be ambiguous, complex, rare and/or imperfectly imitable. Capabilities are defined to be an economy's abilities to integrate, build and reconfigure internal and external assets and competences so that it is enabled to perform distinctive activities. The resource-based approach focuses on the characteristics of resources and the strategic markets from which they are obtained.

Based on the resource-based theory, economies cannot gain sustainable competitive advantage by merely owning and controlling resources. They should be able to acquire, develop and deploy these resources in a manner that provides distinctive and unique sources of advantage in the marketplace. Having the financial resources to acquire top of the line ICTs will fall short of achieving a sustainable competitive advantage in the absence of deploying those resources effectively. The traditional conceptualization of the resource-based view has not addressed or examined the process of resource development, however, be it tangible or intangible. In addition, the traditional resource-based view is to a certain degree or other applicable in fairly stable environments, which is not usually the case in developing and emerging countries.

Another theoretical base used in this book was deterrence theory. Deterrence theory falls in the behavioral approach category and it is based on the understanding that people will engage in malicious or criminal acts considering factors such as the likelihood that they will be caught and the severity of punishment associated with committing the crime (Son, 2011). In a nutshell, deterrence has to do with minimizing the likelihood of adversaries launching cyberattacks or engaging in cybercriminal activities, and in the event that they do, the theory highlights the punishment associated with the crimes committed.

When we apply deterrence theory to cyber space, the main objective is centered on making criminals intending to commit malicious activities think twice about partaking in these activities. In doing so, it draws their attention to the consequences associated with their actions, as well as the penalties that might come from any legal responses. As covered in Chapter 3 of this book, five different approaches to deterrence were identified and discussed. Deterrence by punishment and deterrence by denial are the two classical approaches. Deterrence by punishment is based on a cause–effect relationship; in other words, if a crime is committed then an appropriate punishment is levied on the perpetrator. This will be effective only if the would-be criminal believes that the punishment is upcoming and costly. The second classical approach, deterrence by denial, is based on either minimizing the perceived gains from a criminal activity, or making it difficult to even go through with the crime.

Three additional approaches were added recently in the literature: (a) deterrence by association; (b) deterrence based on norms and taboos; and (3) deterrence through entanglement. These three approaches are still not well tested empirically but are gaining importance in the literature.

Our content analysis of the national cybersecurity policies of the countries in our sample assessed the degree and type of deterrence woven in the countries' policies, specifically through punishment or denial.

SUMMARY OF THE RESEARCH

This book proposed an empirical/theoretical framework for understanding the level and degree of the quality and comprehensiveness of National Cybersecurity policies and associated strategies in a sample of developing and emerging economies. A framework that is grounded in resource-based and deterrence theories was developed. Based on the framework, a set of hypotheses was developed and tested. The analysis used fundamental constructs that appear central to resource-based, deterrence, institutional, economic and technology diffusion literature and provided an understanding of cyber space adoption processes by public and private sector entities in developing and emerging countries.

Chapter 1 of this book established the context of the research. It highlighted the importance of the subject in hand and the importance of the digital economy, including the impact of cyber adoption on economic growth and development, and the various impediments and obstacles facing developing and emerging economies during the adoption and diffusion phases of cyber activities.

Chapter 2 reviewed the literature on cyber security and trust in cyber space and the main drivers to engaging in cyber activities in developing and emerging countries. The chapter covered the role that consumer trust plays in ensuring success in cyber space; consumers are unlikely to support commercial online activities that fall short of creating a perception of trust. Trust can only exist if the consumer believes that the provider has both the capability and the motivation to deliver goods and services of the quality expected by the consumer, and if they are confident that their cyber activities are safe from hackers and cybercriminals. In this respect, a NCS policy fulfills two roles; on the one hand, it is perceived as a compass for economic agents, both individual and commercial, to follow in creating a cyber culture in an economy; and on the other hand, it creates a sense of security for consumers, in that they know they are protected by the highest levels in government and by the laws that are governing cyber activities, as they are spelled out by the policy.

The trust concept may be more difficult to establish in cyber space than in the bricks-and-mortar world. In cyber space, providers depend on an impersonal electronic storefront to act on their behalf. Additionally, the Internet lowers the resources required to enter and exit the marketplace, making it difficult for consumers to have confidence that the commercial entity is here to stay. In many developing and emerging countries, the Internet is fairly quickly displacing older media such as television and newspapers as the prime source of important information for younger people. It can be fairly stated that compared with developed countries, the use of cyber space in developing and emerging countries has been relatively slower due to obstacles in the online use of credit cards, inadequate marketing strategies, and a relatively smaller online population. The lack of interest in e-commerce adoption of several consumer groups is also due to unclear price advantages and a poor supply in this commercial mode. Cyber activities in the majority of developing and emerging economies are currently afflicted by impediments such as low level of bandwidth, lack of independent gateways for Internet Service Providers (ISPs), an inadequate telecommunications infrastructure, low rate of personal computer (PC) penetration, and low tele-density, among others. Looking at our sample, we identify countries such as Zimbabwe or Mauritania, who developed National Cybersecurity policies but have Internet diffusion rates of 21 percent and 17.1 percent, respectively. However, the expected higher PC or Internet access device penetration levels, current trend of entry of private ISPs, availability of greater bandwidth, and the coming together of technological infrastructure will hopefully lead to some kind of growth in the number of Internet users in developing and emerging countries.

Assessing the socioeconomic influences of cyber space is difficult because it requires the use of methods capable of revealing often complex and unpredictable intangible traits and values. However, the growth of online activities in the public and private sectors has created an enormous influence on services, market structure, competition, and restructuring of industry and markets. These changes are transforming all areas of society, work, business and government. However, the use of ICT deepens and intensifies the socioeconomic divisions among people, businesses and nations. It is often reported that there is a complicated mixture of varying levels of ICT access, basic ICT usage, and ICT applications among socioeconomic groups, and many of these disparities are getting even larger. Disparities in the location and quality of Internet infrastructure, even the quality of phone lines, have created gaps in access among the various economic groups of a country's population. Gaps exist in the adoption of digital technologies among different social groups and firms; the former depending on income levels, education and gender, and the latter depending on industry structure, business size (large firms versus SMEs) and location. Chapter 2 also covered the threat of cybercrime in the financial industry, considered to be the prime target for cybercriminals. With respect to the state of the regulatory environment, the modus operandi for countries at this point is playing catch-up. Cybercrime law and regulation, especially when it comes to the financial/banking sector, are not moving at the same pace as the development of technology that has taken place within the past ten years.

The chapter also covered cybercrime activities in the four countries deemed to harbor a large percentage of criminal activities. These are China, Russia, North Korea and Iran. Although the coverage of cyber-criminal activities in these countries is scant, the chapter highlighted the role nation states play in embracing cybercriminals to help them achieve political or military objectives.

Chapter 3 covered the theories used in the research, including the resource-based view (RBV), and deterrence theory literature. As an economic theory, the RBV addresses the impact of resources at the micro, firm level; the authors adapted the theory and used it at the macro level of the economy. Simply stated, the RBV of the firm is one of the latest strategic management concepts to be enthusiastically embraced by information technology and information management scholars. This book and the empirical analysis carried out maintain that the RBV holds much promise as a framework for understanding strategic information/knowledge economy issues with the caveat that it needs to be fully understood before it can be embraced effectively in the cybersecurity literature.

Chapter 3 also outlined the development of the RBV from its origins in early economic models of imperfect competition, through the work of evolutionary economists to the contributions of strategy economics scholars over the past two decades. The chapter also differentiated between and defined the two categories of resources: firm specific and country specific. In addition, the relationship between RBV and institutional theories was covered, along with the few attempts to evaluate the experiences of developing economies from a resource-based perspective. It is apparent that research using resource-based theory and examining macro strategy difference in the social context of developing economies is almost absent. Similar to most resources that create competitive advantage at the micro level, resources for competitive advantage at the macro level in developing economies are mainly intangible.

The economics literature has paid attention to the revenue-generating promises of developing economies, and as such, has focused, mainly, on big developing and emerging economies such as China, India and Russia. Consequently, the authors concluded that it is essential to understand the relationship between economic experiences and the changing nature of the institutional environment.

Chapter 3 also discussed deterrence theory and its effectiveness in reducing cybercriminal activities through either punishment or denial. A brief discussion of the newer deterrence approaches was also covered in this chapter.

Coverage of the sample countries' ecosystems and the different types of resources available and their relationship to a healthy cyber environment and the role those resources play in the development of a quality and comprehensive of national cybersecurity policies were the subject of Chapter 4. This chapter covered the situation on the ground for the various economic blocs of the countries in our sample. Content analysis of national cybersecurity policies of the sample countries was also covered in this chapter. The content analysis was performed based on five constructs we created: economic, technical/technological, policy, political and social aspects of the policies of the countries in question. In addition, the chapter discussed the role the legal system plays either as a deterrent of cybercriminal activities, or as a means to punish perpetrators. As far as the legal system is concerned, it was argued that the battle against cyberattacks is principally contingent upon the legislative/legal structure of every country. In particular, cybersecurity is contingent upon every economy first having effective laws that criminalize attacks that cause damage to systems and networks, and make certain that law enforcement officials have the authority to look into and take legal action against crimes made possible by technology. Secondly, economies must have laws and policies that facilitate international collaboration with other parties in the fight against Internet-related crimes. Given the nature of cybercrime, these laws have to be coordinated across borders in order for them to be effective and successful. In order to reach a global synchronization of cybercrime legislation and a common understanding of cybersecurity and cybercrime among countries developed, emerging or developing, a global agreement at the United Nations' level should be established that incorporates resolutions designed to tackle the global challenges.

The content analysis based on the above-mentioned constructs was used to develop countries' indices measuring the quality and comprehensiveness of their national cybersecurity policies. In that chapter, we also developed the set of hypotheses dealing with the determinants of a quality and comprehensive national cybersecurity policy. These determinants were identified as the human resources, the financial resources, the diffusion of the Internet (access), technical capabilities of an economy, the strength of the rule of law, and the strength of the economic base of a country as measured by the per capita income. The first hypothesis highlighted the soft sector of the economy, stating that the QCNCS policy is positively correlated with the repository of technically skilled people in the country. It was stated that a well educated and trained population will require and develop a better policy document dealing with cyber activities. The second hypothesis has to do with the financial resources available to the country. Evidence of a positive relationship between the strength of the financial base of a country and its economic growth has been presented in previous studies; in the Information Age and with more reliance on cyber space, financial investment in Internet-based technologies is to be positively correlated with economic growth, and this consequently leads to more emphasis on policies guiding and/or controlling cyber activities. The third hypothesis dealt with access to Internet-based resources and technical capabilities. Without access to Internet connections at a reasonable cost, citizens in developing and emerging economies will be unable to migrate from traditional markets to electronic markets based on cyber space. Consequently, a more mature technical infrastructure is assumed to be positively correlated with the quality and comprehensiveness of national cybersecurity policies. The fourth hypothesis assesses the importance of the strength and transparency of the rule of law and the role it plays in facilitating the use of Internet-based technologies in a developing country. Law plays a vital role in the transformation and development of societies. A number of reasons have been advanced in the resource-based literature to highlight the role a strong rule of law plays in affecting transactional integrity in an Internet-based society, and thus investment in such markets. Because of the unique nature of the Internet, its use creates legal issues and questions, especially in areas related to intellectual property rights and cybercrime.

Based on our analysis it was shown that less than 50 percent of the sample of countries in the emerging/developing world have drafted comprehensive cyber laws, and those that have are still struggling to perfect the enforcement of those laws. In this book, we argue that the level of maturity of a country's cyber law will be positively correlated with the quality and comprehensiveness of national cybersecurity policies. The fifth and last hypothesis set forth has to do with the level of government digitization and the QCNCS policy of a country. It was hypothesized that the level of (maturity) quality and comprehensiveness of national cybersecurity policy is positively related to the level of government digitization in the country. This in turn has to do with the strength of the economic base of a country as measured by its per capita income. It is hypothesized that the more advanced the country is as measured by its per capita income, the more mature is the country's national cybersecurity policy.

Chapter 5 covered data collection and statistical analysis to test the five hypotheses formulated in the previous chapter. This chapter presented the first systematic study on the level of QCNCS policies in a number of developing and emerging economies. Based on the computed QCNCS index for the countries in our sample, the authors classified them into five different categories. These were the *cheetahs*, countries with a QCNCS between 5 and 6 inclusive. Topping the *cheetahs* are Estonia and South Korea, with a QCNCS of 6 each. The *gazelles* are countries with QCNCS less than 5 but more than or equal to 4. Bahrain, Bulgaria and Chile topped the *gazelles*, with a QCNCS index of 4.5 each. The *bears* are countries with QCNCS less than 4 but more than or equal to 3, and in this category, Argentina, Columbia, Mexico and Turkey were the top *bears*, with an index of 3.5 each. The *koalas* are countries with QCNCS less than 3 but more than or equal to 2. The top performers among the *koalas* are Bolivia, Ecuador and Vietnam. The last category, the *tortoises*, includes countries with QCNCS less than 2; here Cambodia and Lebanon were the leaders among the *tortoises*.

Based on the statistical analysis performed in Chapter 5, the three significant variables identified through the stepwise regression analysis carried the expected sign. Our statistical model showed a positive relationship between the quality and comprehensiveness of the country's National Cyber Security policy and the rate of a country's Internet penetration, the level of maturity of cyber law in an economy, and the human development index. The three variables were significant at the 95 percent level. Our statistical analysis, however, failed to support the hypothesis of a positive relationship between the quality and comprehensiveness of a cybersecurity policy and the index developed by the ITU as a measure of a comprehensive ICT development of a country. As discussed earlier, this demonstrates that having the financial resources to buy the information technology infrastructure is not a sufficient condition for the efficient and effective use of the technology, or the creation of high quality cybersecurity policy and the necessary soft constructs associated with it. As we discussed earlier, some of the Gulf Cooperation Countries (GCC) have created superb information technology infrastructures but have failed to invest in their human resources or create a quality cybersecurity policy to help users and decision makers implement a safe cyber environment. Further, our statistical model did not support the hypothesis of a positive relationship between the quality of cybersecurity policy and the level of e-government diffusion. To reiterate, countries can build the physical ICT infrastructure to move their public activities online and send a message to the private sector to do the same, but fail to develop the necessary controls to ensure their systems operate in a legal, moral and equitable manner.

Finally, following is the concluding portion of this book, which consists of a summary and recommendation for future research.

CONCLUSION AND RECOMMENDATIONS

Based on our research of the sample of emerging and developing countries and their experiences with National Cybersecurity policies and cyber governance, the following challenges are identified in addition to the generic challenges cited by economic growth and development authors.

A major issue is the lack of understanding of the importance of the strategic implications of a national cybersecurity policy and associated strategies in a large percentage of the developing and emerging economies we studied. This was demonstrated by performing content analysis of their national cybersecurity policies where we found these lack lots of substance. Close to 50 percent of the countries we investigated have an Internet diffusion rate of less than 50 percent. In addition, and as we have seen in our analysis in Chapter 5, less than 50 percent of the countries have developed some kind of legislation/laws to deal with cybersecurity infractions and crimes. Some of the countries though have amended their existing laws in bits and pieces as a reaction to incidents and crimes that have taken place within their borders.

Very few of the countries have developed comprehensive, mature national cybersecurity policies and associated strategies as measured by the QCNCS Index developed in Chapter 5. Measuring the QCNCS index on a scale from 1 to 6, we found the average to be 3.8 with a standard deviation of 1.1. To put this into perspective, that is a C–/D+ grade for the countries viewed holistically. This is not surprising though, since many of the countries, faced with cybersecurity challenges, are still at the early stages of drafting and/or implementing National Cybersecurity policies and associated strategies. In a number of those countries, the process has taken on more of a political perspective than a cultural/social/legal perspective. Researchers, practitioners and policy makers have always maintained that while cybersecurity is a technical issue on the surface, it is viewed by many in the developing and emerging economies as an overwhelmingly economic and political consideration. As such, the public and the private sectors in those countries have been unwilling and/or unable to coordinate policies across the various stakeholders who might have conflicting objectives and concerns. It is particularly imperative to recognize the political and economic motivations of national cybersecurity policies and strategies in order to be able to coordinate among policy makers in the various countries. If we take China and Russia, major powers in global cybersecurity, we notice that they differ from other emerging economies in both the relationship between their public and private sectors and their ownership of critical infrastructure. In addition, the cyber policy of China is focused mainly on the use of information warfare tactics and hacking foreign sites, while the cyber policy of Russia emphasizes two aspects: (1) safeguarding information security for its citizens; and (2) securing its physical information infrastructure (Kulikova, 2015). Moving to Latin America, and as far as Brazil is concerned, although cybercrimes are a major threat to the state of Brazil, its National Cybersecurity policy focuses more on the military aspects in the country at the expense of cultural, economic and social aspects. In addition, there is less emphasis on reinforcing its legal infrastructure to deal with cybercrimes (Diniz et al., 2015).

On another front, the exercise of drafting and implementing national cybersecurity policies and strategies is definitely a new form of activity for policy makers in most of the developing/emerging world. It is still questionable whether these countries consider the development and implementation of national cybersecurity policies and strategies as a necessity that warrants developing expertise and investing resources or whether it is only an exercise required by large international NGOs! Having said that, the development of national cybersecurity policies and strategies is a hot button and many NGOs are placing a lot of emphasis in making this a reality for most countries. Several organizations have created a *cookbook* for developing national cybersecurity policies strategies; an example is the International Telecommunication Union (ITU). It is debatable though if the recommendations listed in the form of *one-size-fits-all* can be effective across the board. Countries need to adapt their policies and strategies to their own needs and emphasize certain areas depending on their resources and capabilities. Most of the National Cybersecurity policies and associated strategies developed in emerging economies have taken place in the past few years. The main question as to the success or lack of success is the enforcement of the policies and the implementation of those policies; as far as we are concerned, the jury is still out.

In summary, contents of the National Cybersecurity policies and associated strategies are somewhat all over the place in what they cover, what they regulate, and what kind of penalties are levied against offenders.

A number of countries around the world are planning and developing their own information society and the policies and strategies that govern it. The move in various countries is operationalized to differing degrees, at different speeds, and in different ways. For National Cybersecurity policies and strategies to make the transition from theory to actual enforcement and implementation requires not just the development of feasible policies and strategies but the willingness and desire of the decision makers to implement those policies and strategies, coupled with the ability to support them. In addition, the existence of appropriate institutional mechanisms to facilitate the adoption and diffusion is a must. A number of measures geared toward the promotion of cyber use in developing countries have been identified. The most important include establishing a common digital platform to enhance cooperation and knowledge sharing among emerging/developing countries. This may require the setting up of support centers or 'incubators' to facilitate suitable country-specific cybersecurity policies and strategies. However, the path to and into cyber space may be filled with hurdles, particularly when decision makers remain skeptical about the efficacy and usefulness of this medium to the overall development and growth of their economies.

One of the most severe constraints on wider Internet use in low-income developing countries is their limited access to international 'bandwidth', the high-capacity connections required to transmit the large quantities of information required for full Internet services. Until this jam is eased, email is likely to remain the prevailing use of the Internet in those countries, many of them in the 'black continent', Africa. Developing countries and regions have started to leapfrog traditional copper- and fiber-based landlines and are moving directly into the use of leading-edge wireless technologies that blend voice and data over the same networks.

In recent years economists have assessed the impact of a technology developed in an industrialized country that is copied by a developing/ emerging country. They have shown that the rate of growth of the developing/emerging country depends on its original base of knowledge and the costs associated with replication. A country's readiness for cyber activities depends on hard network-based infrastructure and technology diffusion. The growth of cyber space use, it is argued, is nurtured by strong growth in infrastructure, including broadband access, hardware investment, and Internet use; but it depends also on growth of mobile applications, cost of telecommunications, service improvement, speed and consistency. This is not relevant to the legal aspects of cyber space, since Internet activities transcend borders and cyber space should be regulated by synchronized laws and regulations, laws developed jointly by the various countries.

To facilitate the introduction of the Internet and eventually electronic commerce/services, the necessary and sufficient condition is the creation of the communication infrastructure. This has been demonstrated by one of the authors in her previous work (Karake-Shalhoub and Al Qasimi, 2007).

For developing/emerging countries, in addition to the absence of the regulatory and institutional environments to govern cyber space, investment is one of the main obstacles since most countries rely on foreign aid. In addition to developing the necessary infrastructure, there is a need to create a sustainable supply of Internet services including training of human resources, extension into rural areas in an effort to narrow the digital divide, as well as support and training for small to medium sized businesses.

Furthermore, to facilitate the diffusion of cyber activities, a necessary condition is the development of e-policies and e-strategies, or what we refer to in this book as a National Cybersecurity policy. Telecommunications infrastructure is clearly a necessary but not a sufficient condition for the development and entry of a developing country into the cyber marketplace. In the continent of Africa, for instance, the Internet is growing fast. Internet penetration levels are about 29 percent and rising. Mobile subscriptions are just shy of 80 percent, and mobile broadband access accounts for more than 90 percent of Internet subscriptions. But the aggregate indicators disguise blatant differences. At one end of the spectrum, countries such as Morocco have an Internet diffusion rate of close to 50 percent, and at the other end we have countries such as

Somalia, with a diffusion rate below 2 percent. As a matter of fact, the Internet diffusion rate of the majority of the countries in Africa hovers around 10 percent and this presents a problem for those countries in their efforts to jump on the bandwagon of the information revolution.

Despite the technology used, the central objective for developing countries is to encourage investment and partnerships with vendors, suppliers and telecommunications companies outside their borders. This requires an organized, focused approach using tools and strategies of an open and fair marketplace; but above all it requires a mature regulatory environment as represented by the existence of mature national cyber-security policies and strategies.

As discussed above, in addition to the hard-side technological resources being considered by many developing/emerging countries, a host of soft-side resources have to be cultivated and emphasized. A chief requirement is the establishment of national policies dealing with the information and telecommunications sector. As noted earlier, hard communications infrastructure is clearly a necessary, but by no means a sufficient condition for successful adoption and diffusion of cyber activities. The repository of soft factors necessary for successful adoption of cyber space in developing economies includes appropriate legal norms and standards, and laws dealing with consumer protection, privacy protection, cybercrime and intellectual property rights. All these factors are essential for the successful implementation of online activities in the public and the private sectors alike. Additional issues that countries have to consider embrace the recognition of digital signatures and electronic documents, and collection of taxes and tariffs. Our content analysis of the National Cybersecurity policy documents found very few countries where these soft factors were addressed. It is important to state here that the experience of the sample countries in developing a national cybersecurity policy and associated strategies addressing the digitization of their economies has not been homogeneous. A number of countries are much more advanced than others in this respect; mainly the Eastern European countries such as Estonia, Slovakia, Hungary and the Czech Republic; the Latin American countries such as Peru, Mexico and Brazil; and a number of Asian countries including the UAE, Israel, Qatar, South Korea and Singapore. Many of these countries have recently established a national infrastructure for digitization. Many countries in Latin America have benefited from the diffusion of the Internet, but a significant imbalance still continues in terms of where countries stand in their cybersecurity strategies. Some strategies have called for more cohesive technical and investigative competencies, and have the necessary laws in place to utilize those capabilities when strategies are implemented.

Others remain at or adjacent to the starting point, wrestling with the challenges intrinsic in determining the content and emphasis of their strategies. It is imperative for the latter governments to cooperate with their more advanced counterparts, and 'initiatives to encourage and facilitate this kind of horizontal cooperation and capacity-building must advance and increase' (Symantec, 2014).

Privacy and information security continue to be one of the most important topics when operating in cyber space. As the number of transactions over the Internet increases, so does the number of security breaches including data theft, vicious file corruption, and even e-commerce site shutdown. Privacy issues would discourage people from using the Internet as a transaction medium, hence reducing telecommunication activities and cyber activities. For many developing/emerging countries, the privacy and information security issues are complicated by the lack of security systems, such as trusted third parties, encryption procedures, and secure telecommunications that would provide the protection needed for their e-infrastructure. The ability to realize a high level of e-commerce diffusion, then, will largely depend on the climate of confidence e-businesses are able to create in their relations with consumers. The most important aspect of e-commerce is trust. Most likely, a product will fail if it does not have market trust. Usually the foundation of trust is based on risk assessment, while confidence is based on familiarity. Society may become reliant on the product when confidence is achieved; however, not all products achieve this level. Establishing trust in the eminently impersonal environment of the Internet is not straightforward. People are unwilling to give their credit card numbers over the Internet. Also, fraud has increased in online transactions and cybercrime is on the rise. Consumers also worry that their private data will not be valued or respected by the company they are dealing with. National Cybersecurity policies and strategies must address the issue of privacy and levy a high penalty on hackers. Few of the countries in our sample have addressed the issue of privacy genuinely. Karake-Shalhoub (2002) recommends a number of solutions to this problem. First, there have to be certain trust policies to establish trust. If governments try to implement certain policies preventing theft of identity, then fraud can be reduced in cyber transactions. A number of difficulties faced are related to the technical area; to deal with this issue, trust enhancers were identified by Karake-Shalhoub in her 2002 book on trust and loyalty in electronic commerce, including the seal of approval from a trusted third party, the appointment of a chief information officer (or a high-level privacy officer at the federal level), and the development of a comprehensive clear privacy statement. In addition to these tools, the development and implementation of cyber laws seem to be the most important drivers in the diffusion of cyber activities. It is simply the stick and carrot approach.

Since the private sector is the engine of growth in any economy, the involvement of the private sector in cyber space in the form of adopting click-and-click business models should be one of the main objectives of developing and emerging economies because it is the private sector that can create additional jobs and enhanced revenue. Having said that, it is vital for the private sector to be an active participant in developing and implementing a national cybersecurity strategy. Yet many cyber space initiatives in developing and emerging countries are initiated by the public sector and financially supported by the government, as demonstrated by all the e-government initiatives taking place around the world. A number of these programs have been very successful, though. The governments of Chile and the UAE have implemented e-government models that are rapidly diffusing to their private sectors. In Chile, for instance, the government's website began as an information portal to the public but rapidly became a facilitator and instigator of e-commerce. In 2001 the Chilean government began its e-procurement portal where smaller businesses compete for public sector contracts, and both private and public-sector entities can conduct transactions over the portal. The portal has since become a meeting place where the government provides, free of charge, a cyber market for buyers and sellers to gather and conduct business. This program has enhanced government services through the upgrading of back office systems and the transparency of its processes. The program has motivated businesses to partake in the Internet's development while increasing their transaction cost efficiency and widening their markets. From our analysis, it is estimated that almost 45 percent of Chile's population are active users of the Internet. Notwithstanding the above, there is no national or sector-specific governance roadmap for cybersecurity in Chile (ITU, 2015).

As e-commerce and e-government require technical knowledge and understanding, a lack of education of these technologies is a serious impediment to their adoption. Certain countries lack key elements of education: Internet awareness, understanding of the implications of the Internet, and skilled workers in IT. Even when people are aware of the Internet, often the population does not understand how the Internet might improve their lives and they therefore oppose it. The erosion of local culture is a prominent issue when discussing the move to and adoption of cyber space. It is therefore the responsibility of regional governments to foster the development of e-culture to give people the sense that they are protected in cyber space. Culture influences how people perceive certain things, what they value, and how they interpret the graphical images and lines of text they encounter on a website.

Cyber space promises great potential to create and reveal new business opportunities; to reduce all types of costs, especially search and trans-action costs; to increase business efficiency and effectiveness; and to improve the quality of life in adopting countries. Given the enormous benefits cyber space can provide to help the growth and development of any economy, developing and emerging economies should create the necessary conditions to move their economies into the digitized phase, and this includes creating a mature national cybersecurity policy and associated strategies. Those national cybersecurity policies must take into consideration the level of digitization strategies in an economy and align them with existing resources, taking into account the different stages of economic development; the heterogeneous regulatory environments; and the diverse social, economic and cultural frameworks. It is fundamental to state here that enhancing capability in cyber space and harmonization of cybersecurity policies among regional economies (such as the GCC), through economic and technical cooperation, are needed to enable all developing and emerging economies to reap the benefits of the *new normal*. It is recommended that the private sector play a primary role in developing the technology, applications, practices and services. Also, it is advisable that governments promote and facilitate the development and uptake of cyber space policies by providing a favorable environment and the necessary hard and soft resources, such as the legal and regulatory aspects, which are predictable, transparent and consistent, and creating an environment that promotes trust and confidence among cyber partici-pants. These are the main elements of a national cybersecurity strategy. In addition, governments should promote the efficient functioning of cyber space internationally by aiming, wherever possible, to develop their national cybersecurity strategy frameworks which are compatible with evolving international norms and practices, and becoming leading-edge users in order to catalyze and encourage greater use of electronic means.

Cyber activities cannot flourish without the cooperation of business and governments to ensure the development of affordable, accessible communication and information infrastructure. Further, government and private sector businesses should cooperate to develop and instigate policies that build trust and confidence in safe, secure and reliable communication, information and delivery systems, and which address issues including privacy, authentication and consumer protection. National cybersecurity policies will not be effective unless the private sector is involved in the development process from the start. Cooperation between the public and the private sectors is a necessity. In addition, and in order to benefit fully from the cyber revolution, regional developing and emerging economies should strive to work together in developing their national cybersecurity policies; this will help build trust and confidence in digital means, and enhance government use. Cooperation will also help intensify community outreach; promote technical cooperation and experience exchange; where appropriate, work toward removing barriers to the adoption of cyber space; and help develop flawless legal, technical, operating and trading environments to facilitate the growth and development of cyber space adoption.

To accomplish the above, when developing mature national cyber-security policies, governments of developing and emerging economies must consider the measures and indicators on the level of adoption, use and flows of cyber activities in their economies. They must also identify the economic costs that inhibit increased adoption and diffusion of cyber activities, including those imposed by the regulatory and market environment, in an effort to deal with those factors. In addition, they need to consider additional economic and technical cooperation among regional economies to facilitate and encourage cyber activities, and mainly try to encourage and ensure the involvement of the private sector from A to Z.

As our research has demonstrated, many developing and emerging countries are deficient in the area of cyber legislation. Many have not even amended their existing laws to reflect the new reality of cyber space, let alone develop independent national cybersecurity strategies that take cyber laws into consideration. With the exception of a few countries, developing and emerging markets still lack appropriate legislation that deals directly with cyber-related topics. This might be associated with a number of factors, including the underestimation of the magnitude of cyber space, the challenges presented by this new world, and/or the lack of the required judicial expertise in this area.

In those developing and emerging economies where the practice of developing national cybersecurity policy and associated strategies has begun and/or has been completed, there is an indication that such moves are associated mainly with an increase in foreign investment in the country where such investment has increasingly used electronic means. That has driven those countries to develop national security strategies as indicated by our research. A key to success in cyber space is proactively to develop and enact cybersecurity policy that is associated with a country's strategic objectives in terms of economic growth and social development.

On another front, given that cyber space is a global challenge and opportunity at the same time, there is a critical need for international cooperation in the development of cybersecurity policies governing this new world. Cyber space is borderless, and offenders and criminals in one country can commit a crime affecting economic entities in other countries without even leaving their domicile. This borderless nature of cyber space gives rise to cyberattacks independent of time and place, and makes it possible for cybercriminals to abuse 'loopholes of jurisdiction', making it very difficult to prosecute offenders (ITU, 2015).

A number of ways for countries to cooperate in developing cybersecurity policies and fight cybercrime are proposed. Regional cooperation tops the list of our recommendations; coordination covers areas dealing with exchange of information, sharing best practice, and training of legislative and policy-making personnel and law enforcement officers. A number of economic blocs have already demonstrated their leadership in this area, led by the European Union, the ASEAN countries and APEC. The countries in the Middle East and North Africa (MENA) region, as well as the African countries, tread behind. This is a call for those countries to learn from the experience of the avant-garde and start their regional initiatives (ITU, 2015).

On the international level, a number of frameworks have already been developed by the ITU and the European Union. The ITU agenda on cybersecurity and Europe's Convention on Cybercrime are exemplary models for developing countries to follow; however, we still do not have a global governance system of cyber space. There is a need for adopting appropriate procedural laws and procedures for bringing cybercriminals to justice, and policies for implanting the strategies. These implementation mechanisms should take into consideration the country's requirements at the national and international levels.

The success of building and implementing national cybersecurity strategies is partly contingent upon creative forms of partnerships of public and private sector entities. Sharing of information, building frameworks, and cooperating in the areas of training and development of personnel would be a good start. Another possibility would be to cooperate in building awareness of citizens, and especially youngsters, of the dangers, both social and economic, associated with cybercrime. Helping to create understanding in this area is essential to developing beneficial policies, strategies and laws to, possibly not eliminate, but reduce the multifaceted costs of this growing problem.

Building awareness of cybersecurity culture is a key success factor in cyber space. An appropriate culture for cybersecurity should be developed both at the national and global levels, through a global framework for end-users, technologies and content providers, policy makers, and law enforcement officials. This process should be compatible with the different economic, political, social, technical and legal dimensions of cyber space. This cultural awareness should translate into better training of policy, legal professionals and enforcement personnel; these should undergo training and professional education to cover more technical skills. Our research clearly shows soft skills are lagging and countries are in dire need of creating an army of professionals dealing with cyber-security policies and strategies.

A final recommendation has to do with the policy itself in terms of content coverage and enforceability. No one can deny the positive role of cyber space in today's world, be it in the political, economic, cultural or social sphere of life. But everything has its pros and cons; cybercriminals are using the technology to their advantage. A number of countries have developed cyber laws that have many advantages as they give legal recognition to electronic records, transactions, authentication and certifi-cation of digital signatures, and the prevention of computer crime. Those countries have aligned their cyber laws with their cybersecurity policy and associated strategies. At the same time, however, they have various shortcomings, in terms of lack of coverage of certain crimes and/or the weight and severity of the penalty associated with the crime; the UAE Cybersecurity policy, published by the Supreme Council for National Security, for instance, while it emphasizes the cooperation between the public and private sectors, does not cover the protection of intellectual property rights, domain name, or cybersquatting (UAE, 2015).

Many of these policies lack efficient enforceability mechanisms. A challenge many of these countries face in fighting cybercrime is that most of them lack the expertise and the enforcement agencies to combat crime relating to the Internet. Many of the policies fail to address the penalties associated with the various cybercrimes, and hence, fail to deter criminals from committing cybercrimes, punishment in many instances being ineffective and inefficient. Countries need to enact tougher laws to deal with cybercrimes and they need to align their policies and associated strategies with the laws, especially when those crimes pose a threat to national security or the security of funds, information, or destruction of computer networks.

FUTURE RESEARCH

The growth of the cyber economy has been tremendous. According to a study done by IDC, the Internet of Everything (IoE) is possibly the leading business opportunity in the history of mankind (Nedeltchev, 2015). The IoE will have wide-ranging implications, affecting everyone in the world, businesses and individuals. IDC's research expects that this gigantic shift will create approximately US$9 trillion in annual sales by 2020. Another study conducted by General Electric concluded that the IoT will add close to US$15 trillion to the global gross domestic product of the world over the next 20 years. Of the US$19 trillion in profits and cost savings estimated over the next two decades, US$14.4 trillion will be new private-sector profits, and US$4.6 trillion will come from public-sector cost savings and new revenues (Nedeltchev, 2015). A major recommendation here is to study the impact of the IoT at the country level. Some countries, especially those in Africa, are getting their feet wet with the IoT; it would be of great value to undertake studies at the country level to examine the impact of the IoT there and the effectiveness of that country's national cybersecurity policy.

Cyber users emerge as the key beneficiaries: they use the Internet as a way to gather information and increase their search efficiency and effectiveness. However, more reliance on the Internet will increase the need and necessity to develop comprehensive, mature national cyber-security policies to tackle cyber-related attacks and crimes, and to increase users' trust in a not so new world. Unfortunately, not many emerging and developing countries have jumped on the bandwagon of developing comprehensive, mature national cybersecurity policies, which has led to a widening *cyber strategic divide* in the digital world. Another recommendation here is the study of the impact on a mature national cybersecurity policy of narrowing the cyber divide among countries and within regions in the same country.

In general, research on developing and emerging economies faces a number of obstacles. As a starter, theories deducted and/or applied to developed countries may not be suitable to apply in emerging and developing countries. Sampling and data collection are a big problem in addition to difficulties researchers face in developing and applying performance measures. Issues have to be addressed concerning the replication of tests and hypotheses used in developed economies in developing and emerging countries. Developing and emerging economies are dynamic and changes occur at a very fast pace in the institutional environments. As a result, cross-sectional studies may produce mis-leading results concerning the impact of specific policies. To get around this limitation, there appears to be a need for longitudinal studies.

To address the limitation of this study which is associated with looking at emerging and developing countries as a homogeneous entity and recognizing that those countries are heterogeneous, a study is needed in comparing the performance of the countries at the regional levels. One recommendation for future research would be to study the relationship between economic structure and the level of maturity and comprehensiveness of national cybersecurity policies, on the one hand, and the diffusion of cyber activities in particular countries, on the other hand. Excellent candidates would be countries in Latin America, the Gulf Cooperation Council, and countries in Asia. This recommendation, however, is more difficult to bring to life in the near future because of the less than perfect data collection methodologies and the less than acceptable coverage of existing economies. For any study to be fruitful and professionally acceptable, information and data have to be collected through questionnaires over a long period of time. This is a lengthy and costly process, and while it is professionally challenging, it is rewarding.

In addition, one limitation of the study is that in the current research the analysis was cross-sectional. Static data were used to test for what are, without doubt, dynamic relationships. Longitudinal analysis would have been beneficial, but unfortunately, given the novelty of the subject in hand, the lack of comprehensive longitudinal data precluded such analysis. Studying economies at different points in time may help identify how changes in the independent variables affect the decisions on both behavioral and non-behavioral constructs. A profound analysis might be made on an individual country level, when and if data are available. Studies could be conducted at the sector or industry level, such as the banking industry, in some economies; such industry-level studies help in the isolation of industry-specific resources, characteristics and peculiarities of diffusion of electronic commerce and its impact on growth and development of these industries, as well as isolating the impact of the quality of the cybersecurity policy in that context.

If we accept the New Institutional Economics premise that strong institutional foundations in the form of a quality national cybersecurity policy would be conducive to diffusion of cyber activities, then we should find strong support from our statistical analysis.

More work is also needed on the interface between relationship development policy and cyber space strategies. It is the firm conviction of the authors that devising well articulated national cybersecurity policies will lead to a higher rate of diffusion of cyber activities in our sample countries.

Hackers and cybercriminals around the world are taking advantage of the anemic cybersecurity practices in developing/emerging countries, and are launching attacks in so many different directions. Since a large percentage of the countries in the developing world are cash starved, and given that the impact of a cyberattack will affect countries in the developed world, it is in the best interests of developed countries to come up with a global response that encourages and supports organizations in the developing world to formulate policies and a set of strategies to assist them to protect themselves against cybercriminals. Cybercriminals are not going to go away, and all countries, at the highest levels of government, need to make it difficult for those cybercriminals to achieve their purposes by exploiting vulnerabilities in systems and infrastructures.

Many developing countries have recently moved to develop cyber-security strategies, cyber laws and cybersecurity policies. Many prac-titioners in this area are advocating the development of global and regional initiatives emphasizing the creation of public–private partner-ships. It is imperative to emphasize the fact that one size does not fit all in this domain. Cybersecurity policies have to be designed in a way to fit the cultural, social and political norms of each society. While the cybersecurity policy constructs identified in this book create a common ground, the relative importance of those constructs varies from one country to another. Just as an example here, in countries where remedial and response measures are weak (lack of a CERT team for instance), a major effort should be made to strengthen the response and remedial constructs before a country moves to emphasize the public–private partnership construct. A major force here is the role of the top level of government in getting involved in the development and implementation of cybersecurity policies and strategies. A shining example in this domain is India, where Prime Minister Modi has been personally involved in the development of cybersecurity policies, strategies and laws in his country. He has also been very active in creating partnerships with other countries in this domain; just recently he inked a cooperation with Israel and Sweden (Roy, 2018). Other initiatives that merit a mention here are the efforts by some governments directed at allocating accountability for cybersecurity in one agency and/or one person, as is the case in Australia where an Ambassador of Cyber Affairs position was created back in October 2017. The role of the new Ambassador is to lead Australia's international engagement to advance and protect its national security, foreign policy, the area of the Internet and cyber space. The five pillars that the new ambassador is tasked with are national cyber partnerships, strong cyber defense, global influence, growth of innovation and the creation of a cyber smart nation (Abbott and Whittaker, 2018). Countries in the emerging and developing world can follow the lead of Australia in creating a top-level position to centralize the responsibility and account-ability of a specific agency as far as cybersecurity is concerned.

To improve the state of cybersecurity policy development in develop-ing countries, governments and decision makers in developing countries need to share experiences, success stories, challenges and working practices. This is a must to reduce the likelihood of cybercriminal activities and create a more secure cyber space. There are a number of necessary conditions to the success of cooperation among the different countries: topping those conditions is for governments to be proactive through early engagement in developing national cybersecurity policies with the necessary constructs, political, social and cultural, in addition to the necessary measures of deterrence, both through punishment and denial. This is becoming of vital importance as more and more countries are adopting the smart city initiative.

NOTE

1. Maturity is defined by two constructs: quality and comprehensiveness.

REFERENCES

Abbott, C. and Whittaker, G. (2018). Australia government releases cyber security strategy, accessed 11 May 2018 at https://www.cyberwatchaustralia. com/tag/cyber-ambassador/.

Diniz, G., Muggah, R. and Glenny, M. (2015). Deconstructing cybersecurity in Brazil: Threats and responses, accessed 10 June 2016 at http://www.slideshare. net/CesarMRibeiro/strategic-paper-11cyber2-deconstructing-cyber-security-in-brazil.

Hale, T. (2017). How much data does the world generate every minute?, accessed 22 February 2018 at http://www.iflscience.com/technology/how-much-data-does-the-world-generate-every-minute/.

International Telecommunication Union (ITU) (2015). Global Cybersecurity Index & Cyberwellness Profiles, accessed 22 December 2015 at http://www. itu.int/dms_pub/itu-d/opb/str/D-STR-SECU-2015-PDF-E.pdf.

IT Governance Institute (2006). Information security governance: Guidance for boards of directors and executive management, accessed 5 July 2016 at www.isaca.org/Template.cfm?Section5HomeandTemplate5/ContentManagement/ ContentDisplay.cfmandContentID524572.

Johnson, L.J. and Hall, S. (2009), 9 habits of highly successful CISOs, accessed 2 February 2016 at http://searchsecurity.techtarge.com/magazineFeature/ 0,296894,sid14_gci1257074,00.html.

Karake-Shalhoub, Z. (2002), *Trust and Loyalty in Electronic Commerce: An Agency Theory Perspective*, New York: Quorum Publishing.

Karake-Shalhoub, Z. and Al Qasimi, L. (2007), *The Diffusion of E-commerce in Developing Economies*, Cheltenham, UK, and Northampton, MA, USA: Edward Elgar Publishing.

Kulikova, A. (2015). China–Russia cyber-security pact: Should the US be concerned?, accessed 20 May 2016 at http://www.russia-direct.org/analysis/ china-russia-cyber-security-pact-should-us-be-concerned.

Nedeltchev, P. (2015). The Internet of Everything is the new economy: It is inevitable. It is here. Are we ready?, accessed 2 September 2016 at http://www.cisco.com/c/en/us/solutions/collateral/enterprise/cisco-on-cisco/Cisco_IT_Trends_IoE_Is_the_New_Economy.pdf.

Organisation for Economic Co-operation and Development (OECD) (2008). OECD Guidelines for the security of information systems and networks, accessed 2 January 2015 at www.oecd.org/dataoecd/16/22/15582260.pdf.

Ponemon (2015). 2015 Cost of cybercrime study: United States, accessed 2 April 2016 at http://www.ponemon.org/blog/2015-cost-of-cyber-crime-united-states.

Price, D. (2015). Facts and stats about the big data industry, accessed 11 March 2016 at http://cloudtweaks.com/2015/03/surprising-facts-and-stats-about-the-big-data-industry/.

Roy, S. (2018). India, Sweden to step up cyber security and defense ties, accessed 8 May 2018 at https://indianexpress.com/article/india/india-sweden-to-step-up-cyber-security-defence-ties-5141694/.

Royal Geographic Society (RGS) (2017). 21st century challenges, accessed 30 November 2017 at https://21stcenturychallenges.org/what-is-the-digital-divide/.

Son, Y. (2011). Out of fear or desire? Toward a better understanding of employees' motivation to follow IS security policies. *Information & Management*, **48**(7): 296–302.

Symantec (2014). Latin American and Caribbean Cybersecurity Trends, accessed 12 December 2015 at http://www.symantec.com/content/en/us/enterprise/other_resources/b-cyber-security-trends-report-lamc.pdf.

UAE Supreme National Council (2015). The UAE cybersecurity strategy, internal document.

Ula, M. and Fuadi, W. (2017). A method for evaluating information security governance (ISG) in the banking environment, *Journal of Physics: Conference Series*, **812**(1).

United Nations (2008). *UN Resolution 57/239 on the Creation of a Global Culture of Cybersecurity*, accessed 7 May 2016 at www.itu.int/ITU-D/cyb/cybersecurity/UN_resolution_57_239.pdf.

United Nations (2015). Transforming our world: The 2030 agenda for sustainable development, accessed 11 February 2018 at https://sustainabledevelopment.un.org/post2015/transformingourworld.

Index